# Prisoner Subcultures

Lee H. Bowker
University of Wisconsin-Milwaukee

**Lexington Books**
D.C. Heath and Company
Lexington, Massachusetts
Toronto

301.293

**Library of Congress Cataloging in Publication Data**

Bowker, Lee Harrington.
    Prisoner subcultures.


    Includes index.
    1. Prisoners. 2. Subculture. I. Title.
HV8665.B68        365'.6        77-6182
ISBN 0-669-01429-X

Second printing, November 1978.

Published simultaneously in Canada.

Printed in the United States of America.

International Standard Book Number: 0-669-01429-X

Library of Congress Catalog Card Number: 77-6182

To three great teachers who have influenced my professional and intellectual development: Morris Greth, who introduced me to the complexities of sociological analysis; Otto Pollak, who taught me the methods and value of theorizing; and James F. Short, Jr., who showed me how to integrate theory and methodology into a total professional commitment.

# Contents

# Acknowledgments

This book would not have been possible without the cooperation, interest and support of my wife Dee, who participated in the development of many of my ideas on prisoner subcultures. At the Washington State Penitentiary, Superintendent B.J. Rhay and Associate Superintendent Bob Freeman gave freely of their time and support over a period of years. Jack Struck and Dennis Lehman were instrumental in introducing me to the inner workings of prisoner subcultures. The superintendents, staff, and prisoners of men's and women's prisons from Alberta to California to Florida cooperated fully in my on-site visits designed to ascertain whether changes in the prisoner subculture at the Washington State Penitentiary were also occurring in other North American institutions.

Research for my first prison study was carried out under the kind direction of John Lillywhite at Washington State University. The Aid to Faculty Scholarship Committee at Whitman College funded field trips and manuscript typing costs. Additional field trips were supported by a Ford Foundation Venture Grant and a Wilkins Fund Grant, both administered by Whitman College. The library staff members at Whitman, headed by Arley Jonish, were untiring in their willingness to help in any way they could. Lorraine Reed, reference librarian, offered particularly outstanding services over a period of many years. My departmental colleagues, Ely Chertok and David R. Norsworthy, were unusually tolerant of the problems that my research activities caused for the smooth running of departmental affairs. Finally, this project would never have come to its conclusion without the typing and research skills of Joy Pollock at Whitman College, the editorial assistance and personal encouragement given me by Margaret N. Zusky and the staff at Lexington Books, D.C. Heath and Company, and the kindness of many fine scholars who sent papers, articles, and unpublished dissertations for my study and eventual inclusion in this book.

# Introduction

My interest in prisons began when I started teaching sociology night classes in the community college program at the Washington State Penitentiary. After a few years, B.J. Rhay, the administrator in charge of the institution, asked a group of college professors and other interested citizens to develop a program to help violent drug abusers. We did so, and I took responsibility for the direction of the unit named the Social Therapy Program. Because this unit was an isolated therapeutic community—a prison within a prison—I was forced to cope with all the pressures and problems of a prison warden, though on a reduced scale.

Problems of dealing with staff, volunteers, and the general public were bad enough, but even greater was the problem of combatting the negative influence of the prisoner subculture and substituting a positive therapeutic subculture in its place. The program had convict leaders to supplement the free world staff, and they helped us to understand not only the normative requirements of the convict code but also the intensely political character of personal, clique, and intergroup relations among prisoners. Simultaneously, I began to collect as much academic material as possible, partially to use in staff training and partially to try to make sense of the flood of confusing observations that I made in my hours behind the walls each week. As I became aware that the prisoner subculture at Walla Walla was dynamically changing rather than stationary, I developed an interest in whether these structural and normative changes were being duplicated in other prisons around the country. Thanks to a number of modest grant awards secured through Whitman College, I was able to satisfy that curiosity by completing on-site visits to penitentiaries in most of the western United States, plus additional institutions in the southeast and the Canadian province of Alberta.

When I began my service at the Washington State Penitentiary, I was a "bleeding heart liberal" on prison affairs. I was horrified at the suffering of the prisoners and readily believed their stories of line staff cruelty and administrative misuse of funds. As I became more sophisticated, I began to see that what the prisoners were doing to each other was far worse than anything staff ever did to them. In the third stage of my prison education, I found out that many stories about staff were myths instead of realities and others that were true were based on custody problems of which I had been previously unaware. I then came to realize that most long-term line staff members and many administrators were only slightly less prisonized than the prisoners themselves. My conclusion was finally that certain structural conditions in the prison caused most of the negative facets of prison life on both the staff and prisoner sides of the battle. I was delighted when Zimbardo's research at Stanford offered convincing evidence of the same genesis of prison problems.

As I now see it, prisoners, staff, and administrators are caught in antagonistic yet reciprocal webs of meaning that are largely structured by social forces beyond their control. Many of these forces operate through organizational and physical characteristics of the prison setting that have been ossified through centuries of penological tradition. I continue to be disturbed by the suffering of prisoners and to be convinced that no fully developed civilization could tolerate prisons as we now know them, but I no longer agree that this needless suffering is forced on prisoners by line staff and administrators. Quite to the contrary, prison conditions are an expression of the will of the general citizenry, and they will not change significantly until the public develops a different conception of what to do about crime and criminals.

In this volume my intention is to summarize what is known about prisoner subcultures in institutions for men, women, and adolescents. My hope is that correctional administrators, middle-level staff members, and students of prisoner subcultures will be able to use the book as a kind of mini-encyclopaedia in which they can use the index to look up the most important studies on any given topic related to prisoner subcultures in just a few minutes time. I also intend to provide a general summary of the field for those interested in an overview of prisoner subcultures, to indicate recent and projected future changes in prisoner subcultures, and to make some modest theoretical suggestions and policy recommendations. If these efforts justify the time donated to the project by hundreds of prisoners, staff members, administrators, and professional criminologists, I will be satisfied.

# Prisoner Subcultures

# 1

## Pioneering Studies of Prisons for Men

### Early Studies

The scientific study of prisoner subcultures in maximum security institutions for adult males began in 1934 with the publication of Joseph Fishman's book, *Sex in Prison.*[1] Fishman had visited most of America's prisons over the years in his position as a prison examiner for the U.S. Department of Justice. Most of his prose is not specifically about prison subcultures, but there is quite a bit of relevant information scattered throughout the book.

Fishman believes that homosexuality is practiced by between 30 percent and 40 percent of all prisoners. He describes homosexual behavior in prison and relates some of the argot terms commonly used; for example, the prisoners who take the active role in homosexual relations are called "top men" and "wolves" and the passive participants are called "punks," "girls," "fags," "pansies," or "fairies." Through a series of case studies, Fishman shows how men are made into homosexuals in prison—that is, through "turn outs" and gradual reorientation, as women fade in their memories. Fishman's book is an amazing one for its time; it is very accurate and fearlessly realistic.

Shortly thereafter, there appeared a brief article on prison language by James Hargan who was a psychologist at Sing Sing Prison at the time.[2] In addition to providing a censored list of Sing Sing argot, Hargan made some insightful observations on the functions of this specialized jargon. He felt that the use of argot terminology helped prisoners to acquire a sense of group solidarity, thus neutralizing many of the negative feelings they had about themselves. According to Hargan, argot terms typically understate and soften the harsh realities of prison life and perhaps convince prisoners that things are not quite as bad as they seem.

Hans Reimer delivered a brief paper at the 1937 conference of the American Prison Association on socialization in prisons.[3] He had managed to get himself incarcerated for four months without any prison administrator or fellow prisoner knowing that he was a participant observer rather than a criminal. He found out that those prisoners who most closely followed the convict code became leaders, and he delineated the roles of "politician" and "right guy": "Politicians" were excessively self-serving, but "right guys" upheld the convict code with great rigidity. As the moralists of prisoner life, the "right guys" were the true leaders of the prisoner society, and their leadership had a great deal of legitimacy within that society.

1

At this time, the idea that criminal behavior was biologically caused was still respectable. The case studies of the Kallikaks and the Jukes were still influential, as was the work of Lombroso.[4] Brown and Hartman reported on the intelligence of 13,454 Illinois adult male prisoners in 1938.[5] They found the prisoners to be approximately as intelligent as Army draftees, though there was a higher proportion of subjects who were retarded or mentally defective. The same conclusion was reached in a more detailed study by Tulchin.[6]

Studies such as these are typical of early research on prisoners. They either ignored sociological factors completely, or at best limited themselves to the consideration of a few demographic variables. Erbe managed to compare the social backgrounds of murderers, property offenders, and sex offenders in the Iowa State Penitentiary without making any analysis of how the different backgrounds of these three types of offenders impacted prisoners' social relations.[7] Similarly, Tolman did not consider the implications for the prisoner society of her finding that Los Angeles County recidivists were more hostile or dissatisfied than first-time offenders on every one of fifteen dimensions tested.[8] The same can be said for Hanks' comparison of one hundred prisoners in solitary confinement at the Wisconsin State Prison with the general population and a matched group consisting of individuals who had never been in solitary confinement.[9]

Although a student intern rather than a secret participant observer like Reimer, Rasmussen became familiar with many aspects of the prisoner society at the Joliet-Statesville Penitentiary in Illinois during the two summers he spent there.[10] In fact, he became so immersed in the prisoner subculture that he internalized some of its values and beliefs. Rasmussen detailed the bitterness about prison life and the parole board that was held by most prisoners, but he was too busy being outraged at the suffering of the men to closely examine how they used the adaptive tool of social organization to cope with this suffering.

*Hayner's Studies of Washington State Penal Institutions*

In 1936 Ellis Ash, a student of Norman Hayner's, spent four months as a participant observer in the Washington State Reformatory at Monroe. Together, they produced an insightful analysis of the prisoner society at Monroe in "The Prisoner Community as a Social Group."[11] Perhaps the combination of an uninvolved professor with the field worker was the reason why their article was objective rather than strongly proprisoner. They did write a polemical article later, but even this one was not visibly influenced by prisoner values and beliefs.[12]

Hayner and Ash found that the basic social process among Monroe prisoners was "conniving." "Conniving" consisted of a variety of sub rosa activities, including gambling, food and drug (coffee, tobacco, and alcohol) smuggling, and commercial transactions involving a wide range of implements and services. Commerce was carried on by barter or with any of three forms of money: tobacco, "white" money (U.S. currency), or "hickeys" (tokens used within the prison, where U.S. currency was illegal). Economic activity was an essential component of social organization, for the primary function of the prisoner society was to provide these illegal items and services, and the division of labor among prisoners was largely based upon differential opportunity and ability to succeed in the various forms of "conniving."[13]

The prisoner upper class was called "politician's row," which always included many of the men who were central to the "conniving" system. If the prison administration was lax in enforcing prison regulations, "rangatangs" became "politicians," which probably added to the brutality of the system because they could not even be expected to respect other prisoners who followed the convict code. When the administration tightened up, the "rangatangs" were controlled and more stable prisoners were able to move into the top spots in the "conniving" network.[14]

In 1941, Hayner was asked by the Interim Committee on Penal and Charitable Institutions to make studies of all four Washington penal institutions: the School for Girls, the Training School (boys), the Reformatory at Monroe, and the Penitentiary in Walla Walla. He placed students in all four institutions in following the model he had established with Ash at Monroe five years earlier. Hayner passed up the chance to make a comparison between Monroe in 1936 and the same institution in 1941, but he did compare all four institutions studied at the same time. He concluded that the prisoner social system became increasingly crystalized, and there was a sharper definition of social roles as one moved from girls to boys, young men, and finally older men.[15]

The man who did the field work at Walla Walla was Clarence Schrag, who was the classification secretary on the prison's staff at the time. His report delineated five major prisoner roles—"outlaw," "right guy," "politician," "square john," and "ding"—and a number of more informal secondary roles such as the "old time con" and the "rapo."[16] His observations at the Washington State Penitentiary will be discussed in detail in a later section of this chapter.

## The Father of the Sociology of the Prison

Donald Clemmer was a sociologist at the Menard Branch of the Illinois State Penitentiary during the 1930s. He used his position there to collect information on the prisoner society between 1931 and 1934. He first published his findings in 1938 in "Leadership Phenomena in a Prison Community"[17] and followed that in 1940 with his celebrated study, *The Prison Community*.[18] Two decades later, he was Director of the Department of Corrections in the District of Columbia and still involved in research on prisoner subcultures.

*The Prison Community* was the first detailed sociological study of a prison, and its wealth of data remains unmatched today after six hundred additional publications on the topic have been produced. It is similar to the great ethnographic classics of the Chicago school, many of which were written at about the same time. Clemmer makes clear that his interest is ethnography rather than theory building.[19] He was only concerned with theory when it served the function of more clearly describing the phenomena at hand. A methodology that included over 30,000 conversations with prisoners, more than 50 biographies, 200 prisoner essays, 190 interviews utilizing six batteries of questions, and 174 questionnaires was admirably suited to the collection of ethnographic data in depth.[20]

The amount of data in *The Prison Community* defies summary, so we will be content to discuss its major contributions to the study of prisoner subcultures. The first is Clemmer's analysis of language in conversation and written in "kites" (notes). His findings resemble those of Hargan at Sing Sing mentioned earlier, but his analysis is more complete. He compiled a dictionary of 1,063 argot terms (many of which are listed in an appendix) and then analyzed them to see what categories of human experience they referred to. Eleven percent referred to sex, 30 percent to crime, 32 percent to prison, 8 percent to descriptions of individuals, 6 percent to body parts, 5 percent to "vagabondage," 3 percent to alcohol, 3 percent to other drugs, and 1 percent to gambling.[21] Could the number of argot terms reflect the importance of a given category of experience in prisoners' lives? If so, we could draw useful conclusions from the fact that sixty-four argot terms referred to homosexual behavior and but fifty-two to heterosexual behavior, or that twenty-two referred to food while only nine referred to clothing. Surely, modern prisons see more than the thirty-seven argot terms referring to drugs and narcotics that were known in Clemmer's day.

More important than Clemmer's analysis of prisoner argot is his portrayal of the group structure of the prison population. He found three general classes of prisoners: the elite, the middle class, and the "hoosier" class. Only one-fifth of the men were members of primary groups, with the others equally divided between those who were friendly with others and those who were socially isolated. The prisoners' own opinions of prisoners' social relations tended to be negative, with 72 percent believing that prison friendships are short, 77 percent that familiarity breeds contempt among prisoners, and 70 percent that prison friendships are based more on mutual help than on personal attraction. Those who "made it" socially in prison tended to be younger, more criminalistic, and more intelligent than the socially isolated prisoners. Some of the isolated prisoners stayed aloof from others because of close ties to family or friends outside the prison; others did so because they were antisocial and some because they were what Simmel called "strangers"—that is, men who never got involved with anything, yet were "good cons."[22]

Altogether, Clemmer cites nine structural dimensions along which social differentiation and organization occur in prisons. These are (1) the prisoner-staff dichotomy, (2) the three general classes of prisoners, (3) the work gangs and cellhouse groups, (4) racial groups, (5) offense, (6) the role of the politician versus the common man, (7) degree of sexual abnormality, (8) recidivists versus noncriminalistic offenders, and (9) personality differences due to preprison socialization. The prisoner-staff dichotomy and the primary group structure that arises out of work gangs and cellhouse groups were the two most important structural factors that Clemmer found at Menard. These multiple cleavages, combined with the asocial personality traits of many Menard prisoners, produced an atomized society in which conflict and opposition between prisoners was only slightly less than that between prisoners and the staff or society at large.[23]

A third major contribution of *The Prison Community* is the analysis of sexual behavior in prison. With much greater detail and honesty than most recent studies, Clemmer portrays the imposition of homosexual behavior upon prisoners, not so much by gangs of "wolves" as by the state. Clemmer estimated that approximately 60 percent of the prisoners made a "normal" adjustment to their sexual needs while in prison, 30 percent were quasi-abnormal, and 10 percent were severely abnormal. In order to remain reasonably normal, a prisoner had to have a fairly short sentence plus continued contacts with one or more heterosexual love objects outside the prison. With a longer sentence, even these normal men might resort to anal intercourse, but only in the active role and with heterosexual fantasies.[24]

Clemmer classed playing the active role in anal intercourse (a "wolf," "jocker," or "daddy") or in its close approximation, "leggins," as quasi-abnormal. These men would occasionally find fellow prisoners to perform fellatio upon them. At the very least, they would masturbate to relieve their sexual tension. Those who were sexual inverts (with feminine body characteristics), who performed fellatio on others, or who took the passive role in anal intercourse were classed as abnormal. Some of this abnormal behavior was guessed to be constitutional. In other cases, the prisoners were believed to have been forced to regress to an earlier stage of sexual maturity by the conditions of their incarceration, and a third group were considered prostitutes who performed sex acts for favors or money.[25]

Clemmer's discussion of the convict code, social control mechanisms, and the prisoner economic system (called "conniving" here as in Washington) is informative, though not outstanding. His outline of the prisoners' use of leisure time is better, particularly when he deals with the administrative limitations on contacts with people and ideas from the outside world. These and other elements in his analysis make up the fourth major contribution of *The Prison Community*—that is, its detailed, objective portrayal of the Menard system, characterized by a brutality that was more social and psychological than physical. Beatings by guards, tiny cells, and horrible conditions in solitary confinement were probably easier for the prisoners to survive than social and psychological dislocations forced by the sexual situation, the silence rule at meals, the strict limitations on writing letters and receiving visitors, and the negative attitudes shown toward many kinds of prisoners by staff and fellow inmates.

The final great contribution made by *The Prison Community* is the concept of *prisonization*, which sensitized the public to the destructive and criminogenic implications of serving a prison sentence. This concept has been the major focus of most of the meaningful studies of prisoner subcultures in the past thirty-five years. Clemmer defined *prisonization* as a particular kind of rapid assimilation characterized by the taking on of the mores, customs, folkways, and other elements of the general culture of the prison.[26] He recognized the role of what Garfinkel later referred to as status degradation ceremonies in shocking the new prisoner into readiness to enter the prisonization process.[27]

All prisoners studied by Clemmer suffered some of the effects of prisonization, such as accepting their inferior role, learning how to get along within the structure and regulations of the prison, and becoming passive about the meeting of their own basic needs, which were taken care of by the prison no matter what they did. The more criminogenic aspects of prisonization influenced some men more than others. Those who became the most prisonized were men who had long sentences; unstable personalities; lack of relations with outsiders; capability; and interest in joining a primary group of prisoners; willingness to accept the mores of that primary group as well as the mores of prisoners in general; placement by chance into situations that favored contacts with other prisonized individuals; and willingness to gamble and engage in sexual behavior while in prison.[28] Clemmer's conclusion that few men will live law-abiding lives once they have been highly prisonized is as true today as it was in the 1930s. The bitter ending is that these men are likely to be "rehabilitated" only when they become too old to continue their criminal careers.[29]

Clemmer's later work in penology continued to evince a unique combination of a scientist's analytic curiosity, an administrator's realism, and a humanist's compassion for suffering. In "Observations on Imprisonment as a Source of Criminality," he repeated his prisonization thesis and noted that 83 percent of the men admitted to the Washington, D.C., jail in 1949 had been previously convicted of a crime.[30]

A more detailed study of prison sexual behavior than appeared in *The Prison Community* reported that 65 percent of the prisoners masturbated, 43 percent admitted homosexual experiences before entering prison on this conviction, and 16 percent admitted homosexuality during the current prison term.[31] Noting the obvious underreporting in these figures, Clemmer estimated current homosexuality at 32 percent. A significant finding of this study was that men who took the active role in anal intercourse sometimes switched to the passive role, contrary to common beliefs on the matter.

In a third study, Clemmer extended his original analysis of reverie using three samples of men from Washington, D.C., institutions in the late 1950s.[32] He found that an average of sixteen hours a week was spent by prisoners in daydreaming, which is perhaps twice as much as spent by people in the outside world. Although daydreaming about the future was generally positive, Clemmer found that prisoners seemed unable, even with urging, to imagine a successful future—that is, one in which the level of their lives was any better than it had been before incarceration. Clemmer's conclusion again echoes his earlier work in *The Prison Community*. Prison life squashes hope and makes realistic and favorable expectations for a better life after release almost impossible for the vast majority of prisoners. The message given so clearly and forcefully by this penological pioneer in the 1930s and then again and again throughout his career was not to be seriously acted on, however, until three decades had become history.

## The War Years

Only six studies of prisoner subcultures appeared between 1941 and 1945. Three of these focused on relations between staff and prisoners. The penitentiary at Menard, Illinois, which Clemmer made famous in *The Prison Community*, was also studied by Weinberg.[33] He emphasized the unity of the prisoner subculture in its opposition to the staff and a corresponding staff opposition to prisoners. Each group developed stereotypes of the other and expounded an elaborate ideology to justify its rejection. For example, the prisoners pointed out that officials were incompetent or they would not be working in a prison, and they alleged that prison officials had committed many crimes outside the prison and engaged in sadistic and cowardly acts within its walls.

Sacks studied a medium security institution, the District of Columbia Reformatory at Lorton, in 1937 to ascertain the differences between twenty-five resistant prisoners and a matched group of twenty-five conformists.[34] In general, he found that resistant prisoners were more criminal and more alienated from their families. Because of the way in which he chose his subjects, and perhaps also because of the nature of the institution, he tended to suggest more of a split in the prisoner population in their attitudes toward the staff than was found by Weinberg at Menard.

Fifty-one recidivists incarcerated at the Iowa State Prison were interviewed by Polansky.[35] They described the characteristics of institutions in which they had "done time" and then ranked them, so that Polansky was able to ascertain which characteristics were most important to the men. He found that the most significant factors were all controlled by the administration, while factors related to other prisoners were the least important. Polansky also found that in institutions in which the administration enforced strict discipline, there was more prisoner dislike for administrators but also more fighting and internal dissension among prisoners. The conclusion he came to was that prisons are counterproductive, and that the more authoritarian they are, the more atomized and socially disrupted they become. This conclusion is completely consistent with the findings of earlier researchers in maximum security prisons.

Two studies completed during the war years examined prison homosexuality. Greco and Wright studied ten chronic homosexuals and an equal number of nonhomosexuals at the Pennsylvania Industrial School at Huntington in 1941.[36] They believed that chronic homosexuals were rare—that is, no more than one in twenty-five or thirty prisoners. Their conclusion was that the chronic homosexual had been seduced at an early age by a homosexual adult and that the institutional conditions were merely precipitating rather than predisposing factors. These findings are not very useful since the sample was so small and in view of the fact that chronic homosexuals are not the major source of prison homosexual behavior. An idea that is hard to resist is that the authors of this article were easily taken in by the self-excusing stories of many of their subjects.

A very different kind of article was stimulated by the discovery that one of two homosexual lovers in the Alabama prison system had committed a crime in order to be transferred back into the institution in which his mate was still incarcerated.[37] In this study, Devereux and Moos initially agree with Greco and Wright that prison life is only a precipitating condition of prisoner homosexuality, but that is where the similarity between their studies ends. Devereux and Moos argue that the prisoner is socially dead and therefore beyond the control of societal norms that forbid homosexuality. Besides, Western civilization has never built systematic social structures to support affection. Only when affection becomes sexual is it fully institutionalized. When prison conditions facilitate an intense emotional relationship between two men, there are few supports in the social organization of the prison for keeping that relationship at a nonsexual level.

The negative picture painted of prison homosexuality by most authors is not duplicated by Devereux and Moos. They see it as performing many valuable functions within the prison, including (1) affirming the integrity of the self, (2) providing new experience and thrills to combat boredom, (3) promoting social stratification through the opportunity for "exploits" in the sense used by Veblen,[38] and (4) allowing a reasonably useful outlet for rebellion against prison rules.[39] The etiquette of prison homosexuality is described by these authors as following the highest ethical rules of romantic chivalry rather than a sordid anarchism.[40]

The best publication on prisoner subcultures from the war years is Farber's study of suffering and the time perspectives of forty prisoners in the Iowa State Penitentiary at Fort Madison.[41] He found that the subjective suffering experienced by prisoners was directly related to (1) the feeling that the sentence was unjust, (2) the belief that the length of time served was unjust, (3) indefiniteness of a release date, (4) having no hope for a lucky break, and (5) seeing the outside world as being unfriendly. More interesting to the student of prisoner sub-cultures are Farber's data on the effects of suffering. His subjects had an inverse relationship between level of suffering and degree of involvement in both cell activities and the recreational activities of the prison.

Farber developed a typology of prisoner types that was not based on social roles, though it was related to role differentiation to some degree. The youthful aggressive offender made a lot of trouble in the institution, experienced high personal suffering, and had the lowest status jobs. The professional criminal was even higher on suffering, but low on troublesomeness and high on job status. The third type was the habitual criminal, who made a lot of trouble in the institution and was average on suffering and on job status. The neurotic prisoner was low on both suffering and troublesomeness, but was likely to occupy the highest status job in the prison. The last of Farber's prisoner types was the situational criminal who was low on job status and troublesomeness, but experienced about average levels of subjective suffering. There was a general nonconformist orientation that was shared by more than half of the youthful aggressive offenders and a quarter of the professional and habitual groups, but not one neurotic or situational offender. Among all these offender types, prison behavior was more oriented toward getting out of prison by any possible means than to any other theme or goal.[42] Although Farber's sample was small and unrepresentative, his findings ring true, especially when compared with more recent studies.

*Schrag's Studies Emerge*

Schrag's involvement with prison research under Norman Hayner in 1941 led to an M.A. thesis in 1944 and a Ph.D. dissertation in 1950.[43] Data from these and other studies were presented and elaborated in a series of publications stretching from 1954 through several decades. His significance in the sociology of prisoner societies is not limited to his own publications, for he and Hayner were the founders of a tradition of penological thought at the University of Washington that is unmatched in the history of prison studies. Among the achievements of this tradition are Ph.D. dissertations by Garrity, Wheeler, Kinch, Garabedian, Rothbart, Mitchell, and Gruninger.[44] Rothbart put it well when he said that Schrag was responsible for developing his interest in prison organization, for encouraging him to undertake his project, and for the intellectual stimulation and guidance necessary to carry it through.[45]

Schrag initially classified prisoners by their crimes into three large groups: violent offenders, sex offenders, and property offenders. He found that there was a tendency for each type to pick its leaders from within its offender group. A second trend was for all groups to select violent offenders as leaders more than would be expected by chance. These leaders had longer sentences, were more likely to be recidivists, and had accumulated more time spent behind bars.[46] Since violent offenders are often the least capable of organizing group efforts, as well as the most negativistic and resistant to improvement,[47] the prisoner body continues to be atomized, and the more positive men are influenced away from improving themselves.

A second and more meaningful classification of prisoners was into the social roles played in the prison society. The "square john," "right guy," "politician," and "outlaw" prisoner types were renamed prosocial, antisocial, pseudosocial, and asocial by Schrag. The prosocial prisoner was positively oriented toward society, relatively uninvolved in the prisoner subculture, and interacted frequently with staff members. He was usually a first offender, often for forgery or a crime of passion. The antisocial offender was just the opposite—that is, negatively oriented toward society, heavily involved in the prisoner subculture, and rarely interacting with staff members. These men were generally multiple recidivists whose criminal records included crimes such as robbery, burglary, and assault. Confidence games, fraud, and embezzlement were more typical of the pseudosocial offender, who had high knowledge and contacts, but low attachment to both legitimate society and the prisoner subculture. These men played both sides for all they could get. The final type, the asocial offender, was low on all social involvement, regardless of object. He had a severely criminal record and showed much evidence of emotional damage. Although unable to cooperate with other prisoners, asocial offenders fought the staff constantly and were responsible for much of the violence and rebellion in the prison.[48]

Each prisoner was likely to choose friends who were the same social type that he was. There was also a trend toward overselecting antisocial and, to a lesser extent, asocial offenders as friends. These friendship choices follow the same pattern as the leadership choices discussed above. Schrag believes that this process is accelerated by increasing tensions and anxieties among the prisoners.[49] If this theory is true, and if we assume that authoritarian institutions produce higher levels of tension and anxiety than institutions in which custody, rules, and hierarchy are deemphasized, then the more authoritarian and custody-oriented the institution, the more antisocial and asocial prisoners become leaders and the more criminogenic the prison becomes.

In a chapter written for Cressey's book, *The Prison, Studies in Institutional Organization and Change*, Schrag points out that prisoners do not merely react passively to prison subcultures, they can also actively produce changes in their social world.[50] Cultural innovators in prisons are likely to be pseudosocial prisoners. By playing both sides and developing a wide range of social skills, pseudosocial men work themselves into positions that allow them to innovate cultural elements that will benefit themselves in some way. In doing so, they inadvertently become the catalysts of sociocultural change. The nihilistic asocial prisoners, rebellious antisocial prisoners, and conformist prosocial prisoners are unlikely to innovate extensively in the prison society.[51]

How do prisoners come to play different roles in the prison society? To some degree, they do so as a matter of personal predispositions and previous experiences, particularly with respect to the general role types of prosocial, pseudosocial, antisocial, and asocial prisoners. The more sociologically interesting aspect of role occupancy is role assignment. Schrag outlines the ways in which members of the prisoner subculture assign roles to newly incarcerated men. First, the older residents decide how loyal the new man is to them, as opposed to the administration. Does he judge his actions by the convict code or by administrative regulations? How well does he understand the complex roles and obligations that structure prisoner relationships? If he qualifies after these deliberations, then the other prisoners contrive a number of empirical situations to test the new man.[52] If he succeeds, he is asked to play a specific role in the sub rosa economic life of the prison. His job may be stealing a needed commodity from the prison, distributing it to others on a wholesale basis, or retailing it to individual prisoners.

In his Master's thesis, Schrag identified focal issues in the prisoner subculture such as sex, food, social contacts with prisoners, staff and outsiders, and health. His observation was that the prisoner subculture allowed alternate roles to exist to deal with each focal issue. Within the subculture doing both "tough time" and "easy time" was legitimate. What was more important was the general set of rules for relating to other prisoners and staff.[53] The finely graded reciprocities between incumbents of the various prisoner roles were central in integrating the prisoner social system and solidifying its opposition to the prison administration.[54] This integration, along with a finely tuned balance between prisoners and staff, attitudes, knowledge, and behavior,[55] produced a remarkably stable social system in the traditional maximum security prison.

## A Decade of Little Progress: 1945-1955

In the decade after the Second World War, the attention of many social scientists was focused on affairs outside the United States. More publications appeared on Nazi concentration camps (a subject that has been excluded from this volume) than on prisons. The items that did appear were generally of little significance. For instance, the publications by Lunden, James, Powelson and Bendix, and Haynes do not really add anything to our knowledge of prisoner subcultures.[56]

### Studies of Structure

One study carried out on a 1936-1941 series of releases from the Wisconsin State Prison examined the relationship between fifteen independent variables and two dependent variables, recidivism and prison conduct.[57] The variables most strongly associated with prison conduct were length of time incarcerated on the present "beef," number of commitments to solitary confinement, total years spent under legal supervision, number of accomplices in the most recent recorded crime, age at admission to prison on this offense, age at first arrest, and type of crime committed. The worst records of prison behavior (as measured by the number of misconduct citations, or "tags") were exhibited by murderers (largely because of their long terms), and those convicted of arson, breaking and entering, burglary, larceny, robbery, assault with intent to rob, and auto theft. In general, this picture is supportive of Schrag's earlier comments about inmate types and the institutional behavior and criminal records associated with each type.

A less empirical but more perceptive view of the prison was put forth by McCorkle and Korn in their famous article, "Resocialization Within Walls."[58] They argue that the main function of the prisoner subculture is to deal with the psychological distress caused by the internalization of social rejection. The more threatening, disruptive, and criminal the offender, the more he gains from the support given by the prisoner subculture.

This subculture is a pressure cooker from which there is little chance of escape except through psychological withdrawal. Its rigid system of social stratification permits little vertical mobility. Nearly all social relationships have an authoritarian quality. Equality between peers is threatening to prisoners, so peer situations are usually resolved into relationships in which one man is subordinate to the other. The possession and use of coercive power is the central value of the prisoner social system. This concern with power and domination is supported by the prison administration, which gives recognition and favors to those men who dominate prisoner groups as a method of social control.[59] This picture of prison life demonstrates how prisoners and administrators prey on each other's weaknesses in a symbiotic, disculturizing, antisocial system.

*Studies of Attitudes*

In 1942-43, Corsini studied the attitudes of fifty prisoners at Auburn Prison in New York.[60] The responses seemed to be more determined by what was appropriate to say under the convict code than by the real feelings of the men. The author replicated his study at San Quentin in 1950, with the same results.[61]

Corsini's finding that most San Quentin prisoners were "reasonably happy" in prison stands in marked contrast to the classic study *The Authoritarian Personality*,[62] which included as one of the groups studied a series of San Quentin prisoners. The naive direct questions asked by Corsini were replaced by the relatively sophisticated, indirect items of the ethnocentrism, fascism, and other scales. San Quentin prisoners were found to be fearful and full of hate toward "underdog" minorities, politically conservative, and authoritarian. There were many men who were unusually threatened by any hint of weakness or femininity in themselves, to which they reacted with a compulsive masculinity that often included criminal acts. The more fascist prisoners tended to conceive of general social events in inappropriately personal terms while at the same time impersonalizing their friendships unduly. This study describes the atomization of prisoners mentioned by Clemmer from a psychological viewpoint rather than Clemmer's sociological frame of reference.

Two other psychological studies focused on adjustment in prison. In one of his many contributions to the literature of penology, Vernon Fox did an evaluation of a new counseling program at the State Prison of Southern Michigan in 1949-50.[63] He found that the counselors were a slight aid to adjustment and that they performed a number of therapeutic functions for the prisoners that included absorbing some of their aggression and providing healthy social contacts. Instead of relating institutional adjustment to a new program, Driscoll compared it with psychological characteristics as measured by the M.M.P.I.[64] Although he only tested 138 prisoners at the Waupun State Prison in Wisconsin, Driscoll's results had important theoretical implications. He found that prisoners with the poorest record of institutional adjustment had the lowest scores on the M.M.P.I. and vice versa. In other words, the psychologically least healthy men were the ones who adjusted best to prison life; sick men did well because they fit well into a sick institution. There have been few studies with results as suggestive of the destructiveness of prison life as this one.

*Homosexuality*

A number of articles were published on prison homosexuality between 1945 and 1955.[65] Karpman's description of the prisoner's drift into homosexuality is the best available anywhere.[66] At first, the prisoner is able to fantasize sexually stimulating experiences from his past while masturbating. This stimulation can be prolonged quite a bit with the aid of photographs, which may soon be replaced by sexy magazine pictures. Gradually, the practice evolves into fetishism, and at this point, overt homosexuality is just around the corner for many prisoners. According to Karpman, if the prisoner's sentence is long enough, his homosexual practices could become so well established that his return to heterosexuality upon release from prison will be unlikely. The fixing of homosexuality is still more likely among juveniles, who have not yet formed a stable sexual identity. Karpman's model is consistent with, but more complete than, what appears in other articles written at about the same time. Lindner points out that homosexual activity without homosexual fantasy and attitudes is not true homosexuality but rather homoeroticism.[67] Smith found about one hundred true homosexuals at the Medical Center for Federal Prisoners, Springfield, Missouri, of whom thirty were judged to be effeminate and seventy masculine.[68] One author suggested that maximum security institutions have less homosexuality than less secure institutions because the prisoners under maximum security supervision are more socially isolated.[69] This idea was not finally refuted until the multi-dimensional comparisons by Akers, Hayner, and Gruninger were made public in the early 1970s.[70]

*The First Replication of Clemmer's Work*

In the mid-1950s, Gresham Sykes spent three years studying the New Jersey State Maximum Security Prison at Trenton, which houses 84 percent recidivists and only 16 percent first time offenders. His methodology was, like Clemmer's, multidimensional; it included interviews, questionnaires, participant observation, and the examination of case files and printed reports. While he was particularly lucky to have a warden like Lloyd McCorkle, himself a scholar in penology, who gave him full access to the institution, on the negative side, his friendship with McCorkle might have made him less sensitive than he might have been to administrative inputs into prison life. Sykes' research led to the publication of three journal articles[71] and a book, *The Society of Captives.*[72]

Sykes' book portrays the entire prison society, not only the prisoner subculture. A considerable amount of effort is directed to relations between staff and prisoners rather than just among prisoners. An entire chapter is devoted to the tasks that prison staffs are asked to perform. These are custody, internal order, self-maintenance of the institution, punishment, and reform.[73] The apparent inconsistencies in these contradictory tasks were resolved by the establishment of a hierarchy of functional importance in the sequence running from custody (most important) to reform (least important).

Sykes has made five major contributions to penology. First, there is an elaboration of the work of Clemmer and Schrag on prisoner roles. Related to this is a careful delineation of the major tenets of the convict code. A third contribution is a description of the ways in which staff members' give up their authority and are forced to bargain with prisoners. Fourth, there is a detailed working out of the mechanisms through which the prisoner subculture functions to reduce the subjectively experienced pains of imprisonment, and fifth, Sykes provides the beginnings of a theory of prison riots.

The role types described by Sykes include the "rat" or "squealer," the "center man," the "gorilla," the "merchant," the "weakling," the "fish," the "pedlar," the "wolf," the "punk," the "fag," the "ball buster," the "real man," the "tough," and the "hipster." The "rat" betrays prisoners to the administration, the "center man" openly adopts the administration's ideology, but the "real man" never gives in to the administration as he "pulls his own time" while the "ball buster" fights back at every step, often foolishly.[74]

The "gorilla" takes whatever he wants from the "weakling" by force. The "merchant" or "pedlar" also manipulates other prisoners to get what he wants, but uses economic pressure rather than force. The "fish" is a first-time offender who is generally fair game for all the prison predators. The "wolf" plays an aggressive, masculine role in homosexual relations while "punks" and "fags" take the passive role. The difference between them is that "fags" are "true" homosexuals, but "punks" are "turned out" by the manipulations of the "wolves." A prison "tough" defends his honor against any prisoner, strong or weak, but if someone pretends to be tougher than he actually is, he is called a "hipster."[75] Through these social roles, prisoners order their relations with each other, map their social worlds, and turn the prison into a meaningful environment in which to live.

A number of the prisoner roles identified by Sykes involve the exploitation of one prisoner by another. In the questionnaire portion of his study, he found that 35 percent of the prisoners used both manipulation (as in the "merchant" role) and instrumental violence (as used by the "tough" or the "gorilla"), 10 percent used only instrumental violence, and 30 percent used only manipulation.[76] Since three-quarters of the prisoners were manipulative, we can appropriately conclude, as Sykes did, that exploitation is a central element in prison life.

According to Sykes, all studies of prisoner subcultures describe the same basic sociocultural system, regardless of the location and characteristics of the institution. The convict code summarizes the behavioral expectations current in the system. Sykes finds five main groups of expectations: "Don't interfere with inmate interests"; "Don't lose your head"; "Don't exploit inmates"; "Don't weaken"; and "Don't be a sucker."[77] Based on these expectations, the perfect prisoner is strongly proprisoner, antiadministration, tough, cool, dependable, and never uses other prisoners unfairly. Obviously, few prisoners approximate this ideal man, but most give verbal allegiance to the model, and for one prisoner to make behavioral demands on another prisoner that are based on these norms is considered proper. Clearly, then, norms function in the prisoner subculture in much the same fashion as they do in the larger society.

Since the prison staff has (at least up until recent court decisions) almost unlimited power over prisoners, why is it that there are riots, smuggling, rapes, and endless other illegal activities in the prisons? In several of his publications, Sykes explains how this comes about.[78] Prisoners have not internalized administrative norms, values, and beliefs. If they follow prison regulations, they do so because they are forced to do so, not because they agree with them. But force works poorly where men are already being punished so severely that they have little else to lose. As a result, staff members have to make "deals" with prisoners—some implicit and others explicit—in order to achieve reasonable compliance with their orders. This corruption through reciprocity is supplemented with corruption by default or friendship.[79] When an officer is lazy, prisoners gradually take over his job. If he becomes their friend, how can he demand their obedience later?

Sykes discusses many of the pains of imprisonment, including loss of liberty and social acceptance, personal autonomy, security, goods and services, and heterosexual relationships. Most of these punishments were openly discussed before Sykes' time, but his listing of the deprivation of security was an important addition to the literature. He found that prisoners suffered because of having to live closely with other prisoners who they defined as dangerous. Today, the prevalence of suits against the state by men who have been robbed, beaten, and raped by their fellow prisoners confirms his perception of the problem. In any case, Sykes' theory is that the more cohesive the prisoner society, the more it is capable of reducing the pains of imprisonment for its members.[80] Even though it is very different in content from the larger society, it functions to provide many of the same comforts and illusions that we take for granted on the "streets."

The final contribution to penology made by Gresham Sykes is his analysis of the prison riots that broke out in the New Jersey State Prison in 1952. Sykes believes that the prisoner social system does not adjust well to disturbances. Instead of being absorbed through equilibrating mechanisms, as Schrag believes, they may cause other disturbances that cycle and explode into a riot. In the New Jersey State Prison, an attempt was made in the mid-1940s to increase the level of the administration's control of the institution. As part of that process, the staff ceased granting favors to what Schrag would call the pseudosocial prisoners. As a result, this group of men gradually lost their control over the prisoner population and were replaced by antisocial prisoners.[81] Once this change had occurred, it was just a matter of time until an insignificant incident became the spark that set off the conflagration.

## A Stirring of Interest: 1955-1960

In the period between 1955 and 1960, there were a number of signs that the study of prisoner subcultures was not going to be disposed of on the academic scrap heap, like so many applied sociology, ethnographically oriented topics pioneered by sociologists at the University of Chicago in the second quarter of this century. Ignoring a number of publications of poor quality, we still have the work of Gresham Sykes, the flowering of the University of Washington school of penology, the introduction into American journals of articles describing prisoner subcultures in other countries, an increased interest in structural studies of the prison as an institution, and the first linkages of prisoner subcultures with broader perspectives in sociological theory.

There was also a continuation of the earlier interest in prisoner adjustment. For example, Hulin and Maher found that prisoners' attitudes toward both the abstract social functions of the law and its concrete manifestations became more negative the longer they were imprisoned.[82] In an unpublished doctoral dissertation, Morello found that Caucasians became more nonconformist while blacks became more extrapunitive as time served in prison increased.[83] By extrapunitiveness, Morello means that black aggression is increasingly turned outward towards the environment as prison time accumulates. Like others before him, he is forced to conclude that the process through which men adapt to prison life is maladaptive and destructive to a normal adjustment in the free society.[84]

## International Perspectives

The information obtained by Cavan and Zemans on the marital relations of prisoners in twenty-eight countries sheds some light indirectly on prisoner subcultures in those countries during this period.[85] In European countries, they found that prison visits were short and infrequent, but were supplemented with home leaves that must have interfered with the process of prisonization to some degree. Latin American countries generally allowed conjugal visits, and Mexico, India, Pakistan, and the Philippines all had penal institutions in which families were permitted to join the prisoners and live permanently on the prison grounds. The general reason given for these positive programs was simple humanitarianism, and while that is enough, they also have the effect of reducing the men's commitment to the prisoner subculture by increasing their involvement with their families.

At Iwahig Penal Colony in the Philippines, men could have their families join them or marry and form new families. They served the first one-fifth of their sentences in a maximum security facility for observation, and only those judged fit for open living were sent to Iwahig. The government not only completely equipped the families for subsistence farming while under sentence, but gave them land elsewhere on the island after the sentence was completed if they wished to continue in this pattern of life.[86]

In another article, Jewell describes Mexico's Tres Marias Penal Colony, which he believes to be one of the world's most humane prisons.[87] Other Mexican prisons sent men and women with very long sentences to Tres Marias if they had demonstrated adequate control over their behavior. Tres Marias had much the same structure as Iwahig, but in addition had an elaborate business economy. Men and women could work for a private industry that was located on the island, they could do subsistence farming, or they could set up businesses of their own. There was minimum supervision by the authorities and a humane pragmatism in the regulations. As an example, if two prisoners were married and one's sentence terminated, the other had to stay behind but was free to marry another prisoner. Presumably, the freed partner could also choose to remain in the colony to avoid breaking up the family unit.

## Structural Elements

While incarcerated in Norway's largest prison as a conscientious objector, Johan Galtung performed an interview, questionnaire, and participant observation study of the prison social system.[88] The article that grew out of this experience contains an insightful analysis of a dozen manifest and latent functions served by the prison. In addition to its comparative aspects, this study presents a convincing argument that accomplishing resocialization at the same time as meeting the other eleven functions served by the prison is structurally impossible. This theme is carried out in three different ways in three other studies.

McCleery analyzes the change from an authoritarian custody orientation to a liberal treatment stance at Oahu Prison in Hawaii.[89] Under the authoritarian system, information flowed vertically, with higher officials always knowing more than lower officials and all staff knowing more than prisoners. The information given to certain prisoners by the staff permitted these men to be the leaders of the prisoner subculture. The transition to a liberal administration was a gradual one, with much intrastaff conflict along the way. One of the first changes was to use disciplinary actions in a justice rather than a control framework, thus decreasing staff discretion and according prisoners due process rights.

Knowledge became democratized when rules, policies, and punishments were published. The establishment of an inmate council further undermined the traditional prisoner leaders and a group of younger prisoners with reform school upbringings took control of the prisoner population. As norms weakened, an increasing number of disputes were settled by force. The prison sank into anarchy and almost had a major riot.[90] Unfortunately, McCleery is less than clear about how equilibrium was restored, although he does mention some meetings between the warden and prisoners. In a footnote to a later version of this article, Donald Cressey mentions that a major riot broke out at the Oahu Prison in 1960, about five years after the period described by McCleery.[91]

Another approach to looking at the conflict produced by a change from custody to treatment within one institution would involve comparing two institutions, one oriented toward custody and the other toward treatment. Cressey did just that while working at the Center for Education and Research in Corrections of the University of Chicago. He found that the treatment-oriented institution protected prisoners more from tourist groups of outsiders, but subjected them to more ridicule than the staff did at the custody-oriented prison.[92] Even though the official policies of these two institutions were clear, the staffs still had to deal with the problem of a conflict of function. At the treatment-oriented institution, guards were expected to allow prisoners a wide range of self-determined behavior, but still enforce the rules, a complete impossibility. In a similar conflict, guards at the custody-oriented institution were expected to enforce the rules rigidly, yet they had to make many concessions to prisoners in order to obtain their cooperation (Sykes' corruption by reciprocity).[93]

At Camp Davis, a small prison camp in the California system, Oscar Grusky identified prisoner leaders via sociometric techniques and then compared them with nonleaders.[94] He found that the leaders were more prostaff than the followers and that they probably aided rather than hindered the therapeutic process, just the opposite of Schrag's findings at a maximum security facility. This difference between prisoner leaders and followers did not reach statistical significance under the treatment-oriented administration, but it strengthened greatly when a new custody-oriented camp supervisor took office. Leaders in the camp tended to become more prostaff as time spent in the institution increased, while followers became more antistaff over time.

The switch from treatment to custody led to a number of incidents including increased escapes, damage to state property, and the necessity of increased transfers of trouble-making prisoners out of the institution. As the rules became formalized and pressure on staff for staff enforcement increased, they experienced increased role conflict.[95] Grusky does not explain how this conflict was dealt with by the administration, nor does he relate what the final results of the change were. The reader is left hanging as to the details of the resolution of this conflict.

*Broader Theoretical Applications*

To the extent that an area of applied social science is isolated from general theory, knowledge in that area will tend to be descriptive and uninformed. Only when that applied area is linked to broader scientific concerns can the operation of the scientific mode of seeking knowledge reach its fullest potential. In the study of prison subcultures, one major dimension along which this has occurred is the comparison of prisons with other closed institutions in an attempt to build a general theory of total institutions. Two early examples of this movement are Cressey and Krassowski's comparison of American prisons and Soviet labor camps[96] and Garfinkel's study of degradation ceremonies.[97]

Cressey and Krassowski hypothesize that in order for the administration to control an American prison, most prisoners must be anomic or individualistic, and there must be a leadership structure among the prisoners that can be coopted. They set out to see whether inmates of Soviet prison camps had these same characteristics in a preview of Solzhenitsyn's *The Gulag Archipelago.*[98] Their conclusion is that these same conditions do obtain in the prison camps, though there are considerable differences in the details of both procedures and ideology. In the Soviet Union, inmate labor is emphasized more than in the United States, so much so that prisoners who do not work hard will starve. The split between "real" criminals, who are considered essentially innocent of offenses against the state, and political prisoners, who are the guilty ones to be oppressed in any way possible, is the crucial fact of the prisoner status structure. The camp administrator is able to make nonpolitical prisoners into leaders who have a stake in preserving the status quo and in the continuing oppression of the political prisoners.

Instead of a cross-cultural comparison of one type of institution, Garfinkel's analysis of degradation ceremonies links together different kinds of institutions, in this country or others. A status degradation ceremony is a segment of social interaction, not necessarily a formal ceremony, through which a person is demoted from his present status position to a lower one. In addition to the characteristics of the participant and the event itself, the degraded person must be separated from his or her place in the status structure. In our society, the ultimate degradation is a trial in court, and the final separation is incarceration in prison.

## The U-Shaped Curve of Prisonization

Stanton Wheeler empirically evaluated Clemmer's prisonization hypothesis using prisoners age sixteen through thirty in Washington's Monroe Reformatory.[99] His initial analysis confirmed Clemmer's findings, for the longer the men were confined, the more antistaff they became. Those men who were more involved in social relations with other prisoners became prisonized more quickly and more intensely than men who were relatively uninvolved. When prisonization was crosstabulated with phase of institutional career instead of years in prison, a U-shaped curve emerged. This was due to changes in high and medium conformity to staff expectations, for the percentage of antistaff prisoners continued to rise throughout the career phases the same as it did by years incarcerated on the present sentence. As a whole, men in the first six months and the last six months of their terms were more prostaff, while those in between were more proprisoner subculture.

This prostaff change toward the end of a prisoner's sentence may be interpreted as a resocialization effect. Highly involved prisoners also experience this effect, but to a smaller degree than prisoners who are relatively uninvolved with the prisoner subculture. Possibly, the prisoner subculture delays the impact of social rejection rather than solving any of the problems that derive from that rejection.[100] If so, these may become increasingly prominent as the release date approaches, and this may be the cause of the resocialization effect.

Another segment of Wheeler's research at Monroe (originally his doctoral dissertation) focused on differences in norms and perceptions between prisoners and staff. Staff and prisoners only agreed on the value of one of six items tested—therapeutic programs. In all six cases, the staff saw prisoners as being more antisocial than they were by their own reports. Likewise, in tests on staff expectation, prisoners saw them as being more antiprisoner than they actually were. Wheeler concludes that part of this mutual misperception is due to the visibility of a highly antistaff group of prisoner leaders who largely control the interaction between staff and prisoners because of their central position in the communications network.[101]

## Differential Opportunity and the Prisoner Subculture

Few scholars are aware that much of the brilliant theory contained in Cloward and Ohlin's *Delinquency and Opportunity*[102] was originally developed in Cloward's unpublished doctoral dissertation, "Social Control and Anomie: A Study of a Prison Community."[103] In this volume, Cloward united the anomie tradition of Durkheim and Merton with the subcultural tradition of Sutherland and the Chicago school of thought.[104] The anomie tradition described the effects of limited access to legitimate goals, and the subcultural tradition explained how deviant orientations to goal attainment developed in subcultural areas. In Cloward's concept of illegitimate means,[105] these traditions are united. Not only legitimate means, but illegitimate means may be differentially available to reach culturally prescribed goals. Illegitimate opportunity structures may replace legitimate ones in subcultural areas where legitimate means are in short supply. This situation produces a huge strain toward deviance. Where neither is available, or where an individual is a failure in both systems, modes of withdrawal such as drug abuse are common, as are incidents of violence.

Interviews with ninety prisoners in a large Army prison provided data with which to test this theory. The prisoners were interviewed five times at intervals of six weeks in a panel design. The prison publicized the goal of restoration to duty, but awarded this achievement to only about one in every fourteen prisoners. Would this limitation on legitimate opportunity produce increasing deviance and withdrawal? Cloward found that the number of conformists (of eighty-seven men) decreased from sixty at the first interview to thirty-one at the fifth interview. Ritualists who had maintained a commitment to the legitimate means while giving up the goals completely rose from fourteen to thirty men. Rebellion and retreatism also rose, as did innovation, but ritualism was the mode into which most men drifted if they gave up conformity.

In prison terminology, the "merchant," the "politician," and the "right guy" are all innovators who develop illegitimate means to reach the legitimate goals of wealth, power, and status, respectively. By regulating the availability of illegitimate means, the prison administration can determine the proportion of prisoners who will adopt these innovative roles. Administrators can also determine who becomes a prisoner leader by the distribution of favors to prisoners who display conservative attitudes and a propensity for accommodation. For the prisoners to whom access to this adaptation is closed, either withdrawal or aggression is adopted.

An additional contribution by Cloward is his theory of prison riots. He believes that a riot arises as a planned action by the prisoner leaders in reaction to a threat to their control over the other prisoners. In essence, they are demonstrating their power over the prisoner subculture and blackmailing the administration into restoring whatever privileges were originally taken away, undercutting their position and leading to a crisis of leadership. Riots occur when both legitimate *and* illegitimate means of reaching goals are closed off.[106]

# 2

# A Period of Maturation in Institutional Studies

## Studies of the Early 1960s

### The Concept of Total Institutions

In institutional sociology, the concept of the total institution inevitably brings to mind the name of Erving Goffman. His book *Asylums* is mostly about life in mental hospitals, but his introductory essay, "On the Characteristics of Total Institutions" relates mental hospitals to prisons, concentration camps, monasteries, orphanages, and many other organizations.[1] According to Goffman, total institutions are institutions in which all elements of human life occur in the same place and under the same authority. An individual in a total institution does everything with a large group of other inmates, all of whom are doing the same thing at the same time under a tight schedule imposed by some higher authority. All activities are rationally organized in the service of the institution's goals. The advantage of Goffman's concept is that it sensitizes us to the similarities and differences between these various institutions, thus forging a link between penology and general sociological theory.

Every page of Goffman's essay contains comments of interest to the student of prisons. Among the most valuable points are disculturation, mortifications, "looping," the privilege system, inmate adaptations, the "sad tale," release anxiety, the cycle of staff-inmate contact and withdrawal, and differences among total institutions. The degradation ceremonies described elsewhere by Garfinkel[2] are only the beginning of a long series of mortifications.

According to Goffman, long-term mortifications include the circulation of embarrassing facts about inmates among staff members, who may bring them up at any time, and contamination of the self by undesired material items and social relations. In looping, the inmate's reaction to an institutional abasement is used by staff as an excuse for additional abasements.[3]

Inmates are reoriented by these abasements and other techniques to the life of the institution. They are induced through a complex organization of privileges and punishments to conform to the house rules, the institutional regulations. Their secondary adjustments to these conditions make up the inmate social system. Goffman concentrates more on individual adjustments to the total institution than on the adjustments made in common through the inmate social system. As he sees it, inmates may withdraw from the situation, adopt an intransigent line, colonize the institution, or convert to the staff's world view.[4]

23

The colonizers make themselves so much at home in the institution that they may go to great lengths to avoid release.

Inmates try to reduce their stigmatization within the institution by telling "sad tales" that claim their innocence, healthiness, and so forth, and explain that they are where they are by accident. Their sense of exile and wasted time is acute. As they near their time of release, they become increasingly sensitive to the stigma of being an ex-inmate when they return to free society and to the fact that the disculturation they have suffered has decreased their ability to cope with free society.[5]

There is a constant tension in staff relations with inmates between a caste model of social relations and normal human interaction. The caste model demands staff withdrawal from inmates with reciprocal negative stereotypes. In contrast, staff members feel a strain toward normalizing their interaction with at least a few of the more appealing inmates. According to Goffman, they react to this conflict by cycling between contact and withdrawal.[6] As contact increases, a staff member becomes increasingly sympathetic toward an inmate. Eventually, he gets in too deep, gets "burnt," and withdraws into the safety of the caste model of staff-inmate relations.

Goffman claims that these and other processes are common to all total institutions, but he admits that there are differences between them. He analyzes these differences along three dimensions: degree of role differentiation, mode of recruitment, and permeability.[7] Role differentiation refers to the division of the inmate population into differing but interlocking roles. Some total institutions have a much more fully developed inmate subculture than others. Inmates volunteer to enter some institutions but must be forced to join others. Permeability refers to the degree of contact between inmates and free people from outside the institution. As compared with other total institutions, prisons are high on role differentiation and forced recruitment but low on permeability. In recent years, however, permeability has sharply increased.

Goffman's view of total institutions is negative. He does not expect even treatment-oriented mental hospitals to do much rehabilitating, to say nothing of prisons. *Asylums* has some critical weaknesses, including the looseness of Goffman's empirical observations, his confusion of literature with social science, his fuzzy view of the human personality, and his questionable use of total institutions as an ideal type. In addition, the basic elements of his definition of total institutions are somewhat ambiguous and do not clearly differentiate this concept from other constructs current in the behavioral sciences.[8] These points notwithstanding, *Asylums* introduces a valuable comparative perspective and contributes a number of conceptual tools to the analysis of prisoner subcultures. The general implication of Goffman's work is that many of the negative effects of prisons are due to structural properties that are common to all total institutions, not just to prisons in general, to specific prisons, or to the actions of individual administrators.

A careful typological comparison of total institutions with villages and cities was carried out by Hillery[9] two years after the publication of *Asylums*. He identified nineteen traits as major components in the folk village and the city, but found that prisons and mental hospitals were similar to them on only three. To Hillary, the total institution is a system containing a bureaucratic staff and a localized collectivity, with the former compelling the latter to behave in certain ways in order to achieve specified ends. Thus defined, total institutions were similar to villages and cities in degree of interpersonal contact, member awareness of the unit as a unit, and longevity. Among the more obvious differences, Hillary emphasized dissimilarities in the use of space, familial organization, and cooperation between members. Out of this discussion, Hillary concludes that total institutions are *not* communities; they are complex organizations. On the basis of this analysis, he fully supports Goffman's concept of the total institution and his model of their functioning characteristics.

## Brief Studies of Attitudes and Adjustment

In the early 1960s, studies of prisoner attitudes, personal adjustment, and sexual behavior continued to appear. For the first time, these were outnumbered by the study of the prisoner subculture as a social system. The studies of attitudes and adjustment need not be individually mentioned, except for an unpublished doctoral dissertation by Rosenblatt.[10] This author compared the effects of mild, moderate, and severe punishment upon matched groups of prisoners at Rikers Island Penitentiary in New York. He found that mild or moderate punishment did not improve prisoner attitudes toward authority-oriented behavior and that severe punishment actually led to significantly more negative attitudes and behavior.

## Sex in Prison

Reports of prison sexual behavior in Canada, Illinois and Mississippi were added to the literature in the early 1960s. Huffman[11] indicated that sexual practices in Illinois prisons had not changed since the time of Clemmer's work (see Chapter 1) and that young offenders often developed schizophrenic reactions to homosexual attacks. Huffman found in a five-year period that 786 young men age eighteen and under were admitted to *adult* Illinois prisons. Some of these boys were as young as fourteen or fifteen years old.[12]

At "a Canadian reformatory located in the Midwest," boys age sixteen and older were mixed with adult first-time offenders.[13] In this study of a prisoner population of nearly one thousand inmates, twenty to forty men were known to be "keeping" younger boys in sexual relationships called "lugging." The boys exchanged sexual favors for consumer goods and protection from exploitation by other prisoners. Since anyone caught in a homosexual act was immediately segregated, the known total of fifty to seventy-five overt homosexuals must be considered a considerable underestimate.

The Mississippi State Penitentiary at Parchman helped to combat homosexuality by legalizing conjugal relations between husband and wife, which Hopper first publicized in an article in the *Journal of Criminal Law, Criminology and Police Science*.[14] Hopper later expanded his analysis of the program into a monograph,[15] and if we can believe him, it is one prison program that is inexpensive, useful, and without any negative effects. Since no pretest and posttest data are available, we cannot tell what the actual impact of the conjugal visit program was on prison homosexuality when it was instituted.

### Prisoner Roles and Social Structure

Norman Hayner, founder of the University of Washington tradition of penological studies, has continued to be active in the field down through the years, though his publications have not always been directly relevant to the subject of prisoner subcultures. For five years, he was a member of the Washington State Board of Prison Terms and Paroles, during which he interviewed over six thousand prisoners. As a result of this experience, he developed a classification of five types of offenders: the con forger, alcoholic forger, "rapo," "heavy," and "graduate."[16] In this model, the "con forger" was serving time for forgery or grand larceny by check. The alcoholic forger was defined the same, except that he had less criminal skills and wrote bad checks while drunk. The "rapo" was incarcerated for sexual relations with children and had no other criminal offenses. "Heavy" offenders were older violence-prone property offenders, while "graduates" were younger property offenders with reform school backgrounds.

Hayner took a 20 percent systematic random sample of parole board sentence cases from a two-and-one-half-year span beginning January 1, 1955 to illustrate the relative numbers and characteristics of his five offender types. More significant for our purposes, he cross-tabulated his types with Schrag's prisoner social roles (see Chapter 1). "Con forgers" were almost all "right guys" or "politicians"; alcoholic forgers were mostly "right guys"; "rapos" were nearly all "square johns" or "dings"; and "heavys" and "graduates" were primarily "right guys," with a smaller number being "outlaws." More than a third of the cases Hayner reviewed were residuals that did not fit into any of his five offender types. These residuals were largely "square johns" or "right guys."[17] Seen in a larger perspective, Hayner's work suggests that the assignment of prisoners to roles in the subculture is not random, nor is it based merely on personality characteristics. Preprison criminal career is an important determinant of prisoner role occupancy.

One of the more informal roles that is mentioned in all intensive studies of prisoner subcultures is the "rat" or "snitch." Elmer Johnson studied fifty "rats" who had been considered for transfer out of a prison where they had been openly accused of carrying tales to the administration.[18] He notes that the prisoner subculture uses the "rats" to dramatize the loyalty of other prisoners to the convict code and as a sponge for free-floating aggression that might otherwise erupt into collective actions that would upset the power balance in the prison. Some "rats" had betrayed the prisoner subculture after being assimilated into it, but others never had pretended to accept the convict code. Both received high levels of aggression as a result of their reputation as "rats." Interestingly, "rats" of all types greatly reduced their number of infractions after being labeled, presumably to court official protection from other prisoners.

The topic of staff influences on prisoner role occupancy was treated by several articles published in the early 1960s. The Louisiana State Penitentiary's change from a custody to a treatment orientation in the 1950s was described by Mouledous.[19] He traces this change and demonstrates how each system produced just the reverse of what it intended (which is often the case in the sociological literature—that is, we can always expect to find that something produces its opposite). Under the traditional Louisiana system, prisoners performed almost all staff functions. There were only fifty paid staff members to supervise 18,000 acres divided into eight prison camps. Prisoners became gun-carrying guards, bookkeepers, secretaries, and practically everything else. In return, skilled trustees were freed from most custodial requirements, allowed limited home visits and unofficial conjugal visits, and given a wide range of material rewards. The less-favored prisoners were little more than slaves (called gunmen) who toiled long hours in the fields. An intermediate role was also created by the staff. Analogous to the foreman, this role was filled by gunmen who showed they could be trusted, but not to the extent of the trustees. They received smaller, but still substantial rewards, including permission for cooking, drinking, gambling, and homosexual affairs. This system of three classes was very real to the prisoners, and was maintained by the reward hierarchy, which was adequate to motivate the entire status system. Prisoners were socialized to work hard for their rewards, in a fashion similar to life in free society.

When the change was instituted, the new administration increased the staff to four hundred, emphasized a treatment ideology, gave away most of the privileges of the old system as rights that all prisoners shared, and banned the rest of the privileges as immoral. Did prisoners respond to this treatment orientation with better performance? Apparently they did not. Farm production decreased because there were not sufficient rewards to encourage hard work. To gain any cooperation at all, lower-level staff had to join with the prisoners in a system of illegal "conniving." This practice reinforced the prisoners' antisocial attitudes ("staff members are all crooks") and removed any administration control over prisoner role occupancy. Prisoners now achieved status by exploiting each other in a classic prisoner subculture rather than by pleasing staff through prosocial behavior and economic productivity. Mouledous comments that either an egalitarian or an authoritarian prison administration will tend to turn control of the penal environment over to the prisoners. Only through a vigorous distribution of material rewards and other privileges on the basis of prosocial behavior can a prison administration hope to make a prisoner subculture go its way.[20]

Support for Mouledous' position comes from the Draper Correctional Center in Alabama, where Warden John Watkins pioneered a technique for turning the prisoner subculture into a prosocial influence.[21] At Draper, Watkins rewarded prosocial behavior by promoting prisoners to influential positions. In response, prisoners even worked to become "dog boys" who tracked escapees. Watkins' technique was to identify the "right guys," whom he called the "solid convicts." He then singled them out for special attention, manipulated their environment to isolate them from other prisoners, and convinced them that he was a dependable father-friend. Once the "solid cons" were on his side, swinging the other prisoners away from a completely antisocial stance was fairly easy.

At Draper in the 1960s as at the Louisiana State Penitentiary in the 1940s, a strong reward system allowed the administration to have a considerable degree of control over the prisoner subculture. The unanswered question that remains, however, is whether Warden Watkins was able to exercise such control without violating standards for prisoner treatment now established by the courts?

## The Beginning of the Importation Model–Indigenous Origin Theory Debate

Cloward, Sykes, and others held that the prisoner subculture was largely a response to conditions within the prison, or the pains of imprisonment, so to speak. This view is the indigenous origin theory of prisoner subcultures, which remained essentially unchallenged until 1962 when Irwin and Cressey first published their opposing theory, the importation model.[22] They point out that the convict code is part of a more general criminal code that exists outside the prison and is imported into the prison from the streets by newly sentenced felons. There is also a more general utilitarian and manipulative "hard core," lower-class culture in free society, from which most criminals are drawn. The indigenous theory, they say, has more to do with the maintenance of the prisoner subculture than with its origin.

In fact, according to Irwin and Cressey, there are really three prisoner subcultures, not one. These are the thief subculture, the convict subculture, and the conventional subculture. The thief subculture is inhabited by various professional criminals who share with their friends, who are loyal to other thieves, and who do not seek leadership within the prison. In contrast, the members of the convict subculture manipulate others for their own gain and seek maximum power and status while incarcerated. Conventional subculture people are "square johns" who bring the legitimate culture of the streets into the institution with them.[23]

This challenge to the theoretical hegemony of the indigenous origin model was not long unanswered. Roebuck was quick to point out that Irwin and Cressey offered no real evidence for their model, that their theory was contradicted by much of the penological literature, and that it was inconsistent with his own prison experience and research.[24] Roebuck argues, for example, that the prison experience is what teaches thieves how to "do easy time" and that the "right guy" image of nonmanipulative sharing is a prisoner-created myth. Some support for Roebuck's position was shortly forthcoming from a study of a hospital serving imprisoned narcotics addicts by Tittle and Tittle. In the first of a long series of reports derived from this study, the Tittles reported that belief in the convict code increased directly with time incarcerated for first offenders and that the more prisoners accepted the convict code, the less they subjectively experienced the pains of imprisonment,[25] and the less likely they were to reach a satisfactory therapeutic adjustment.[26] Not all the predicted relationships were found at statistically significant levels, but the general trend of the data was supportive of the indigenous origin theory.

*More About the U-Shaped Curve and Prisoner Roles*

At approximately the time that Stanton Wheeler was studying prisoner social roles at the Monroe Reformatory in the state of Washington (see Chapter 1 for a discussion of Wheeler's research), Peter Garabedian was doing the same thing at Washington's State Penitentiary at Walla Walla. While Garabedian's doctoral dissertation was never published,[27] the results of his research were disseminated during the 1960s in various journal articles and papers given at professional meetings.

Garabedian had administered questionnaires to a random sample of 380 prisoners and an availability sample of 141 staff members. Both groups evaluated five contrived situations derived from prison life. Staff members showed a high degree of consensus on their evaluations of these situations, and this consensus was used as a standard against which the scores of individual prisoners were compared. This comparison yielded an estimate of prisoner conformity to staff norms.[28]

The prisoners also responded to a set of fifteen attitude statements in a Likert scaling format. These statements were divided into five groups, with each containing three items that were designed to identify one of Schrag's role types (see Chapter 1). Garabedian was able to assign 73 percent of the prisoners to a particular role (the remaining men gave mixed responses).[29] The occupants of the different roles had systematically different delinquent and criminal records before entering the institution and equally different behavior within the prison. For example, none of the "square johns" had three or more institutional infractions, as compared with 14 percent of the "politicians," 16 percent of the "right guys," and 22 percent of the "outlaws." Exactly the reverse order, ranging from 62 percent of the "outlaws" to 84 percent of the "square johns," was found for participation in staff-sponsored programs. In short, those prisoners who were already most strongly committed to the conventional society were the ones most likely to join groups designed to change deviants into conventionals.[30]

Garabedian also analyzed social contacts by role types. For all roles, he found the modal pattern was one of low social contacts with both staff and fellow prisoners, which supports Clemmer's picture of prisoners as socially isolated individuals. Very few prisoners of any role type were high on staff contact and low on contact with other prisoners. For "square johns" and "politicians," the second most popular social pattern was to be high on both staff and prisoner contacts, but for "right guys" and "outlaws," the second most popular pattern was to be high on contact with other prisoners but low on contact with staff.[31]

At the time of this study, prisoners commonly believed that one way to gain a speedy release from confinement was through "programming"—that is, joining various programs in order to "look good" at the next parole board hearing. For the "square john" and the "politician," this practice presented little problem, since both were often seen in association with staff personnel. The "right guy" could hardly do so and retain his reputation. How could he "program" and still be recognized as a "right guy?" The answer was to start an inmate-sponsored therapy group for which participation did not have prostaff implications. Garabedian found that "right guys" were almost twice as likely to join an inmate-sponsored group as a staff-sponsored program. "Outlaws" were also infrequent in staff-sponsored groups, but almost nonexistent in the inmate-sponsored group.[32]

Garabedian replicated Wheeler's crosstabulation of prosocial attitudes (conformity to staff norms) and prison career phase (early, middle, late) and found exactly the same pattern. Forty-one percent of the men in the early phase were high on conformity to staff norms, as compared with 21 percent in the middle phase and 41 percent again in the late phase. When this crosstabulation was calculated separately for each prisoner role type, only the "square johns" and "right guys" showed true U-shaped curves. The "outlaws" declined in conformity to staff norms at each successive stage of incarceration, thus approximating the prisonization model of prisoner socialization. "Politicians" were stable and relatively prostaff throughout their careers, and "dings" gradually improved at each successive stage. Variability in conformity to staff norms among the role types was least during the long, middle phase of incarceration,

31

which thus indicates a rise in the consensual support of the convict code during this period of greatest distance from the free society. Isolation was the rule in the early phase of incarceration. The fact that it dissolved into a consensus around proprisoner norms in the middle phase is supportive of the indigenous origin theory of the prisoner subculture.[33]

## Three Case Studies of the 1960s

At this point in the history of studies of prisoner subcultures, enough research reports began being published to make a basis for comparison and generalization. In this section, we will discuss three of these studies that are all book-length manuscripts.

The first study we shall consider is reported in *Pentonville, A Sociological Study of an English Prison* by Terrence and Pauline Morris.[34] Pentonville is a large, overcrowded maximum security prison located in an urban area of Great Britain. Although not all the sentences are long, the prisoners there are generally recidivists and often severely inadequate in their social functioning. Morris and Morris used nonparticipant observation and interviews to collect their data, which resulted in a qualitative rather than a quantitative picture of prison life. For example, the sexual behavior of prisoners was judged to follow the pattern described by Clemmer (see Chapter 1) almost exactly, but a percentage breakdown of the normal, abnormal, and quasi-abnormal types was not computed.

The convict code was also quite standard, and Morris and Morris believe that this characteristic was more due to its problem-solving qualities than to negative selection. They favor the indigenous origin theory over an importation interpretation in which the prisoner subculture is largely an outgrowth of the pooled criminal backgrounds of the men.[35] The economic underlife at Pentonville was much less standard. There was no equivalent of Sykes' "merchant" role (see Chapter 1 for a discussion of the various roles defined by Sykes). Commercial transactions were mostly carried out in tobacco, rather than by direct barter, and followed the principle of balanced reciprocity. The "barons" who sold tobacco and loaned it out at interest often had it smuggled in to them in much the same fashion as marijuana and other drugs are smuggled into American prisons today. "Fiddling," the supplying of food, services, or miscellaneous goods at cost, was the approved method of what Hayner and Ash (see Chapter 1) called "conniving."[36]

The "robber baron" was a violent man, sometimes a tobacco dealer, but often just a bully. He was sort of a combination of the "gorilla" and "merchant" roles described by Sykes. This man was a leader of sorts, but was feared rather than respected by other prisoners. A more ideal leader was the "Robin Hood," who was strongly committed to the convict code of prisoner reciprocity and noncooperation with staff. Because he was willing to fight to uphold the code, he was a troublemaker from the staff's viewpoint, but a hero to fellow prisoners and an altruist to Morris and Morris.[37]

It's a long way from urban England to rural California, where Rudoff studied prisoners at the Deuel Vocational Institution. This facility houses young adult delinquents and older prisoners judged to be relatively prosocial. It is fairly well staffed with treatment personnel and equipment for vocational training. Many goods and services that are in short supply in other institutions are abundant at Deuel. Rudoff studied this unusual institution via formal and informal questionnaires and interviews, direct observation, and the general, well-known method of Weber's *verstehen* (empathetic understanding). Rudoff's work is reported in the unpublished doctoral dissertation "Prison Inmates: An Involuntary Association."[38] This study is sophisticated and descriptive, but not nearly as quantitative as most prison studies of the 1960s and 1970s.

Three topics treated by Rudoff should be considered modest advances. These are (1) the description of the hard core prisoners and their differentiation from other prisoners, (2) a cursory look at the Chicano and black groups within the prisoner subculture, and (3) a discussion of the economic underlife of the prisoners. At Deuel, only about one-fifth of the prisoners comprised the hard core of men who identified fully with the convict code. The remaining four-fifths often supported the code in public, but privately believed in the values of "straight" society. The hard-core prisoners were more likely to be young, property offenders, black or Mexican-American, and with more previous commitments than the other prisoners. All prisoners tended to equate manhood with manipulation, aggression, and exploitation, but the hard-core prisoners did so much more than the other men.

Quoting some of the attitude statements used by Rudoff to show how differently hard-core and other prisoners responded to them is worthwhile. For example, 90 percent of the hard cores and only 35 percent of the others agreed that "Where ever one is, the strong take from the weak—that's the way life is." The statement "In an institution, an inmate can't trust anybody, not even his friends" was agreed with by 67 percent of the hard cores and 25 percent of the others. As a final example, 86 percent of the hard cores but only 10 percent of the other prisoners agreed that "If an inmate has a chance to beat the system without getting caught, he should take it."[39]

Most of the studies of prisoner subcultures published before the mid-1960s paid little attention to the minority groups that lived within the walls. Prisoner subcultures as they were known in the literature were Caucasian. For this reason, even the cursory treatment of racial differences in prison by Rudoff represents a contribution to social science. He emphasizes the machismo theme among Mexican-Americans, but does not talk very much about their social organization in prison. He found that they were relatively unsuccessful at recreating their gang structure and had loosely connected cliques that joined together only when involved in a riot or similar collective behavior. In contrast, blacks stayed isolated from each other most of the time and were more interested in improving themselves as individuals than in maintaining their group structure.[40]

The underlife at Deuel was limited by the considerable success the administration had in preventing contraband from entering the institution. Drugs obtained or made from institution supplies, homemade weapons, and pornography written by prisoners were the most interesting categories of contraband. Drugs were obtained from the hospital (tranquilizers and other pills), kitchen (nutmeg), or other parts of the prison (gasoline, airplane glue, carbontetrachloride). Marijuana and heroin were only sporadically available. Most prisoners had a "shiv" or perhaps a "zip gun." They were owned more for self-protection than for offensive use. Typed copies of pornographic stories circulated on a rental basis and reaped large profits—in cigarettes and other commodities—for their writers. Cash was very limited, with perhaps as little as three hundred dollars circulating in the entire prisoner population at one time; thus cigarettes were a major money substitute.[41]

Rudoff collected much of his data while he was a research associate in the Inmate-Staff Community Project, which was later discussed in detail in *C-Unit: Search for Community in Prison* by Studt, Messinger, and Wilson,[42] as well as a subsequent journal article by Wilson.[43] Because the C-Unit project was a therapeutic change-oriented project rather than a scientific study of the prisoner subculture, it is not directly relevant to the task at hand, but it does include some valuable material. Studt, Messinger, and Wilson recognize the importance of the prisoner subculture in the resocializing process. As a result of their experience, they conclude that the prisoner subculture need not be a barrier to resocialization, and to make it more prosocial, staff and prisoners must work together on projects of interest to both groups and develop a unitary normative system through this interactive process.

In Wilson's article, he compares C-Unit with two other housing units at Deuel, an honor and nonhonor unit. Men in the honor unit received more privileges than men in the nonhonor unit, but both bureaucratically controlled units contrasted with the participative political process in C-Unit. In general, the prisoners exposed to C-Unit's participative program formed closer social relations with both staff members and their fellow prisoners. Wilson concludes that task performance will be little modified by participative management unless the subordinates (prisoners in this study) are allowed to exercise a high degree of discretion in their behavior.

The third case study to be examined in this section is another dissertation produced by a student of Clarence Schrag at the University of Washington. Rothbart's study of the Reformatory of Monroe lay unpublished for a decade, but has now been reprinted by R & E Research Associates.[44]

Rothbart started out by soliciting cooperation from a reasonably representative sample of 356 prisoners. Only 48 percent completed the first in a series of three questionnaires, and 26 percent of this group were lost by the third questionnaire, for a final return rate of 35 percent. A large number of variables were measured in these questionnaires and the analysis of the results is complex. Unfortunately, the small number of cases (125) and the low final response rate leave much of the author's effort at data interpretation open to question. The design should be praised despite this weakness, for few panel studies are conducted in correctional research and the advantages of a true process analysis over a cross-sectional design with its mere inference of process are considerable. A reasonable degree of case mortality is to be expected in any panel design. Rothbart did well in limiting this mortality to 26 percent. Where he fell down was in his loss of 52 percent of the cases on the first questionnaire.

Rothbart found that prisoners who engaged in protesting behavior were careful to defy prison personnel in such a way as to avoid a strong counter-attack. They were very dominance-oriented, and tended to perceive staff as not sympathetic to prisoners. Protestors did not like their fellow prisoners any more than nonprotesters, but they identified more strongly with them. A moderate degree of concern about negotiating with staff for rewards led to decreased protest, but extreme concern about it increased protest behavior.

## Comparative Studies of the 1960s

In this section, we will consider a number of studies, mostly published as journal articles, that have particular value for the comparative study of prisoner subcultures.

### Prisoner Subcultures in Five Federal Institutions

We begin with Glaser's classic study, *The Effectiveness of a Prison and Parole System.*[45] Glaser studied five federal institutions in 1959: Leavenworth, Terre Haute, Milan, Chillicothe, and Ashland. The first three housed adult criminals with an average age around thirty, and in the last two were incarcerated young men with an average age near twenty. The order in which the institutions are listed above denotes their rank in the seriousness of the offense for which sample members were incarcerated, with Leavenworth containing the most serious offenders.

Most of Glaser's work is an evaluation study, but the within-institutions panels were asked some questions on prisoner subcultures in a lengthy question-naire administered verbally. Some prisoners in each of the five institutions were selected into one of three panels—entrance, mid-term, and near-release—which correspond to Wheeler's institutional phases on the U-shaped curve (see Chapter 1). In addition, the entrance panel was interviewed in their fourth and sixth months of incarceration. This complex design permitted comparisons between institutions and between phases of institutionalization at one point in time or developmentally for the entrance panel by comparing the initial, fourth-month, and sixth-month interviews.

Glaser shows a comprehensive grasp of the literature on penology and relates it effectively to his own findings as he goes along. The superiority of the design of the study was limited only by severe deficiencies in the techniques used in the field. The interviewers were not sufficiently differentiated from staff personnel to give prisoners confidence that their responses would be kept anonymous. The effect of this was to keep prisoners from giving honest answers to some of the more delicate questions. While separating reality from respondent biases in situations like this one is difficult, in Glaser's case the total pattern of the evidence suggests that his findings are valid in general though not in specific details.

The data analysis in *The Effectiveness of a Prison and Parole System* leads to a number of general theoretical statements: Prisoners, particularly the older men, are more likely to isolate themselves from other prisoners than to join the prisoner society wholeheartedly. For very young prisoners, the reverse may be true. Prior incarceration and the heterogeneity of the prisoner population also correlate with the voluntary isolation of prisoner from prisoner. There is a U-shaped curve in which voluntary isolation decreases in the middle phase of imprisonment and rises again near release, which is consistent with Wheeler's findings at Monroe.[46]

Advice is often given from one prisoner to another, with the giver tending to be older than the receiver. When trouble occurs between prisoners working on an institutional job, the job is likely to be one involving many men who were rejected for job assignments elsewhere, a great deal of contact with prisoners in general, a large number of prisoners assigned to that particular job, and the availability of items or services that other prisoners desire to obtain through the contraband network. Dependence of one prisoner on another for material aid and psychological support increases throughout the period of incarceration, but dependence for protection of self or property decreases. This aid comes primarily through a few friends rather than through larger social units in the prisoner subculture. Prisoners have a strong interest in staying out of trouble while in the institution and generally have aspirations to reach socially accepted goals via legitimate means. There is a condition of what Cloward called "pluralistic ignorance,"[47] in which prisoners see each other as being more antisocial than they actually are.[48]

Glaser also developed a number of propositions about prisoner-staff relations. An authoritarian staff depresses staff-prisoner interaction. The more it is depressed, the more prisoners place a high value on unusual access to staff information. Depressed staff-prisoner interaction and depressed prisoner-prisoner interaction vary together. Prisoners seem to be influenced by the same kinds of staff behavior that influence people on the streets: fairness and predictability, friendliness, and respect for the other's rights. Positive cycling in prisoner-staff relations is enhanced by comprehensive and nonritualized staff contacts. Staff members who believe in a prisoner's potential for rehabilitation are more likely to have a reformative influence on him. This effect is maximized if the staff member shows interest or gives assistance in ways that go beyond the minimum standards of his or her job description.[49]

These propositions aspire to being valid for prisons in general. Are they really contributions to a general theory of prison behavior? Being based on a careful comparison of five institutions strengthens their claim considerably. If Glaser has approached the prisoner subculture from a number of methodological perspectives rather than the structured interview format, and if he had gathered a wider range of data, he might have succeeded in creating a comprehensive theory with a wide range of validity.

Almost as an afterthought, Glaser created a prison panel supplement that included prisoner respondents selected from fourteen institutions. Because of the limitations on time and funding at this late stage of the project, Glaser did not fully develop the possibilities inherent in his design. He found that older prisoners were lower than younger men on the criminality, criminal identification, and inmate loyalty scales. Time spent in prison affected inmate loyalty more than the other two scales, which leads to the conclusion that prison experience produces specific prison adaptations more than it does general criminalization. Esteem for staff was inversely related to procriminal orientation, but not to inmate loyalty, which shows the other side of the coin.[50]

In this survey, Glaser also replicated Garabedian's operational measure of Schrag's prisoner role types that was described earlier in this chapter. He found that 87 percent of the men scored high on the scale items for at least one of the role types, but most of these were high on more than one. Only 34 percent were high on a single role type. Aside from the possibility of methodological inadequacies, his findings suggest that the role types are overlapping, bell-shaped distributions of attitudes rather than discrete types. The men who were high on only a single role scale were 304 "square johns," 178 "outlaws," 112 "right guys," and 145 "politicians." Their characteristics followed Schrag's model (see Chapter 1) quite well and support his findings more than Garabedian's formulation of scales for identifying prisoner role types.[51]

*Scandinavian Studies*

Thomas Mathieson spent a year of participant observation at Ila, an institution for mentally abnormal, but not insane, criminals in Norway. Ila is a small, medium security institution with a strong treatment orientation. Its capacity is only 110 prisoners, for whom 80 staff are provided. Some of the men there are thought to be "psychopaths," while others are considered neurotic or feeble-minded. All have sentences of about five years, but most are paroled before serving their full sentences.

There was little inmate cohesion at Ila, according to the findings of Mathieson's study.[52] Instead of adopting the convict code, the prisoners largely accepted the cultural system of the prison staff. Prisoner opposition to staff behavior was based on the argument that staff members did not conform to their own norms, rather than on the concept of antisocial rebellion of the prisoner subculture. Mathieson termed this behavior "censoriousness." Through the careful use of censoriousness, prisoners could force staff members to adhere closely to the regulations, thus reducing their discretionary powers and largely substituting the rule of law for the rule of men. Mathieson concluded that the study of a large sample of prisons might show an inverse relationship between censoriousness and the strength of the prisoner subculture.

Most authors would be happy to stop at this point, but Mathieson goes further. He develops theoretical principles and then compares prisons to mental hospitals and the family in order to gain a wider comprehension of the uses of censoriousness as the "defense of the weak." He hypothesizes that censorious-ness increases to the extent that prisoners see themselves as being in a weak bargaining position in their battles with staff members. It will also increase as the sense of honor among the prisoner group decreases and to the extent that a criminal subcultural tradition is lacking in the larger society (as it is in Norway).[53] Brief discussions of industrial workers, mental hospital inmates, and children in families suggest that these principles may have a wider range of validity than the limited universe of correctional institutions.

A truly comparative study was performed by Cline in a sample of fifteen correctional institutions scattered over Norway, Sweden, Denmark, and Finland.[54] Data collection was by questionnaires that were reproduced in four languages. The percentage of prisoners estimating that at least three-quarters of their fellow men would approve of opposing the staff in two of three hypothetical situations varied from 78 percent down to 28 percent. Prisoner opposition was then correlated with median age at first arrest, percentage of prisoners with a previous commitment to an institution for children, percentage with a previous commitment to an adult institution, and level of institutional social deprivation (one of the pains of imprisonment). The correlations that Cline obtained were $-.80$ for age at first arrest, .49 for juvenile commitments, .73 for adult commitments, and $-.36$ for institutional social deprivation.[55]

In Cline's sample, youth institutions had the highest level of opposition to the staff, although this finding is somewhat misleading because the treatment characteristics of the institutions varied greatly. His overall findings may be taken to support the importation over the indigenous origin model of prisoner subcultures. Institutions in which prisoners had the greatest amount of previous criminal experience were the ones in which the highest levels of opposition to the staff existed. There was a tendency for the more depriving institutions to have less antistaff prisoners, which is just the opposite of what would be expected under the indigenous origin theory.[56] Possibly, the social deprivations measured by Cline were not experienced as crucial by the prisoners, but the more likely conclusion is that the indigenous origin theory does not apply very well to Scandinavian prisons.

### Life in a Canadian Reformatory

W.E. Mann was a volunteer chaplain for eleven months at Guelph Reformatory in Ontario. This experience later led to the idea of doing a sociological study of the prisoner community at Guelph. Mann's study depended on his memories of experiences within the reformatory plus detailed interviews, some of which were as long as ten hours, with thirty prisoners. At the time of the study, most Guelph men were under age twenty-one, a quarter were between twenty-one and twenty-nine, and a tenth were age thirty and over. The majority of the prisoners had served three or more sentences before coming to Guelph. Mann's preliminary conclusions were published in 1964 without identifying the institution studied.[57]

After a careful rethinking of the data, he published *Society Behind Bars: A Sociological Scrutiny of Guelph Reformatory* in 1967.[58] In this volume, Mann establishes himself as one of the most astute observers of prisoner subcultures in the history of penology. Mann understands that since most prisoners come from the lower classes, they are accustomed to many of the kinds of social interaction that normally occur in the prison. Some of the settings in prison life are also familiar. For example, social interaction during recreation periods in the "yard" closely approximates gang behavior on the street corner.

In his earlier report, Mann linked "lugging" specifically to homosexual behavior. Now, in an exciting observation pregnant with theoretical implications, Mann reports that "lugging" only occasionally goes as far as kissing. Although some "lugging" relationships do lead to overt homosexuality, others are characterized by a father-son relationship.[59] This finding is reminiscent of the pseudo-families created by incarcerated women and is the only direct link in the literature between the socio-sexual forms of behavior in male and female correctional institutions.

Two other high points of *Society Behind Bars* are Mann's description of the prisoner economic system and the social roles hierarchically arranged in the status structure. Economic transactions at Guelph were carried out with "bales" of tobacco. Street money was in short supply, and even a few dollars enhanced the social status of a prisoner. Again following the norms of lower-class street life, economic transactions were rarely planned, but were impulsive and informally organized. To be successful in the economic world of "wheeling and dealing," a prisoner needed to have good social status and contacts, the opportunity to obtain contraband items, and the willingness to take risks in order to make a profit. When Mann observes that one reason the upper-class prisoners prefer to gamble with "bales" of tobacco is because they can easily out-smart "fish" and "goofs,"[60] he is recognizing the central dynamic through which societies became organized: The structuring of conditions by the upper classes in such a way as to facilitate their continued and increased dominance over the lower classes.

The stratification system at Guelph was rather fluid due to high prisoner turnover, but six classes of prisoners were clearly recognized by Mann's respondents. "Real wheels," comprising about 3 percent of the Guelph men, were at the top. They were followed by "fifth floormen" (3 percent), "wheelers and dealers" (10 to 15 percent), "solid cons" (15 to 20 percent), "goofs" (40 to 45 percent), and "rats" (5 to 10 percent). Men being "lugged" and men with very short terms were not included in this more stable status system.[61]

The role played by the "real wheels" was found to be similar to upper-class behavior in straight society, "solid cons" to the middle class, and "goofs" to the working class. The "real wheels" were characterized by higher than average intelligence, size, strength, boldness, social contacts, and self-confidence. They often were "lugging" a younger prisoner. Like the members of the upper-middle class on the streets, "wheelers and dealers" were intensely upwardly mobile— that is, sacrificing anything to move into the upper class but being unable to do so because they were always overdoing their efforts. "Fifth floor men" worked in the administration tower, which gave them power because of their access to staff and administrative information. This same access made them suspected of not being loyal to the prisoner subculture and left their status rather ambiguous. "Solid cons" were loyal to the convict code, but also had to maintain a certain style of life and acceptance by the in-group in order to retain "solid con" status. In contrast, "goofs" did not have the necessary characteristics to be accepted as "solid." They were exploited in various ways, just like the lower class on the streets, though they were rarely subjected to the violence or social ostracism directed toward "rats." "Rats" and those known to have sexually attacked children were the criminals of the prisoner subculture at Guelph and often had to be locked up in a jail within the reformatory for their own safety. They were considered socially dead and would never rise again.[62]

### Other Studies with Comparative Implications

Further insights into the variations possible in total institutions are provided in articles by Wulbert, Martinson, Denzin, and Berk.[63] Wulbert and Denzin compare prisons with mental hospitals; Berk compares three minimum security institutions arrayed along a treatment-custody continuum; and Martinson reports his prison observations while incarcerated as a "Freedom Rider."

Wulbert studied male patients on two wards in a psychiatric hospital serving the greater Chicago area. These wards were essentially integrated into one functional unit. The wards went through a brief period of disorder during which nine deviant acts were committed by individual patients. The aggression was not directed toward the staff in any of these incidents. There was no social organization at all during the periods of disorder, and little more than that in times of high stability. Wulbert theorizes that mental patients have low inmate pride, for which reason they avoid any form of inmate social organization that would identify them with other patients. He contrasts this with the organization, leadership, role differentiation, and group identity demonstrated by prison inmates during the riots of 1952 and 1953 and argues that prisoners have much higher inmate pride than mental patients—high enough to permit this kind of social organization.[64] This interpretation explains much of what Mathieson found at Ila prison in Norway.

Denzin cites previous research to show that Wulbert's theory of inmate pride is not consistent with many reported observations of inmate behavior in mental hospitals. Instead, he supports the application of Turner and Killian's[65] civil society perspective to total institutions. In this interpretation, collective behavior arises in response to situations in which the social order has become temporarily unstructured. These situations develop when significant changes in the norms, patterns of communication, and the division of labor upset the regularized functioning of the social system.[66] Denzin provides additional conformation for his thesis from the prison literature by briefly recounting the reports by Hartung and Floch, Sykes, and McCleery that we have reviewed in Chapter 1 of this volume.

Berk's comparison of three institutions replicates Grusky's earlier study, "Organizational Goals and the Behavior of Informal Leaders,"[67] and his findings are completely supportive of Grusky's. In Berk's study, prisoners at the treatment-oriented institution were more positively oriented toward the prison, the staff, and the programs in the institution than prisoners at the custody-oriented institution, with prisoners at the intermediate prison falling in between in every case. Furthermore, the longer a prisoner was in the treatment-oriented institution, the more positive he became, and the longer he was in the custody-oriented institution, the more negative he became. Involvement in the prisoner social system followed the same pattern—that is, it was related to positive attitudes in the treatment-oriented institution and to negative attitudes in the custody-oriented one.[68]

Berk also confirms Grusky's conclusion that leaders are more positive at a treatment than a custody institution. This finding reinforces Grusky's point that Schrag's finding of a pattern in which the most negative prisoners rise to the top is not necessarily true of all prisons. Berk's analysis goes beyond Grusky's when he examines the centralization and authoritarianism of prisoner leaders at the three institutions. He reports that leadership in the treatment-oriented institution was spread out among a larger proportion of prisoners, that leaders were personally less authoritarian (both in comparison with their followers and in absolute terms), and that their styles of leadership were more friendly and open.[69] These findings paint a very positive picture of treatment-oriented institutions. In contrast, a careful reading of Mathieson's work discussed in an earlier section of this chapter suggests that they may be even more devastating than custody-oriented prisons.

Martinson's contribution to the comparative study of prison subcultures is his relating of the behavior of a group of unusually prosocial citizens who were suddenly plunged into prison life. Martinson and his fellow "Freedom Riders" were confined in the maximum security unit at Parchman Penitentiary for periods ranging from one to six months. They were effectively isolated from the other prisoners at Parchman. After a time in the two-man cells, the men lost the ability to clearly separate sleeping, fantasy, and what Martinson calls "irritated awakeness." An essentially lawless society existed in the unit, which was due to the ambiguity and lack of legitimacy of all rules, the ecological disruption of prisoner communication by the geography of the facility, and the extent to which all behavior was relevant to relations with the staff.[70]

The men attempted to bring social order out of the imposed anarchy by forming a grapevine democracy, but this was not accepted by the guards. Staff routines also introduced a certain amount of predictability and therefore order. An emotional rather than rational order was achieved by the singing activities of the group. Martinson sees this "ecstatic solidarity" as an indigenous solution to the problem of anarchy in the unit. The extent to which the group was influenced by the physical environment of the isolation unit can be seen by the fact that when they were relocated to a dormitory setting, the ecstatic solidarity collapsed and the "Freedom Riders" became individuals again.[71]

## Brief Studies of the Late 1960s

A number of the dissertations and journal articles that appeared between 1965 and 1968 are isolated studies that do not fit into any particular framework or theoretical tradition. The others either focus on homosexuality or on the sociological dimensions of the prisoner subculture.

### Homosexuality Comes Out of the Closet

Few American citizens other than prison employees were aware of the type of sexual behavior that characterizes jails and prisons until Alan Davis authored a *Transaction* article entitled "Sexual Assaults in the Philadelphia Prison System and Sheriff's Vans."[72] As Chief Assistant District Attorney of Philadelphia,

Davis joined with Police Commissioner Rizzo in a detailed investigation of forced homosexuality in incarceration. They used 3,301 interviews with prisoners (plus interviews with almost all staff), written statements, and polygraph-supported testimonies to study the period from June 1966 through July 1968. Their conclusion was that prison rapes were at an epidemic level. The only men who escaped forced homosexuality were the few locked up for their own (sexual) protection and those so tough as to be able to fight off their attackers.

Most victims of homosexual attack were fearful of admitting it officially, but 156 sexual assaults by 276 aggressors were documented and supported by polygraph testimony, institutional records, or other corroboration. A conservative estimate of the total number of sexual assaults in Philadelphia during the 26-month period is 2,000. Of 129 cases studied in detail, 15 percent involved white aggressors and white victims, 29 percent black aggressors and black victims, 0 percent white aggressors and black victims, and 56 percent black aggressors and white victims. Other significant findings were:

1. Most sexual aggressors do not consider themselves to be homosexuals.
2. Sexual release is not the primary motivation for sexual attacks.
3. The conquest and degradation of the victim are the main goals of the aggressors.
4. Many aggressors must continue to participate in gang rapes in order to avoid becoming victims themselves.
5. The aggressors have themselves suffered much damage to their masculinity in the past.[73]

Two general treatments of homosexuality in male and female prisons are "The Social Meaning of Prison Homosexuality" by Gagnon and Simon[74] and *Problems of Homosexuality in Corrections* by Vedder and King.[75] The latter publication contributes no new information to the literature, so it will not be detailed here, but it is a good source of information for the beginning student of prison homosexuality. It also includes a discussion of conjugal visits. Gagnon and Simon's article is also a good introduction to the field without any new empirical data, and it is informed by Kinsey's[76] early work on the sexual behavior of prisoners. Claghorn and Beto's finding that homosexual and sexually inadequate prisoners are more likely to mutilate themselves than men with adequate sexual adjustments points up the seriousness of this problem in prison life.[77]

*Modest Contributions to Theory Development*

The accumulation of new social facts enables theory to move forward. At the same time, the creation of a new theory or the extension of an old one leads to the reinterpretation of facts (actually reported findings) already established in the literature. An example of the extension of a well-established theory is Wallace's[78] application of Burgess'[79] concentric zone theory of social ecology to a maximum security prison. This prison had four large housing units that the administration had organized into a system of custody grading. Newly admitted prisoners entered the worst housing unit and earned their way upward into the best housing unit through good behavior. Wallace charted the prison and showed how the different housing units and other areas were analogous to Burgess' ecological zones in Chicago. Wallace makes the point that it is the zones that determine the men's behavior rather than the reverse.

Two studies suggest that prisoner status is more important than the offender's race. In one study, differences between Caucasian and black prisoners on a fifty-item scale of moral values were much smaller than differences between white laborers and white prisoners.[80] In the other study, prisoner infractions were analyzed by age, race, and rate of recidivism. Younger men and those with more criminal records committed more infractions than average, but there was no significant difference by race.[81] Both of these studies may be taken as supportive of the idea that race is not a significant differentiating variable in the prisoner subculture. Later research tends to reject this position, but no comprehensive examination of the question has ever been carried out.

Stratton studied 351 youthful offenders in the Federal Correctional Institution, Ashland, Kentucky, to test Glaser's reformulation of Sutherland's differential association theory of criminalization.[82] He found that attitudes favoring the violation of the law were related to two of three indices of procriminal reference group orientation: criminal identification and associational preference. There was no relationship at all with the third index, inmate loyalty. This finding may be because the values transmitted by the prisoner subculture are more related to institutional adjustment than to general criminality outside the prison.[83] It could also be related to the unusual nature of the Federal Correctional Institution at Ashland, where more than three-quarters of the prisoners studied were incarcerated for the interstate transportation of stolen automobiles.

A similar federal institution with a high proportion of stolen vehicle offenders was the site of a replication of Wheeler's work on prisonization (see Chapter 1). Not one of Wheeler's findings was supported by data collected by Atchley and McCabe.[84] Neither the rising trend of prisonization nor the U-shaped curve of conformity to staff role expectations were found. In their article, Atchley and McCabe do a lot of looking around to find explanations for these differences. They show how the criminal records of men studied differed from Wheeler's subjects and produce Glaser's data on role types at their institution to show that their subjects were less committed to the more negative prisoner roles than Wheeler's were. The institution studied by Atchley and McCabe was oriented toward re-education, personal development, and treatment. They observe that linear and U-shaped prisonization models apply only to custody-oriented institutions. This conclusion could have been reached more quickly had they been aware of Mathieson's work discussed in an earlier section of this chapter, or if they had made a wider search of the comparative literature on inmate subcultures in total institutions.

A second replication of Wheeler's study was conducted by Wellford at a Washington, D.C., institution housing 1,500 prisoners in dormitory facilities.[85] At this prison, 85 percent of the prisoners were black. There was no relationship between prisonization and amount of time served, but Wheeler's U-shaped curve showed up when phase of institutional career replaced flat time as the independent variable. Antisocial prisoners were much more likely to be highly prisonized that prosocial men, with the mixed types falling in between. Wellford believes that both individual characteristics and situational variables must be included in any comprehensive theory of prisonization. Characteristics that prisoners bring into the institution with them determine the level of prisonization, but men at all levels experience the U-shaped shift during their institutional careers. Wellford's institution seems to be midway between Wheeler's and the prison studied by Atchley and McCabe on the custody-treatment continuum and other variables. Should we be surprised to note that his findings are also intermediate between these two extremes?

# 3 Contemporary Approaches to the Study of Prisoner Subcultures

In the period from 1969 through 1976, more material has appeared on prisoner subcultures than in all previous years combined. After culling out the less valuable contributions, we are left with a number of categories of publications. These fall into two groups: categories identified by the nature of their approach, and those characterized by attention to one particular dimension of prison life. In some cases, both factors are combined in a single category. For instance, the economic approach also focuses specifically on the "conniving" underlife of the prisoner subculture.

In this chapter, we will first consider publications in the main line of prison research running back to Clemmer. This tradition is largely sociological, with a bit of anthropology thrown in. Four additional approaches will be presented: the total institutions perspective, the economic approach, the psychological approach, and innovative sociological perspectives in ecology and micro-sociology. Finally, four topics will be singled out for special attention. These are sexual behavior, racial and cultural minorities, violence, and prisons in an international perspective.

## Culture and Structure—Traditional Sociological Approaches

Traditional sociological studies of prisoner subcultures have examined dimensions of culture such as values, norms and beliefs, and elements of structure such as roles, social status positions, and groups. The focus on cultural elements involves a certain amount of anthropology, while the structural analysis is more clearly sociological. This mix is also typical of traditional sociological approaches in fields other than penology, including the sociology of mental health, leisure and recreation, intergroup relations, and the family.

The foundation of any field is its doctoral dissertations, which are largely produced by young, promising scholars in the best universities under the direction of the top senior professors in the area. We would be reasonable to expect that the best dissertations would be published and the less valuable ones unpublished, and at the very least, the best dissertations would be summarized in one or more journal articles. Unfortunately, this is not the case in sociology. Many fine dissertations are never circulated because their authors take positions in fields that do not reward publication. Xerox University Microfilms can provide Xerox copies of most of the dissertations completed in the last decade or two, and R & E Research Associates has entered into an extensive program of dissertation publishing and already has several hundred items in print. Except for these two sources, availability of dissertations is poor. Most university libraries no longer send out dissertations in response to interlibrary loan requests. For this reason, one purpose of this book is to summarize the results of dissertation research that has hitherto been unavailable in the profession.

*Hidden Gems*

Between 1969 and 1976, five unpublished dissertations utilizing traditional sociological approaches were completed. Four of them will be discussed in this section, with the fifth, by Mark Hansel, reserved for a later section on criticisms of sociological prison research.

The first of the dissertations to be discussed is "Prisonization and Self Conception: A Study of A Medium Security Prison," completed under the direction of Oscar Grusky in 1970 by Will Kennedy.[1] Kennedy studied men incarcerated at California Men's Colony East, a medium security prison that had already been the subject of studies by Glaser and the team of Ward, Kassebaum, and Wilmer.[2] Kennedy's sample was random, but Chicano prisoners sometimes refused to participate, so that they were underrepresented in the final sample. He generally found no significant differences by race, but perhaps that would have been different had more Chicanos been surveyed.

Kennedy ascertained that prisonization was related to offense, unemployment, and involvement in a criminal subculture before commitment.[3] Highly prisonized men were sought out for advice by other prisoners, but mostly on topics related to prison life rather than nonprison topics such as family problems. Some of these highly prisonized men withdrew from staff members and "did their own time," but others interacted often with staff. These two groups seemed like the "right guy" and "politician" prisoner role types.[4]

A number of roles were rated on a semantic differential test by prisoners who were low, moderate, and high on prisonization. Kennedy also compared all prisoners with a control group of forty-four college students. Unfortunately, this group was not a true control group, and any results found cannot be assumed to be due to the prisoner-"straight" differences. Social class, education, and other factors cannot be ruled out as confounding variables. Among the prisoners, the ideal friend received the highest percentage of favorable ratings, followed by the businessman. Inmates and criminals were ranked at the bottom, with roles such as the average citizen, teacher, and politician receiving more moderate ratings. Highly prisonized offenders tended to give lower ratings in general, and they rated criminals above inmates while the reverse was true for men who were only slightly prisonized.[5]

A number of other variables were crosstabulated with degree of prisonization, which led to the conclusion that highly prisonized inmates at California Men's Colony East were more oriented toward a general criminal subculture than a specific prisoner subculture. There was much evidence that prisoners were greatly affected by the larger society despite their incarceration. The semantic differential responses of Kennedy's subjects suggest that the prisoner subculture was not able to protect these men from the negative self-images derived from society's rejection of them. Interestingly, on questions rating various criminal activities, the college student group was very similar to the criminal groups.[6] Often, only the highly prisonized men, rather than prisoners in general, were different from the college group.

Kennedy found that the highly prisonized inmates tended to be younger and less educated than their fellow prisoners. In addition, they had been incarcerated for offenses such as robbery, burglary, and assault. Apparently, their high prisonization was related to higher than average criminalization before incarceration on the present sentence. This finding seems like more of an influence from outside the prison than it actually is, for these highly prisonized men may have picked up their high criminalization on previous prison terms. The cycle of arrest, trial, and imprisonment apparently has a much stronger negative impact on felons' self-conceptions than imprisonment alone.[7]

"Prisonization and Self Conception" represents a challenge not only to the indigenous origin theory of prisoner subcultures, but also to the idea that prisoners form a unitary system in opposition to the prison administration. The large amount of sexual and material victimization that characterizes prisons could not possibly occur if prisoners were tightly organized into an oppositional subculture. By showing the extent of social differentiation along the dimension of prisonization, which is only one of a number of significantly differentiating characteristics in the prisoner population, Kennedy convinces the reader that at least at California Men's Colony East in the late 1960s, there was no unitary prisoner subculture to speak of.

Additional questions about traditional theories of prisoner subculture arise in another dissertation, "The Prison Social System: An Analysis of Consensus and Normative Structures."[8] Ellis conducted interviews with prisoners, staff members who supervised prisoners, and work-release supervisors at the Louisiana Correctional and Industrial School, a medium security prison for male first-time offenders. Most prisoners at L.C.I.S. at the time, of the study were under age twenty-five.

Ellis was not overwhelmingly successful at supporting his theories. Of eighty-nine hypotheses tested in his dissertation, only thirty-three were supported by the data. He was forced to conclude that consensus among prisoners was no greater during the middle phase of incarceration than during the early phase. Furthermore, conflict between prisoners and supervisors declined rather than increased with time served, thereby indicating that colonization rather than antistaff socialization was a dominant process. Prisoners were able to agree on the norms specifying correct behavior toward other prisoners more than they did on norms about interaction with supervisors. Consensus between prisoners and supervisors did not follow the U-shaped curve predicted by Wheeler (see Chapter 1). Instead, the greatest need for consensus was shown by prisoners in the early and late phases of imprisonment, and these men, rather than middle-phase prisoners, were the ones who perceived the greatest amount of conflict between staff and themselves. This finding is just the reverse of the U-shaped curve hypothesis.

How could it be that Ellis came up with such unexpected results? There are many reasons that could be cited, but there is one general point that stands above all others. Maximum security institutions of the type studied by Clemmer, Sykes, and Wheeler (see Chapter 1 for a review of their studies) are located at the far end of the treatment-custody continuum as well as the security-level continuum and are extreme along other dimensions such as length of sentence and criminal career, age of offender, and type of crime committed. The model developed in their studies really only applies to the kind of institution they studied. Treatment-oriented institutions, those incarcerating very young or less criminalized men, and the ones with a minimum or medium security rating may approximate the Clemmer-Sykes-Wheeler model in some ways, but they are likely to differ in many significant details. As with criminal behavior in general, the hope that a single theory would explain all cases of the phenomenon of "prisonization" has been dashed on the rocks as the research reports have accumulated.

A sample of prisoners at the Terre Haute Federal Penitentiary was surveyed by Guenther following extensive exploratory interviews and a pretesting of the questionnaire.[9] His response rate was 74 percent of the prisoners selected for inclusion in the sample, which is adequate for scientific purposes, but not outstanding. He divided his sample into role types, using Schrag's prisoner role types (see Chapter 1) and a modification of Garabedian's set of attitude scale items (see Chapter 2) as a measurement device. He found that "square johns" and "right guys" were more common in the early and late phases of imprisonment than in the middle stage, but the "con politician" role had the highest number of adherents in the middle phase.[10] Because there were only six "outlaws" in Guenther's sample, he did not include them in his analysis.

The "square johns" were highly prostaff, the "right guys" proinmate, and the "con politicians" almost exactly split in their conformity patterns, based on five questionnaire items. A related measure, loyalty to the convict code, produced the same pattern of differences between the prisoner role types, except that strict acceptance of the convict code was less prevalent than general support for prisoners against staff norms.[11] Alienation, operationalized as powerlessness in this study, was highest among the six "outlaws," followed by the "con politicians," "right guys," and "square johns."[12] Although some earlier data indicated that alienated prisoners learned less information relevant to parole, Guenther was not able to replicate this finding. However, he did find that alienated prisoners were more likely than other prisoners to endorse the importance of parole criteria that were noncontrollable (not subject to modification based on the efforts of the individual prisoner) and less likely to endorse as important a group of items about the prisoner's personal behavior in the institution.[13] In short, alienated prisoners had low faith in their ability to influence the parole process by their own good behavior.

When analyzed by prisoner social role, most variables did not show any statistically significant difference. One that was meaningful was that "square johns" gave high endorsement to manipulable parole-relevant behavioral statements but low endorsement to noncontrollable items. In contrast, "right guys" strongly endorsed the noncontrollable items and were low on the manipulable ones. "Con politicians" fell between the two extremes, but were closer to the "right guy" pattern than the pattern exhibited by "square johns."[14] In general, Guenther found that beliefs about parole (release ideology) were independently affected by alienation and prisoner role occupancy. Aside from its value for its empirical findings, Guenther's dissertation makes a useful contribution to the field by extensively summarizing prisoner roles identified by earlier investigators on the basis of their own observations or prisoner argot.[15]

We commonly hear that most doctoral dissertations are so esoteric as to be useless and are but an exercise in academic futility. This characterization is not entirely inappropriate for some of the dissertations that have been published on prison subcultures, but it is grossly inaccurate as a generalization about such work as a whole. Some of the finest work done in the field has been in doctoral dissertations. One reason why most people are unaware of this is that so few of the best dissertations find their way into print. An outstanding example of this situation is Gruninger's dissertation, "Criminalization, Prison Roles, and Normative Alienation: A Cross-Cultural Study."[16]

Gruninger's study is the most recent product of the penological tradition at the University of Washington. Gruninger's work was carried out with data on twenty-two prisons in five countries collected by Norman Hayner. For Hayner, this project capped a full thirty-five years of research and publishing on prisoner subcultures—a record unmatched in the history of American prison studies.

In each of the twenty-two prisons studied, tape-recorded interviews with administrators were conducted to collect basic information on the prison as an institution, and a random sample (with a few exceptions) of prisoners was surveyed with a questionnaire to gather data on a typical series of variables relevant to prisoner subcultural studies. The institutions were not randomly selected since only prisons to which Hayner had personal access could be used in the study. Of the twenty-two prisons for males, eight were located in Mexico, seven in the United States, three in Germany, two in Spain, and two in England.

The administrative data sets were analyzed separately by three judges and rated on nine dimensions: architecture, administrative goals, classification procedures, prisoner employment, education (vocational and academic), treatment, custody and security, staff characteristics, and outside contact. The judges rated each of the institutions on these nine dimensions on a seven-point rating scale. The final measure of concordance between the judges was .95, which gives us confidence in the classification system used.

Although most of the prisoner samples were probably representative of the populations in their own institutions, comparisons between the national prison groups and federal prison statistics from the various countries on the dimensions of sentence length and age indicate that the prisoners sampled cannot be taken to be representative of the entire prisoner populations of these countries.[17] This result is largely due to the nonrepresentative character of the institutions studied. The comparisons between countries cannot be considered to be valid for all the institutions or all the prisoners in these countries, but just for the specific prisoners and institutions sampled. Despite this limitation, the Hayner-Gruninger data is the best comparative material on prisoner subcultures ever assembled in one volume.

Another dimension along which the prisoners studied seemed to be unusual was the proportion of "outlaws." This role type comprised about half of Gruninger's subjects, as compared with from 7 to 19 percent of the prisoners studied earlier by Schrag, Garabedian, and Garrity (see Chapters 1 and 2). Gruninger thought this increase indicated a true change in prisoner role occupancy—that is, prisoners were becoming more rebellious. He believed that this finding was associated with higher education and younger age among prisoners, but he found no differences in "outlaw" role occupancy by age or education. He also found no difference by race when he compared the American prisons. His conclusion is that diversion and parole have increased the proportion of serious offenders in prisons and therefore the number of prisoners adopting the "outlaw" role.[18]

There may be some truth in this theory, but there is a more subtle possibility. Offenders age eighteen to twenty-four were overrepresented in Gruninger's sample, and we know from many of the other studies discussed in this volume that there is a general tendency for younger prisoners to be more severely antisocial than older prisoners. The Spanish sample included 77 percent under age twenty-five, compared with 27 percent in the entire Spanish prison system. For Germany, the situation was the same, with 38 percent under age twenty-five in the sample and only 15 percent in the prison system as a whole.[19] Gruninger does not give direct comparisons for the other countries, but indirect analysis suggests that the American and British samples may also have been skewed in this direction.[20] The Mexican prisoners were not asked to respond to the role identification questions, so they were excluded from this part of the analysis. Thus, in all likelihood there has been some movement toward "outlaw" role occupancy in many prisons, but not as much as is suggested by Gruninger's data.

If age is inversely associated with antisocial attitudes and behavior across institutions, why didn't Gruninger find this association within the institutions he analyzed? Perhaps because the milieu of an institution is changed by the addition of the younger, more antisocial offenders. The strongly antisocial emphasis they introduce into the institution can spread to the older prisoners within that institution, and the entire prisoner subculture will become more negative. Cloward's description of a situation in which each prisoner overestimates the antisocial qualities of his fellow prisoners explains how this could happen.[21] The new prisoners "up the ante" of the level of antisocial expression necessary to prove that one is both a man and a good convict.

We can recalculate the proportion of prisoners in each role type reported by Schrag, Garrity, and Hayner by allowing for the fact that the "ding" role was excluded from Gruninger's data and then average them together. When we do this, we see that the increase in "outlaw" role occupancy came more at the expense of the "politician" role than any other. "Right guys" also decreased quite a bit, but "square johns" decreased the least, both in absolute terms and proportionately. This result suggests that if the milieu is changed in an antisocial direction by the introduction of many young rebellious prisoners, the "politicians," with their sensitivity to the social scene, are the first to switch to "outlaws." "Square johns," on the other hand, are already fairly isolated from the most antisocial influences in the prisoner subculture, and so resist the change more effectively than other prisoners. Of course, all this is pure conjecture since we do not have the necessary processual data from panel studies spanning the period of change available to test the theory here proposed.

One interesting comparison in Gruninger's dissertation is on the prisoner role type distribution between Britain, Spain, Germany, and the United States. The countries were similar in that the "outlaw" role was the most common one found everywhere, and the "politician" role was the least common (except in the United States, where it missed being the least common by a mere five cases). Larger differences were found for the "right guy" and "square john" roles. "Square johns" were not common anywhere, but they were considerably less frequent in American prisons than in any of the European samples. Just the reverse was true of the "right guy" role, although in this case, Spanish prisoners occupied a middle point between the high proportion of "right guys" in America and the low percentage found in Germany and England.[22] What is outstanding here is not the differences, but the similarities. To some degree, the crossnational correspondence may be an artifact of the methodology used in assigning prisoners to role types, but there is still an impressive similarity in the data that leads us to the observation that people solve similar social-psychological problems by adopting similar social conventions.

Again, we come to the question of the negative effect of imprisonment on attitudes toward society. Gruninger finds that there is only a slight shift in the antisocial direction during a single sentence, but there is a huge shift if we consider the entire criminal career, with its revolving-door cycle of arrest, trial, imprisonment, release, rearrest, and so on. A full 71 percent of the first offenders were prosocial or at least not antisocial, but this declined to 50 percent during the second and third imprisonments and to only 37 percent for five or more prison terms. With successive prison sentences, the felon sees his fellow prisoners in increasingly antisocial terms. Because of confusion between the delayed effects of imprisonment and other influences that impact the felon in his time between sentences, Gruninger believes that "criminalization" is a more appropriate term for this process than "prisonization." Thus, data that seem to favor the importation model of prisoner subcultures may be actually showing little more than the effects of previous imprisonments.[23]

Because the twenty-two institutions were classified on both the custody and treatment dimensions, determining whether a strong treatment emphasis was associated with more positive prisoner attitudes was possible, but did not prove to be the case. The proportion of antistaff prisoners was the same in treatment- and custody-oriented prisons. There was also no difference in the proportion of prisoners perceiving an antisocial climate among other prisoners in general. We might say that treatment facilities as presently utilized have a humanitarian advantage over custody facilities, but no utilitarian advantage in outcomes. Guenther thinks this is due to the unwillingness of prison administrators to segregate prisoners by degree of criminalization. This failure means that criminal learning in prisons can continue to occur, with more criminalized inmates teaching the less criminalized and preparing them for successive reinstitutionalizations.[24]

A final point to come out of Guenther's dissertation is that prison deprivation, like deprivation in other settings, is relative rather than absolute. The pains of imprisonment are apparently felt more severely by the less-criminalized prisoners. The more criminalized men have developed effective defense mechanisms as a result of their previous incarcerations. Men who identified closely with prison staff members were more likely to report severe feelings of deprivation.[25] Again, careful segregation by level of criminalization would benefit mankind by reducing the negative effects of imprisonment.

*Studies Commonly Available in Major University Libraries*

One of the most significant variables impacting prisoner subcultures is the custody level of the institution, though there have been several authors who suggest otherwise. For this reason, the following section is divided into parts concentrating on studies of maximum or medium-minimum security institutions. A third category, studies of state systems, is a mixed type since these systems integrate institutions of diverse custody classifications.

**Maximum Security Prisons.** One of the trends in prison research has been away from studies of maximum security facilities. From 1969 to 1976, less than a third of the traditional sociological studies of prisoner subcultures focused exclusively on maximum security institutions. Several of these are only indirectly about prisoner subcultures. Waldo demonstrates that for the cohort of prisoners admitted to the North Carolina prison system between January 1959 and September 1971, murderers were considerably less criminalized than nonmurderers, as measured by previous incarcerations, escapes, and rule infractions.[26] An excellent list of source materials is included in the discussion of the penal press by Rogers and Alexander.[27]

Wilson and Snodgrass studied the graded tier system at the Patuxent Institution in Maryland.[28] They found that socialization (social maturity) was higher in the most therapeutic tier than in the least therapeutic tier, while adherence to the convict code showed just the reverse pattern. Of various background variables, only age was related to adherence to the convict code, with older prisoners being less committed to the code than younger prisoners.

At a southwestern state prison, Nagasawa and Pfuhl measured prisoner integration by rejection of staff norms and level of contact with other prisoners, rather than convict code adherence.[29] They found that both these variables were inversely related to subjectively defined pains of imprisonment, which supports Sykes' indigenous origin theory of prisoner subcultures. Furthermore, they found that the greatest effect of prisoner contacts on deprivation pains (or the reverse) was in the middle rather than the early or late phases of imprisonment. The fact that deprivation rose in the late phase could mean that the prisoner subculture paradoxically increases deprivation in the long run by stimulating increased staff repression in response to negative prisoner behavior. If true, this situation would be a case of a negative feedback effect that ultimately takes precedence over a positive direct effect.

Faine combined samples from a maximum and a medium security prison to test his hypothesis that self-concept was influential in determining the effects of imprisonment.[30] He found that men whose self-concept indicated a deviant social anchorage became increasingly prisonized from the early through the middle and late phases of imprisonment, but men with a legitimate social anchorage showed no changes in prisonization, and men having low social anchorage became more prisonized in the middle phase of imprisonment but returned to a lower level of prisonization in the late phase. Since the U-shaped curve was found for only one of the three types of prisoners, Faine legitimately concludes that the U-shaped curve can not be applied across the board to all prisoners.

An unusual methodology was utilized by Bowker in examining the perceptions of parole board actions held by prisoners in Cell Block Six of the Washington State Penitentiary.[31] He used pretest prisoner responses as the basis for assembling a list of activities relevant to parole board decision, rather than structuring the list himself based on the academic literature. As Hansel points out, this procedure should be extended to all studies of prisoner subcultures.

Men in Cell Block Six were then surveyed with the scale developed through the pretest procedure. They defined assaulting an officer, attempted escape, and use of narcotics as the actions most likely to result in a "flop" decision (increased time to be served) by the parole board. Surprising were their definitions of educational activities as the most likely to result in a "cut" (decreased time) and of having long hair, being on legal medication, and appealing their cases as leading to "no action" (scheduled time unchanged). Less than a quarter of the men defined parole board decisions in general as fair, which could reflect a common attitude in the convict code or "real" unfairness in parole board actions.[32]

Bowker also replicated Garabedian's role type identification study (see Chapter 2) and found that the proportion of "politicians" in his sample had risen to 48 percent. This increase could be due to sampling differences between the two studies, but an analysis of selected characteristics of the Cell Block Six sample does not support this conclusion. A more interesting possibility arises from the fact that a 1955 law authorized the parole board to reconsider minimum terms anytime after the first year of incarceration. Possibly, prisoners responded to this structural change by increasingly adopting the more sophisticated "politician" role, which allowed them to impress the parole board with their prosocial behavior while at the same time exhibiting a more antisocial side to their fellow prisoners.[33] This process would have already increased the proportion of "politicians" before Garabedian's survey, but not as much as by the time of Bowker's study.

Charles W. Thomas has been the most prolific of all writers on prisoner subcultures. A large number of his articles and papers are based on a 1970 study of prisoners in a southeastern maximum security prison. His initial model was set out in an article published the same year in *Criminology*, in which he suggested that prisoners' adaptations to the institution are influenced by attitudes and values developed in their preprison lives as well as their responses to the conditions of imprisonment.[34] In essence, Thomas was arguing for the integration of the importation and indigenous origin theories of prisoner subcultures rather than their continued conceptualization as necessarily opposed interpretations.

This theoretical paper was followed by articles in *Social Problems*, the *Georgia Journal of Corrections*, *The Sociological Quarterly*, the *Journal of Research in Crime and Delinquency*, the *International Journal of Criminology and Penology*, the *Criminal Justice Review*, and (forthcoming) *Sociological Focus*. These articles do not necessarily build on each other, but rather analyze different combinations of the large number of variables included in the original questionnaire. The structure of the analysis in these articles is extremely advanced. Causal models involving half a dozen variables are proposed and diagramed, with gamma correlations presented for each relationship. The relative influence on the dependent variables of each of two independent (but inter-related) variables is evaluated by computing partial correlation coefficients holding each one constant in turn.

A full exposition of this very important work would take an entire chapter. Instead, we will be content to summarize only the most important points.

1. As prisoners increase their acceptance of the prisoner subculture and adopt antisocial prisoner roles, the negative, criminalizing effects of imprisonment also increase.[35]

2. As prisoners' expectations for their postprison experience become more negative, the negative criminalizing effects of imprisonment increase. This causal influence is both direct and indirect via its effect on acceptance of the norms of prisoner subculture and the adoption of antisocial roles.[36]

3. Prisoners from the lower class and those with the lowest level of contact with the outside world while incarcerated are the most likely to be high in their acceptance of the prisoner subculture.[37] However, the relationship between social class and acceptance of the prisoner subculture is reduced to nearly zero when alienation is introduced as a control variable.[38]

4. Prisoner alienation (operationalized as powerlessness), which Thomas assumes increases as the coerciveness of the prison increases, leads to increased prisoner acceptance of the subculture.[39]

5. Age of first conviction is related to acceptance of the prisoner subculture, and this finding is not modified by the introduction of alienation as a control variable.[40]

6. Alienation can not be explained to any great degree by the influence of sixteen independent variables, whether taken one by one or together in a multiple regression equation. This inability to explain more than 20 percent of the variance in alienation by these characteristics of men within a single prison could mean that much of the alienation is being caused by structural characteristics of the prison itself, which could only be revealed in a comparative study of many prisons at once.[41]

In short, Thomas has shown that preprison, prison-specific, and extraprison variables are all influential upon the assimilation of felons into the prisoner subculture. Prisoner assimilation is then a causal factor in producing a number of negative consequences of confinement, such as opposition to the legal system.[42] At least in his sample, there can be no question about the fact that neither the indigenous origin nor the importation theory of prisoner subcultures can exist alone.

**Studies of State Prison Systems.** Two studies used as their populations prisoners who experienced conditions in various institutions within a state system rather than men in a single institution. Bennett investigated the effect of institutional-ization on the self-esteem of a cohort of prisoners who were admitted to the California system at Vacaville and then dispersed throughout the system over a period of two years.[43] He found that self-esteem increased from the early to the middle phase of imprisonment and then continued to increase at a decreased rate through the final phase of imprisonment. Possibly, the California system had a positive effect on these men, or perhaps they only did better in prison than outside, which had the effect of raising their self-esteem the longer they were inside.

In the other study of an entire prison system, Bowker et al. simultaneously surveyed the staff, prisoners, and parole board members of the Washington State Corrections System.[44] A single parole board serves the entire state, but separate samples of prisoners and staff had to be drawn at each of the state prisons: Treatment Center for Women at Purdy, Washington Corrections Center at Shelton (first offenders and evaluation), Washington State Reformatory at Monroe and Washington State Penitentiary at Walla Walla. Walla Walla receives most of the highly criminalized or serious male offenders, while Monroe takes the less severe cases.

Much of the Bowker et al. material is only indirectly related to the study of prisoner subcultures, but there are a number of points worth mentioning here. In general, the prisoner responses from Walla Walla supported Bowker's earlier study of perceptions of the parole board by residents of Cell Block Six, with a linear decrease in negativism from Walla Walla through Monroe and Shelton to Purdy. Consistent with this pattern, the more often a resident had seen the board (and therefore the more criminalized, on the average), the more likely he or she was to evaluate the board as unfair.[45]

Surprisingly, the prisoners had a more positive opinion of the effects of parole board decision than either staff or board members. The negative staff opinions can be attributed in part to the structural conflict between themselves and the board, but the negative views of board members must be taken to indicate considerable cynicism about and alienation from their own decision-making processes.[46]

There were a number of striking regularities in the data. For example, the same pattern of institutional differences in opinions of the parole board was found for opinions of the intrainstitution classification committees. Even more suggestive, the institutional variation in prisoner responses was exactly paralleled by variation in staff responses.[47]

Could the organizational climates of the institutions be manipulated by officials of the state corrections system both directly by structuring programs, staff positions, and other resources and indirectly by sending different kinds of prisoners to different institutions? The more criminalized prisoners might then contribute to a more negative institutional climate, which in turn affects the staff. Galliher gives us an example of how officials in the central state office can impact conditions in a local correctional institution.[48]

**Medium and Minimum Security Prisons.** In a separate study from his work in a maximum security institution, but using the same basic methodology, Charles Thomas administered anonymous questionnaires to 273 felons at a medium security custody-oriented prison in a southeastern state.[49] His focus was on prisoner drug use, but he included enough additional questionnaire items to replicate his analysis of prisonization in a maximum security setting. He found that stable employment on the streets, the relative absence of feelings of powerlessness, a short period of confinement, and positive expectations of postprison life lessened the impact of prisonization on the men. In comparing the influence of variables derived from the importation theory with the effect of those derived from the indigenous origin theory, he found prisonization and opposition to the prison were much more influenced by indigenous origin variables, but the process of criminalization was more influenced by the importation model variables. When the importation and indigenous origin variables were combined in a single prediction equation, they were able to explain more of the variation in the negative effects of imprisonment than when either model was used separately. This study again argues for an integration of the importation and indigenous origin (deprivation) theories of prisoner subcultures.

Thomas and Cage, in a second paper based on the same data, found that prisoner drug use was only weakly related to powerlessness, prisonization, and other traditionally important variables.[50] The best predictions of prison drug use were preprison drug use and expectations of postprison drug use. Although Akers et al. found that the degree of custody orientation and therefore presumably the level of deprivation experienced by prisoners was directly related to the level of drug use in an international availability sample of prisons,[51] the data presented by Thomas and Cage suggest that the prison does not cause men to use drugs while incarcerated if they did not do so before imprisonment. Prison conditions may, however, increase the chance of drug use among men who were introduced to it on the streets.[52]

Hepburn and Stratton analyzed data on prisonization and criminalization among prisoners at the Federal Correctional Institution at Ashland, Kentucky, and arrived at different conclusions.[53] At Ashland, there was almost no relationship between criminalization and prisonization in the early and late phases of imprisonment and a just barely statistically significant one in the middle phase. Prisonization (commitment to the prison social system) was not related to self-esteem during any of the phases of institutionalization. Criminalization was related to one of two measures of self-esteem in the first two phases, but not in the terminal phase of imprisonment. This study supports the importation model more than the indigenous origin theory of criminal subcultures.

A Midwestern state prison's data for 1970 were examined by Neal et al. in a paper presented at the 1974 meeting of the Society for the Study of Social Problems.[54] These authors found that the alienation variables of powerlessness, normlessness, social isolation, and meaninglessness all decreased the longer men were incarcerated. For powerlessness, meaninglessness, and normlessness, the effect was much stronger for blacks than for whites and for single men over those who were married. This finding may be interpreted as indicating that exposure to the prisoner subculture reduces psychological suffering and thus supporting the indigenous origin model of prisoner subcultures.

Another study, by Faine and Bohlander, focused on the relationship between incarceration and radicalization at a medium security Kentucky facility.[55] Radicalism was broken down into denial of the legitimacy of the system, perceived class oppression, and advocacy of revolution, but since these scales were highly intercorrelated, they could not be considered as independent measures of radicalism. Faine and Bohlander found that prisoners brought a great deal of radicalism to the institution with them, but they became increasingly radical the longer they were incarcerated. This finding is particularly impressive because it is based on reinterviews with prisoners over a nine month period, not on a single cross-sectional sampling. No subgroup or category of prisoners showed any declines in radicalism over the nine months, but those men most likely to stay steady instead of increasing were the older felons who had stable heterosexual relationships outside the prison and had no criminal friends outside or inside the prison. They also were more likely to have extensive criminal records and to be incarcerated for "square john" expressive crimes such as rape and murder.

The studies discussed above are the most significant for theory development. Readers interested in a more complete survey of medium and minimum security institutions should also consult articles by Fry, Brown, Lembro, and Curcione, plus some of the material in the monographs by Brodsky and Eggleson on the military prison and Duffee on prison administration.[56]

### Criticisms of Traditional Sociological Approaches

In their book, *Prison Treatment and Parole Survival,*[57] Kassebaum, Ward, and Wilmer show that the group counseling program at California Men's Colony East did not have a direct positive impact on parole success for the men who participated in it. They also include some data relevant to prisoner subcultures, but the most provocative of their findings was their inability to classify more than a quarter of the men into the inmate roles of "outlaw," "square john," "politician," and "right guy" in using Garrity's operational definitions of these roles. What went wrong? Answers have been given by two sociologists, Robert Leger and Mark Hansel.

Leger administered questionnaires to 88 percent of the prisoners at a medium security institution in a Midwestern state.[58] He supported Wheeler's

U-shaped curve model on four of five measures of socialization and reference group participation and then wanted to see how these patterns held up for prisoner role types in a replication of Garabedian's analysis. His findings did not resemble Garabedian's at all, which he attributed to two major inadequacies in Garabedian's attitude item methodology. First, Garabedian's attitude statements allowed him to classify many more prisoners into a role than could have been justified based on their actual behavior in the prison. In Leger's sample, there was little correspondence between the attitude indicators and behavioral nominations for "right guys" and "outlaws," but a better fit for the more popular role of "politician." The second inadequacy was that a factor analysis of the answers Leger's subjects gave to Garabedian's attitude statements showed that only the "square john" items were unidimensional. In short, the attitude statements for each of the other roles really do not index those specific roles at all, but rather a set of general socialization patterns.

A much more complete analysis of scales for the measurement of prisoner social roles appears in Hansel's doctoral dissertation, "The Measurement and Dimensionality of Inmate Social Roles in a Custodially Oriented Prison: An Ethnographic Psychometric Study."[59] In his first chapter, he analyzes the approaches of Sykes and Garabedian, both of whom see prisoner roles as mutually exclusive, and Schrag and Kassebaum et al., who conceptualize them more in terms of frequency distributions of positions on underlying dimension.

After a highly sophisticated methodological and theoretical critique of their scales plus scales developed in his own study, Hansel is able to show that prisoner roles are all differentially loaded on two general factors. These are solidarity with fellow prisoners and cooperation with staff. In addition, specific roles may include one or more additional dimensions, but these will be relevant only to those roles. Hansel included economic activity as an example, but suggests that additional areas could have been examined. In his conclusion, he gives strong support to the position that prisoner roles overlap on their underlying dimensions. They are not entirely separate, as conceived by Garabedian, but rather differ in the degree to which they are loaded on these dimensions. Interestingly, this most advanced of all analyses of prisoner roles concludes that the early concepts proposed by Schrag are more accurate than any of the more recent formulations.[60]

To summarize, sociologists often find it easier to manufacture data at arm's length through formal methodological procedures than to allow the subjects of the research to speak for themselves, and then to analyze this material phenomenologically. In doing so, they run the risk of producing results that are statistical artifacts—that is, products that are more the concepts of the researcher and his or her methodology than the experiences of the respondents. The work of Leger and Hansel strongly suggests that this has been the case in most of the studies of prisoner roles completed to date.

## The Total Institution Approach

The early work of Goffman[61] and others on a general model of total institutions that would make sense of those characteristics common to prisons, mental hospitals, and certain other social organizations inspired a number of other scholars to examine the fruitfulness of this approach. We will not discuss the people-processing approach used by both Hasenfeld and Shichor here,[62] but we will look at journal articles by Burns, by Karmel, and by Twaddle, as well as Tittle's *Society of Subordinates* and other reports of his study of inmates in a federal narcotics hospital.[63]

Burns makes the argument that a maximum security prison is similar to a totalitarian regime on six dimensions: a totalitarian ideology, a centralized and unified economy, a one-party state with one person as its leader, a monopoly on communications, a terroristic police system (often imposed on many staff members as well as prisoners), and control of all effective weapons.[64]

Twaddle takes a different perspective in comparing the utilization of medical services in prison with that on board naval ships, and both with the general American population. Visits to physicians were much higher in these two situations than in the general population, and the variation within each total institution seemed to follow the same pattern. For example, blacks, young men, and those in prison or on board a relatively short time were more likely to visit the medical unit than whites, older men, and long-termers. Twaddle concludes that stress, socialization, labeling, and administrative policies may explain some of these effects, but there is no reason to believe that differential disease rates were responsible.[65]

Goffman's "soft" research methodology (see Chapter 2) should have had the advantage of bringing him closer to the world of the inmates as they saw themselves and experienced their hospital stays. At least, that is how he presents himself to the reader of *Asylums*—he seems very much like an insider. Karmel set out to test one of his constructs—the self-mortification of inmates that occurs in the early days of institutionalization—with a small sample of inmates at the New Jersey State Hospital, Trenton. She used the Rosenberg-Guttman scale of self-esteem to test her subjects within thirty-six hours of admission and then again after four weeks. Self-esteem decreased for only 14 percent of the patients, and social identity deteriorated in an even smaller proportion. Actually, more patients improved than deteriorated. Karmel comments that what appears degrading to an outsider may not necessarily be experienced as such by the patients.[66] Was Goffman an outsider or an insider? Probably a little of both. The fact that fifty patients at one facility did not conform to his model does not mean that other inmate populations wouldn't if they were studied. Karmel's article is a caution, not a condemnation.

Tittle's research at a federal narcotics hospital included volunteer and imprisoned patients, and both men and women. Although he argues that most patients defined their time at the hospital as imprisonment,[67] it is clearly not the equivalent of a maximum or even a medium security prison. This institution seemed to have an antirehabilitative effect despite it's therapeutic emphasis.[68] Incarceration was related to decreased self-esteem, but only from the early- to the middle-career phase. Self-esteem improved again by the terminal phase of incarceration.[69] Primary group affiliation relieved the psychological pain of low self-esteem for both men and women, but affiliation with the larger prisoner subculture was functional only for men.[70] Women were more likely than men to join small primary groups, but less likely to be closely integrated into the prisoner social system as a whole.[71] In general, Tittle's findings are more supportive of the indigenous origin theory than the importation theory of prisoner subcultures.

In *Society of Subordinates*, Tittle repeats the contents of his earlier journal articles, plus additional material. He is particularly concerned with relating his findings to the traditional sociological literature on prisoner subcultures. The theoretical emphasis is admirable, but the unusual nature of Tittle's sample makes many of his inferences tenuous. He has made as much as he could from a limited data base. Still, readers interested in maximum security prisons should not take *Society of Subordinates* to be typical of the field. It is more valuable as a study of a particular variety of total institution, another point of comparison, than as a contemporary example of the Clemmer-Sykes-Garabedian tradition.

**The Economic Approach**

Two varieties of economic analysis are found in prison studies. One is a formal examination of the costs and benefits of the prison system as a whole, as in *Toward an Economics of Prisons* by Tabasz.[72] While an important policy issue, a cost-benefit analysis is not directly applicable to the study of prisoner subcultures. Economic research on prisoner subcultures is much less formal and abstract. In fact, it relies on "soft" ethnographic data even more than traditional sociological studies of prisoners. Portions of most of the more detailed prison studies have usually been devoted to economic activities, but few publications have focused entirely on this facet of prison life. Journal articles by Strange and McCrory, and Guenther, plus a summarizing monograph by Williams and Fish are the basic sources for this approach.[73] In addition, a dissertation and several journal articles by Huff discuss the phenomenon of prisoners' unions.[74]

Strange and McCrory describe the cigarette barter system at Rahway prison in New Jersey and list the cost of various goods and services. They note that owners of pornographic photographs rarely sell them but instead rent them out at up to five packs of cigarettes a night. At Rahway, the standard of reciprocity applies only within one's subcultural group, while a tougher standard of trade governs relations with men outside the group. The authors correctly point out that participating in the market system keeps many prisoners from completely losing their ability to make decisions for themselves, a skill that is absolutely necessary for survival after release.[75] Guenther also emphasizes the amount of activity that accompanies the distribution of goods and services in the prisoner economy, but his main contribution is a taxonomy of contraband items that are traded and bought in the sub rosa exchange system. Twenty-four categories of items are listed, including gambling equipment, pornography, cooking and eating equipment, firearms, blackjacks, hatchets, chains, knives, bar-spreaders, bar-cutters, keys, digging equipment, explosive devices, street money, drugs, and the equipment for making alcoholic beverages or for injecting drugs.[76]

Williams and Fish summarize all that is known about prisoner economic activities in institutions for both men and women. They do not provide a great deal of information that is new, but they give the best summary of all previous research on prisoner economics that is available anywhere. They emphasize the conceptualization of prison economic activity as a circular flow rather than a simple one-way distribution of goods. In their final chapter, they openly state that much crime could be reduced by the elimination of poverty and ghettos and make some observations on programs that would have an impact on poverty and therefore crime.[77]

Huff's work on the rise and demise of the Ohio Prisoners' Labor Union, and prisoners' unions in general, is economic only in that it describes how prisoners have organized themselves to seek concessions from administrators on economic issues. Because of the relationship between prisoners' unions and the union movement in the larger society, Huff's analysis also has a strong political science orientation. His typology of prisoners' movements as being indigenous (prisoner based) or ancillary (outside based) and oriented toward specific grievances or toward more general ideological change is a good starting point for any examination of the subject.[78] His documentation of the many prisoners' unions that have developed in the United States since 1970 is also important.[79] More significant than these contributions is his case study analysis of why the Ohio Prisoners' Labor Union failed. Although the prisoners made some tactical errors that hastened their demise, the tale Huff tells leads one to believe that the power of the administration in prisons is so great that no indigenous prisoners' union has a chance of surviving.[80] Transfers of prisoners, parole board "flops," punitive segregation, and many other enforced deprivations are too much for a fledgling prisoners' organization to bear. As John Irwin has pointed out, American prisoners are not permitted to actively participate in their own rehabilitation under any circumstances.[81]

## The Psychological Approach

Psychological approaches are used in many of the studies that have been mentioned under different headings in this chapter, either because of the nature of the subject on which they focus or because they are mixed with other approaches in complex research methodologies. For example, attitude scales attempt to measure psychological system variables, but when individual scores are aggregated and crosstabulated with social structure variables, they form a basic part of traditional sociological studies of prisoner subcultures. In this section, three examples of psychological work will be briefly discussed: a dissertation in psychology that is not entirely psychological, one in social work that is very psychological, and a contrived experiment in social psychology that has sociological implications that dwarf most of the traditional sociological studies.

Sociological and psychological approaches differ not only on the system of variables focused upon, but also on the methodological techniques commonly used. Sociological investigators study representative samples of large populations of respondents, except in a small number of microsociological investigations, and prefer to collect data in natural settings. In psychology, samples are much smaller and less likely to be representative of any identifiable population. The research site is more likely to be artificial—as in a laboratory setting—than natural.

Sparger's unpublished doctoral dissertation is a good example of the psychological approach to prison studies.[82] He examined the leadership behavior of three "known" prisoner leaders and twelve other prisoners selected randomly from the general population at the Draper Correctional Center, Elmore, Alabama. Three groups were formed, with each containing one leader and four nonleaders. Each group was asked to formulate a list of prison reform recommendations and to arrange the recommendations in order of priority. The group interactions were videotaped and analyzed in detail by using Bales' system of interaction process analysis. Sparger found that the leaders talked more often, received more positive statements such as agreements and compliments, and asked more questions than the nonleaders. From these limited experimental findings, Sparger concludes that prisoner leaders exhibit the same general behavioral characteristics as leaders in the larger society.[83]

In a more elaborate study, Rotenberg selected prisoner volunteers from the ranch section at San Quentin to participate in role-conflict scenes in front of varying audiences.[84] Prisoners alternately played the roles of prisoner ("right guy"), social worker, and prison captain before three audiences: prisoners, students, and prison officers. Rotenberg was interested in the level of the men's involvement in the different roles. He found that involvement in the prisoner role was highest in front of the prisoner audience and that involvement in the social worker role was highest before the student audience. Involvement in the captain's role was not significantly different between audiences, except that it was higher before the students than the other prisoners. Rotenberg's general conclusion that the "right guy" role in prisons arises as a result of the deprivation of more normal personality roles is an interesting one. He believes (perhaps dangerously on the basis of a limited artificial experiment) that the impact of prison roles on the self-identities of prisoners is largely limited to their time spent behind bars.[85]

One of the most significant prison studies of the last decade wasn't done in a prison at all. Zimbardo[86] and several colleagues set up a pseudo-prison in a basement hall with adjacent rooms at Stanford University. Volunteer subjects were extensively screened and certified mentally healthy and then randomly assigned to play prisoners and guards. Amazingly, despite the artificiality of the facility, the normality of the subjects, and the fact that everyone understood that they were participating in an experiment, prisoners became passive and troubled, guards became authoritarian and sometimes even sadistic, and even the experimenters began to behave irrationally. The experiment had to be called off after only six of the fourteen days scheduled because of the pathological processes being developed by the subjects.

This study shows that an artificial experiment can have significant policy implications. If normal people experience damage from being incarcerated for only six days in what they know is only an experiment, how much damage would they sustain after two years in a real prison? How much worse might this be if they were already severely troubled before they entered prison? If normal people show the symptoms of a "guard syndrome" in just a few days, could they be expected to avoid this influence after years of playing the guard role in an actual penitentiary? These are the kinds of questions that were usually glossed over before the Stanford experiment. Never again will they be so easily dismissed.


## Innovative Approaches—Microsociology and Ecology

Several relatively new approaches have been used in prison studies during the past few years. One of these is the application of ecological insights to prison life. For a brief general summary of the social climate branch of ecological analysis see "Prison Environments, The Social Ecology of Correctional Institutions" by Wenk and Moos.[87] A different ecological slant was taken by Austin and Bates in their ethological study of dominance and territory in a prison camp occupied by forty-five men.[88] Among other things, they found that dominant prisoners controlled more territory and possessed more desirable material goods than prisoners who were lower on the pecking hierarchy.

As a final example of the ecological approach, there is Roth's article, "Territoriality and Homosexuality in a Male Prison Population."[89] At the Lewisburg Federal Penitentiary, Roth identified 107 men known to engage in homosexual acts of whom 14 were homosexual rapists. He then plotted the living areas of each of the men and found that there was only one case in which two rapists lived in the same territory. The others were isolated from each other, but lived near a number of known homosexuals—men that Roth identified as their "prey." Since the administration had not deliberately segregated these men from each other, the assumption is that natural territorial sorting occurred and functioned to reduce the probability of conflicts between the rapists.

Microsociology is not one single approach. It ranges from ethnology and Goffman's dramaturgical system to symbolic interactionism, social phenomenology, and ethnomethodology. What all these schools have in common is their focus on small groups and roles rather than large-scale organizations and mass categories of people, and on reality as experienced by the subjects of the study instead of as prestructured by the researcher. The methodology is participant observation, interviews, and intellectual analysis rather than questionnaire administration and computerized statistical analysis. Sometimes, as in Miller's article "Adaptation of Young Men to Prison" and the pamphlet *Prison Games* by Heise, the results are not very impressive, but books such as Irwin's *The Felon* and *The Time Game* by Manocchio and Dunn have made an impact on the field.[90]

*The Felon* is about men whose careers are in crime and how they do in the system, more specifically the California Department of Corrections. Irwin tries to show how his small sample of felons experienced the system, inside and outside the walls. He is not concerned with hypothesis testing and theory development in any formal sense. *The Felon* does give the reader a good feeling of what being a felon in California would be like, and the book is a corrective to those proadministration studies that are more relevant to managing prisoners than understanding them.

One of the best parts of *The Felon* is not about prisons at all. It is about criminal roles in the outside world: the "dope fiend," the "state-raised youth," the "thief," the "hustler," and so on. For each role, Irwin delineates major themes and a general world view. Some of the best contemporary studies of prisoner subcultures have concluded that it is not prisonization alone, but the entire revolving-door experience with the criminal justice system that produces negative results. From this perspective, another strength of this book is that it gives the reader a fairly complete picture of the impact of the total system on a criminal's attitudes, beliefs, and self-image.

In the section dealing specifically with prisoner organization in the California system, Irwin shows how occupants of each of the criminal roles adjust to prison life. His main addition to the previous literature on the subject is the specification of three modes of adaptation common in the prison world. "Jailing" means adapting so well to the prison that it becomes home. The outside world becomes insignificant. In contrast, "doing time" is making prison life as pleasant as possible without making any personal changes at all. Prison is merely a suspension of the outside life to which the prisoner fully intends to return. Finally, in "gleaning," the prisoner tries to improve himself and to make basic personal changes that will enable him to do better upon release.[91] Irwin's view of the prison is true to the experiences of his subjects to a considerable extent, but it is still a sociological analysis.

In *The Time Game*, Manocchio and Dunn present a prisoner's view, in his own words, contrasted with the same events as seen by a prison counselor (Dunn and Manocchio, respectively). This book does not provide an understanding of the social structure of the prison; it has a different value. It shows the overwhelming difference in perspectives between staff and prisoner—a difference that can not be bridged successfully (at least not in the view of the authors). Both parties to the continued misperceptions are seen to be so involved in their own worlds that they can not reach out to understand each other.

A recent paper by Muedeking is more microsociological than either *The Felon* or *The Time Game*. In "Negotiating Identities In the Prison Visiting Room,"[92] he applies Goffman's insights to interaction in prison visiting rooms. He was able to observe forty visiting sessions in two maximum security prisons and one medium security institution in the California system. Although there are no statistics, his presentation makes a strong case that the visiting room experiences of prisoners tend to confirm their deviant identities rather than to help in the resocializing process. The reason that this and other microsociological analyses are so convincing is that they start with meticulously recorded events of a minor but routine nature and then build from this base to a total conception of the experiences each of the role occupants has in the situation. In this case, the drama is peopled with guards, prisoners, and visitors, each of whom have systematically different definitions of the situation.

At the extreme end of the continuum of microsociological approaches are the methodologically radical techniques of social phenomenology, which imposes no scientific structures on the portrayal of people as they conceive of themselves and their world, and ethnomethodology, which uses linguistic analysis and norm-breaking behavior to reveal the minute shared understandings that make social commerce possible. There is no perfect example of this type of approach in prison studies, but Wieder's study of interaction in the East Los Angeles Halfway House bears on the subject since it uses men just recently released from prison and because it focuses on the convict code.[93] In *Language and Social Reality, The Case of Telling the Convict Code*, he begins by showing how the felons' allegiance to the code inhibits the growth of the therapeutic community and so is linked to the evident failure of the halfway house as a rehabilitative agency. Most studies would end at this point, but Wieder goes on to show that the code is a way of making seemingly unrelated acts meaningful as they are reinterpreted into a recognizable pattern by reference to an extension of the basic convict code.

All humans need a sense of social reality, a feeling that all is right in the world. There must be an order in the social universe as well as the physical universe. When we make a physical facility and a few therapeutic program elements available to prisoners, we cannot expect them to abandon their previous ways of making the world meaningful to themselves unless we provide a new web of meaning. In this sense, we force prisoners to accept some sort of a convict code to the extent that social segregation and administrative regulation or inattention make alternative systems of meaning too remote and meaningless for them to use as functional equivalents for the code. Where therapeutic programs have made available a new frame of reference—an interpretive system expressed verbally to new members—they have been notably successful. Examples of these programs include the Sexual Psychopath Program in Washington State, Highfields in New Jersey, and Alcoholics Anonymous on the streets.

## Topical Approaches

### Family Relations and Homosexuality

Only one American prison system makes a major effort to keep the family unit intact while the man is incarcerated. This is the conjugal visiting program at the Parchman, Mississippi, prison farm complex. Even Parchman provides only minimum facilities for conjugal visitations and has no program of counseling for prisoners and their wives to help them adjust to the problems caused by an extended period of separation. Correctional scholars generally agree that this separation is conducive to the development of prison homosexuality,[94] and Hopper's data from Parchman suggest that conjugal visits do play an important role in decreasing the incidence of prison homosexuality.[95] All sergeants contacted by Hopper indicated that prisoners receiving conjugal visits engaged in less homosexual behavior than the other men. The prisoners themselves rated the primary effect of conjugal visits as keeping their marriages together; the reduction of homosexuality was cited much less often, but considerably more often than other reasons.

Hopper also found that participation in conjugal visits was associated with better work effort, cooperation with staff, trust in staff, and belief in the fairness of staff, but there was no relationship between conjugal visits and the prisoner subculture variables of loyalty among prisoners, trust in prisoner friends, and the number of prisoner friends.[96] Could the effect of conjugal visits make prisoners more prosocial without making them less committed to the prisoner subculture? In *Sex in Prison*, Hopper argues convincingly that the main positive effect of conjugal visits is to enable a prisoner to retain his self-image as a man and husband, not to give him biological release.[97] Doubts about his basic masculinity are what lead him toward committing homosexual rapes and other aggressive acts while imprisoned.

Leo Carroll echoes this argument and applies it specifically to racial conflict in a maximum security prison.[98] He found that most assaults were interracial, with blacks attacking whites repeatedly to reaffirm their masculinity and to express their rage over racial oppression in America. Although blacks were a small minority in the prison studied, they were better organized as a group than the whites. In addition, white leaders cooperated in the raping of prospective "punks" in order to degrade them sufficiently so they would be willing to become "wives" and prostitutes for them after the black gangs had turned to new victims. Carroll believes that the victims are selected not so much because of their feminine characteristics as because they best represent the white middle class toward which the blacks feel the greatest rage. (Some legal action has been by white prisoners to protect themselves against sexual mistreatment, with mixed results to date.[99])

Two other significant empirical studies of prison homosexuality have been published in recent years. In an international study of twenty-five prisons from which Gruninger's Ph.D. dissertation (discussed earlier in this chapter) was drawn, Akers et al. found that the more custodial the institution, the higher the incidence of known homosexual behavior and drug use.[100] They also found that in prisons serving younger felons homosexuality was higher, but the custody-treatment continuum was much more important. The success of this sociological analysis is in contrast with the failure of Porter to find any differences between passive homosexuals, active homosexuals, and nonhomosexuals at the State Prison of Southern Michigan.[101] The .three groups in Porter's study did not differ in their ages, dissatisfaction with body parts, feeling of personal control over their lives, psychological effeminacy, or reaction to underlying femininity in their personalities. This finding suggests that the occupation of sex-related prisoner roles may be determined more by sociocultural system variables than by psychological system variables.

A number of very fine general expositions of prison homosexuality appeared in the early 1970s. Readers desiring a more detailed discussion of the issue than has been presented here should consult Buffum's pamphlet, *Homosexuality in Prisons*, the chapters by both Kirkham and Johnson, or the more popularized treatment of the subject by Kassebaum that appeared in the January 1972 issue of *Sexual Behavior.*[102]

### Race Relations in Prison

The study of race relations in prison has become popular in recent years, partially because of the recognition that the support of racial groups can be useful as a control (called *rehabilitative* by administrators) technique[103] and partially because their potential for radicalizing prisoners and causing riots is considerable in many prisons.[104] In this section, we will examine an analysis of prison argot and a series of publications from the mainstream of the sociological tradition in prison studies.

Kantrowitz analyzed the slang vocabulary of black and Caucasian prisoners at the Joliet Penitentiary in Illinois in 1959-1962, but did not publish his results until 1969.[105] He eventually identified 1,350 argot terms, of which 114 were names the two races had for themselves and each other. Amazingly, only 8 names were used by both groups; 56 were used by blacks only; and 50 by whites only—all of which provides an index of the extreme sociocultural separation of the races despite their physical proximity. Each race had only a few terms for their own group, but many terms for the other group.

Multiple publication being the norm, each of the four mainstream studies on prison race relations are publicized in two or three publications. Jacobs' study of racial conflict at Stateville Penitentiary, a maximum security facility in Illinois, is the subject of articles in three journals. The article in *Urban Life and Culture* describes the difficulties of participant observation in prison and contains a searching discussion of the ethics of prison research.[106] In *Social Problems*, Jacobs describes the operation of four major gangs at Stateville—one Latin and three black—and he shows how close they are to their parent gangs on the Chicago streets, how they protect and nourish their members and corrupt the guards, and how their leaders (who were also leaders on the streets) use wits rather than brawn to maintain their power and to avoid rather than create prison conflicts.[107] The third article, in *Journal of Criminal Law and Criminology*, makes the point that ethnic or gang organization is an intermediate level of prison social organization between the primary group and the general prisoner subculture, and it describes stratification in American prisons in general rather than limiting the discussion to Stateville alone.[108]

Two articles by Harris in the *American Sociological Review* report racial comparisons in a sample of 234 young (average age 22) offenders at Yardville Youth Reception and Correction Center in New Jersey. Harris found that initial limited incarceration resulted in a decreased estimated value of criminal choice and an increased value of "going straight." However, more lengthy periods of incarceration were associated with a decreased value of going straight" and an increased value of criminal behavior. In short, there was a rehabilitation effect for short imprisonment, but a criminalization effect for longer sentences. Blacks switched from the rehabilitation to the criminalization effect at an earlier point than whites.[109] As commitment to crime rose, whites experienced a negative shift in their sense of psychological well-being, but blacks became slightly more positive about themselves. Apparently, being a black is such a master status that criminality does not dent it very much, and it is such a negative status (for lower class young men at least) that what effect increased criminal self-typing does have is generally positive rather than negative.[110]

Davidson, an anthropologist, spent 20 months studying Chicanos in San Quentin as the field work for his doctorate. His subsequent book *Chicano Prisoners, The Key to San Quentin* is summarized in an article, "Family Secrets," by Stocking, published in the magazine *Human Behavior*.[111] Davidson had an ideal research situation until his proprisoner sympathies led to newspaper articles that offended the prison administration, at which point he was cut off from conducting further research. As a result, his 1974 book is weak on details of the 1972 and early 1973 bifurcation of the Chicanos into the "Mafia" and "Familia."[112]

He describes the prisoner subculture well. The structure and social processes of prison life that he reveals are largely the same as those printed in earlier treatments of the subject, but the drugs and other material items are more up to date. Like Jacobs, Davidson sees ethnic leadership as ruling by mental (social) skill rather than physical prowess and contributing much more to stability than conflict among prisoners or between them and staff members. What is unfortunate is that he paints such a positive picture of Chicano social organization that it is not believable. He also seems to slight blacks and Caucasians. While this approach is a fair corrective to correctional writings that are anti-Chicano, it does undermine his claim to objectivity. In addition, the theoretical advances made in the book are minimal. Despite these weaknesses, *Chicano Prisoners* should be read by anyone who wants to understand ethnic group organization in the California prison system. It is an ideal supplementary text for an undergraduate corrections course.

A paper by Carroll on interracial prison rapes was discussed earlier in this chapter in the section on family relations and homosexuality. A second paper plus a book further discuss Carroll's research at a small state prison in New England. Carroll's methodology was similar to Davidson's, but, like Jacobs, he managed to retain an admirable degree of objectivity throughout the research, which is often difficult to achieve when the research becomes aware of the multiple injustices and suffering that needlessly characterize our prisons. Nevertheless, the impact of a completely objective book is greater in the long run than one that is tinged with partiality or protest, and if a list of "classic" studies of prisoner subcultures were to be recommended to a reader unfamiliar with the field, Carroll's *Hacks, Blacks and Cons* would be one of the books.[113]

Carroll's analysis is thorough, his insights are exceptional, and his conclusions are always properly qualified. His investigative procedures, so well presented in his introductory chapter, are a model that no prospective prison researcher should fail to consult. The organization of his study is unique in the prison literature, in that he devotes one chapter each to a description of Caucasian prisoners, black prisoners, and prison officers, then three chapters to different dimensions of the relations between the groups. The economic underlife, social structure, sexual behavior, drug use, racial conflict, and other dimensions of the prisoner subculture (or subcultures) are fully explicated. The amount of attention paid to the prison officers provides a more rounded picture of prison life than does the typical prison study in which officers are dismissed with a passing phrase.

The primary contribution that Carroll makes in *Hacks, Blacks, and Cons* is the wealth of information on the large differences in the way blacks and Caucasians experience imprisonment. His "soft" data are the perfect complement to the statistical analysis of prisoner racial differences in the two articles by Harris discussed above. Carroll's most recent thoughts on the subject are presented in a paper given at the 1976 annual meeting of the American Society of Criminology.[114] In this paper, he argues that blacks are less successful at corrupting the authority of officers than Caucasians, perhaps because they avoid the officers or because of discrimination, or both. Instead, they use direct confrontation tactics. As a result, their leaders are never coopted by the prison administration.[115]

White leaders develop into a conservative elite that has nearly as much invested in maintaining the status quo as the prison administration. They are not nearly as well integrated with their followers as are the black leaders. Strong leadership and a high level of social solidarity make black confrontation tactics rather successful in conflicts with the prison superstructure. White prisoners, being less organized, are more likely to use the ploy of censoriousness as described by Mathieson in Norway (see Chapter 2 for a review of his work). Those whites who choose this course have to admit that they are in need of treatment, which alienates them from other whites who are "solid cons" and from black radicals. When blacks use censoriousness, they do so only from the perspective of themselves as victims of an immoral racist society that is untrue to its own ideals, not because of a defect in themselves.[116] These differences make clear that to ignore racial differentiation in prisoner groups is to seriously distort the reality of the social situation in American prisons in the 1970s.

*Violence behind Bars*

A common psychological phenomenon is that oppression generates aggression that may be turned inward or directed outward toward the external world. If it is directed outside the self, it can be aimed at the oppressors or displaced to others who are safer targets. Among prisoners, direct aggression means riots, attacks on staff, and continued or increased crime after release. Displaced aggression is redirected violence in which one prisoner attacks another. Murder, rape, and assault are primary categories of prisoner-prisoner violence. Finally, aggression may be turned inward toward the self, the safest but most tragic victim. Self-hate, self-mutilation, mental illness, drug abuse, and suicide are examples of internal aggression.

Most of the literature on prison riots has very little to do with the study of prisoner subcultures. However, two of the best sources are individual chapters (discussed below) in two separate books on prison violence. A very general treatment of protest movements, of which riots are one subtype, appears in Lammers' article on strikes and mutinies.[117]

Edith Flynn, in her chapter on sources of violence in prisons, summarizes the history of prison riots and suggests seven factors that have contributed to the recent wave of prison riots.[118] These are disturbances of the prisoner social structure, limited communications that allow problems to get out of hand before reaching the ears of the administration, racial and political tensions originating in the larger society, faulty classification and treatment of military-type revolutionaries, facilitation of the political prisoner ethic as a justification for violence, causing hopes to rise too high by promising more reforms than can possibly be delivered, and perpetuating proviolence ecological conditions.

Wilsnack surveyed forty-eight of fifty-one state penitentiaries (including the District of Columbia) in an attempt to understand what conditions led to nonriot resistance and full-fledge riots between January 1971 and June 1972.[119] Wilsnack cites three broad areas of factors contributing to these disturbances: prisoner deprivation and social disorganization, instability and conflict in the prison administration, and influences from outside the prison. Some of the factors favoring riots were overcrowding, prisoner idleness, increased assaults among prisoners or directed toward staff, heterogeneity of ages, criminal careers, and offenses, major administrative shake-ups, outside agitation for prison reform, and much publicity about poor prison conditions.

Turning to prisoner-prisoner violence, we find some evidence that in one prison, a high level of disciplinary infractions was related more to violent fantasies than to records of habitual criminal violence outside the prison (as recorded in each man's "jacket").[120] In another institution, variations in the density of the prisoner population were directly related to both the number and rate of disciplinary infractions.[121] In a third study, Jacobs argues that many incidents of prison violence are facilitated by administrators who permit low surveillance places (where violence is easily perpetrated) to continue to exist in their institutions and who also tolerate multiman cells and other conditions that are conducive to prisoners' manufacturing knives in prison industries or from metal beds.[122]

Ellis et al. studied violence in 55 North Carolina prisons (29 for felons and 26 for misdemeanants) and collected data on the institutions themselves plus interviews with 278 prisoners at four of the institutions.[123] Young felons in youth-oriented prisons were found to be more violent than adults in maximum-type facilities, for a variety of reasons having more to do with the institutional context than the psychological characteristics of the offenders. This analysis is particularly supportive of the indigenous origin theory of prisoner subcultures.

An even broader comparative perspective was taken by Sylvester et al. in a survey of all the American prison homicides occurring in 1973. They found that deaths from accident and disease were less likely in prison than on the streets. Homicide rates were about the same overall, but when broken down by race, blacks were safer in prison than outside, but whites were less safe. Only one in eight homicides could be classed as interracial. Single-assailant homicides were often spontaneous, but multiple-assailant events were more ritualized, often to maintain social control within the prisoner subculture. Homosexuality, arguments, and debts were the most common factors in single-assailant homicides while gang fights, drugs, and "snitching" were the most frequent factors in multiple-assailant homicides. There was much violence in the victims' histories, but even more in the assailants' records. In general, size, security classification, and (slightly) density identified the institutions most likely to have experienced a homicide in 1973.[124]

Three comprehensive studies of prisoners who turned their aggression inward on themselves have appeared since 1969. The first was Elmer Johnson's report, *Correlates of Felon Self-Mutilations*, in which he analyzed 291 North Carolina prisoners who mutilated themselves from 1958 to 1966.[125] Whites were ten times as likely to mutilate themselves as blacks, perhaps because of greater relative deprivation as compared with their lives in the larger society.[126] Since so few blacks were involved in this study, we'll look only at the findings that apply to white prisoners in the following discussion.

Although some men mutilated themselves because of homosexual fears or general fears of other prisoners, these reasons were less common than mental turmoil or a manipulative or rebellious stance. Even more prevalent than any of these was a dependency complex that was uniquely associated with repeated self-injuries. Of the eleven men who mutilated themselves ten or more times, nine were of the dependent type. Most of the self-mutilators committed only a single act, or perhaps two or three, but a quarter did so four or more times.[127]

Most of the injuries were moderate ones such as cut limbs, but nearly a quarter of the men committed aggravated self-mutilations—that is, breaking bones, taking poison, trying to hang themselves, and burning themselves. Almost another quarter committed gross injuries, which included cutting their heels or Achilles' tendons, removing their fingers and toes, and severely starving themselves.[128] Taken as a whole, these acts appear more as evidence of social manipulation than madness. The more often a person mutilates himself, the less pathological the circumstances of the act seem to become,[129] which may mean that the multiple mutilators are learning how to enjoy the secondary gains of their pathology without as much self-injury.

In Hans Toch's book, *Men in Crisis*, we have the unusual combination of detailed clinical data derived from phenomenologically oriented depth interviews with prisoners and a statistical analysis of the aggregated clinical data in typical social science manner.[130] By using a phenomenological approach, Toch allows the prisoners to speak for themselves. The categories in the statistical analysis are then partially derived from the men's experiences of their own crises rather than from artificial clinical categories lifted from a textbook on abnormal psychiatry.

Toch's sample included all the prisoners in the major facilities of the New York state prison system plus the New York City jails between January 1971 and August 1973 who either attempted suicide or committed acts of self-mutilation. In addition, a control group of 175 prisoners was interviewed. Due to the high turnover in city jails, Toch and his assistants were only able to interview a quarter of the sample from the New York City system, but they were able to reach two-thirds of the prisoners in state facilities who had suicide or mutilation attempts on their records.

By allowing the subjects to speak for themselves, the analytic categories represent the crisis incidents as experienced by the prisoners in their personal lives, not prejudgments by the researchers. The final classification consists of nine categories formed by the intersection of three types of difficulty and three relevant psychological dimensions. The types of difficulty are coping (self and environment), self-perception, and impulse management (both self and others); the psychological dimensions are impotence, fear, and need for support.[131]

The most unexpected finding of all is that suicide-mutilation crises are incredibly common in confinement, if we can assume that the New York data can be generalized to the nation. Toch estimates that one out of every sixteen men and one of every nine women will suffer a self-destructive breakdown while incarcerated. At a prison mental hospital, the odds are even worse: one in three. Those who are younger, single, Latin or white, nonaddicted to drugs and have a record of violence are the most likely candidates for a breakdown.[132]

Toch's book provides a mass of case history material that will enlighten any reader as to what being in prison (and feeling unable to deal with it) is like. In his final chapter, he makes a major contribution to prison treatment programs by suggesting how to handle the crises that arise in each of the nine categories of tragic events. For each category, he gives the goal(s) toward which the therapeutic intervention should be directed, the setting and process of the intervention, and the primary intervention agents recommended.[133]

Robert Johnson was one of the researchers on Toch's team. His doctoral research, subsequently published in *Culture and Crisis in Confinement,*[134] was based on an expansion of the ethnic differences in Toch's sample. Johnson found that psychological impotence was a problem for approximately 60 percent of the crisis subjects in all ethnic groups, but Latins had a higher rate of support problems and a lower rate of fear problems than blacks or whites. By crisis type, there were fewer ethnic differences. Self-assessment was the most common crisis for all three groups. The primary difference was that blacks were significantly more likely to suffer a crisis relating to impulse management.[135]

Black and Latin prisoners seem to experience the same crisis patterns regardless of demographic background and criminal careers, but whites are more diverse. In the case of the former, perhaps this result is one of the marks of oppression. The primary problem for Latins is separation from the interpersonal supports provided by family contacts. Ghetto conditions prepare blacks so well for prison life that few experience personal breakdowns. The few who do break down feel that they are too weak to survive and experience fears not unlike those they may have experienced in the ghetto, but at a heightened level. Whites suffer prison stress partially because they lack the street skills necessary to survive in the lower-class life of the "joint." Problems of guilt and self-hatred are also common among white prisoners.[136] Johnson concludes with some therapeutic recommendations, which are not greatly different from Toch's, but which are more focused on the dimension of ethnicity.

*International Perspectives on Prisoner Subcultures*

In the period 1969-1976 as earlier, few studies of prisons outside the United States were printed in the English language. This isolation is one of the major reasons for the extreme parochialism of American penology. From England, there are Parker's *The Frying-Pan* and Cohen and Taylor's *Psychological Survival, The Experience of Long Term Imprisonment.*[137] Mexico and Scandinavia are represented by one article each, and Canada by a group of articles from the *Canadian Journal of Criminology and Corrections* plus two research reports distributed through the Centre of Criminology at the University of Toronto.

Parker's book on the advanced treatment facility at Grendon, England, should be enlightening, but since he is a writer rather than a social scientist, *The Frying-Pan* is mostly a series of unconnected interviews with prisoners and staff. The other work from England, *Psychological Survival*, is also focused on the day-to-day lives of a small number of men—in this case a group of "dangerous" prisoners in a "max-max" wing of Durham Prison. The authors' approach is phenomenological rather than statistical. Participant observation and informal essays replace questionnaires administered to random samples as the major methodological techniques for data collection. Cohen and Taylor use a style that is more literary than scientific to communicate to the reader the vast oppression of these men on the psychological as well as the physical level. Their prose is filled with references to other studies of extreme deprivation, such as those of concentration camps and disasters. The book makes evident that at Durham the beginnings of a radicalization process enabled the prisoners to organize themselves well enough to resist administration attempts to fragment them and to use collective protests to better their material conditions. This kind of active (rather than passive) behavior also has positive consequences for the growth (or at least the arresting of deterioration) of the prisoners.

The Mexican study is Price's famous article on the free market economy of a prison in Baja, California.[138] It shows that prisons can be structured to encourage active rather than passive behavior, particularly in the economic realm, but it provides neither a full examination of the prisoner subculture at La Mesa Penitenciaria nor an analysis of the effects of this program on recidivism or any other relevant outcome variable.

Hindman was funded by the Canada Council to do a supplementary analysis of the Wheeler-Cline data from fifteen Scandinavian prisons.[139] He found that, in general, prisoners having higher rates of social contact with guards, treatment staff, and inmate friends were more likely to feel more justly treated in prison and more helped by their experience of incarceration. Although consistent, these trends were not strong enough to reach statistical significance. An unfortunate aspect of Hindman's article is that it is so short, since English language readers have much more to learn from the Wheeler-Cline data set.

In brief Canadian research reports, prisoners were found to have more irrational beliefs than a better educated nonprison population,[140] to have a distinctive criminal argot,[141] and to develop more favorable opinions of the prison incentive program if they were exposed to counseling by chaplains or classification officers or if they were members of the residential unit management committees (a sort of inmate government).[142]

Troyer and Frease attempted to replicate Wheeler's U-shaped curve of conformity to staff orientations in the Drumheller Institution in Alberta.[143] They found a steady growth in the proportion of prisoners showing low conformity to staff norms (a prisonization effect) but also a linear increase in the proportion of high conformity response patterns, which is somewhat different from both Wheeler's U-shaped curve and Clemmer's prisonization model (see Chapter 1). Drumheller is not the average prison. It is medium rather than maximum security and has a higher level of cooperation between treatment and custody personnel than most penal institutions. An on-site visit by the author revealed that Drumheller provided facilities for conjugal visits to well-behaved prisoners, which may explain why the proportion reporting high conformity to staff expectations rose directly with time imprisoned.

Two monographs by James are both based on a 1968 study of prisoners at four Ontario penitentiaries. *Prisoners' Perceptions of Parole* confirms that most prisoners do not have an accurate picture of parole regulations or procedures, but tells us little about the prisoner subculture per se.[144] In *Influence in the Prison Environment*, she reports data on prisoner friendships, argot, opinion leadership, and occupational expectations.[145] Her findings support those reported by Clemmer, Glaser, and others, as discussed earlier, in that the Canadian prisoner system is shown to be relatively unintegrated with many isolated prisoners. The major reason given by men for staying away from their fellow prisoners was that they might be a source of trouble. When they interacted with each other, the interaction was more likely to consist of "small talk" or discussion of noncriminal plans than talks about crime or prison life. Use of argot terminology increased from the reception area to the general population and was the highest among the prisoner opinion leaders.[146]

By their own report, prisoners were more likely than their fathers to be blue collar in their occupational status, which implies a degree of downward mobility that may have been a precipitating factor in the criminal careers of some of them. The men were quite pessimistic about their future careers, even more so than Glaser's samples from American prisons.[147] The opinion leaders, defined reputationally, were older, of higher status within the prison, more intelligent, better educated, and more criminally experienced than the prisoners to whom they gave advice.[148] This picture is fairly close to that painted by Schrag (see Chapter 1) on the basis of data collected from prisoners at the Washington State Penitentiary a quarter of a century earlier.

# 4

## Subcultures in Women's Prisons

The numerous empirical research studies that have been conducted within the field of penology from the turn of the century have usually focused on the social world of imprisoned men. The limited research into the female system, while begun in the early 1900s, really only emerged with any impetus in the 1960s. The historical lack of interest concerning women perhaps can best explain the earlier disregard for the study of women's prisons, while the later concern with the field coincides remarkably with the modern feminism movement and the associated increase in the awareness of women by power structures in the larger society. In this chapter, institutions for women and delinquent girls are treated together, partly because of the small number of studies on female prisoners and partly because of the amazing similarities in female prisoner subcultures across different age levels.

### Early Studies

The first article on female prisoners was published in 1913 in the *Journal of Abnormal Psychology*. In this article, "A Perversion Not Commonly Noted," Margaret Otis described the courting process between Caucasian and black girls in a reform school for delinquent girls.[1] Otis also noted that whether the affairs were usually initiated by one race or the other was not clear.

Ford's 1929 article, "Homosexual Practices of Institutionalized Females," continued the same theme.[2] In an Ohio institution for women, considerable nonphysical coercion was used by women to turn newly arrived prisoners into "friends" (homosexual partners). In the simplest kind of "friend" relationship, passing notes was the main overt activity. The exact percentage of "friend" relationships that included physical sexual acts was not ascertained. The women formed pseudo-families complete with parents, children, grandparents, aunts, uncles, and cousins. The homosexual alliances and the kinship bonds, though mutually reinforcing, did not always go together. The familial ties involved some jealousy and passive-aggressive role playing, as in traditional male-female role relationships, but Ford perceived the main function of the kinship ties as emotional instead of physical. The parents played their roles as aggressive fathers or maternally passive mothers, but there were also many "friendships" that did not involve the strict playing of "butch" or "femme" roles. Ford

The coauthor of this chapter is Dee C. Thomas-Bowker.

77

believes that learned sexual habits brought into the prison plus the excitement of breaking rules were largely responsible for the homosexual practices he discovered in the institution.

Pseudo-families were also found by Selling in a study of an eastern institution for women that was 35 percent black.[3] His study showed that homosexuality played a small part in the total inmate family structure. Intimacies between inmates involving one black and one white partner were known among the inmates as "honies." These relationships were firmly rooted in the family kinship network and thus were considered by Selling to be largely social, rather than emotional, in nature. A survey of the backgrounds of the five hundred inmates revealed that only 2 percent had had any previous experience with lesbianism and only 2 percent felt any positive feelings towards lesbianism. When a white girl was given the opportunity to have time alone with her black "honey," she was shocked and refused contact. The prisoners put considerable pressure on new girls coming into the institution to join the "honies," and the social rewards for taking a "honey" and joining a family were numerous. In the small, stable family groups formed within the prisoner subculture, an inmate usually played either a feminine role (such as sister, mother, niece, or wife) or a masculine role (such as husband, father, brother). These roles were not found to be consistently followed from one homosexual alliance to another. In general, however, girls were appointed to be a female or a male depending on what type of personality and appearance they were judged to have by their fellow prisoners.

The only other relevant study completed before 1950 was of the New York State Training School for Girls at Hudson, which was surveyed as part of Moreno's multisample research for *Who Shall Survive?*[4] At Hudson, white girls tended to have "crushes" on black girls and to be aggressive in seducing them into relationships that may or may not have become overtly homosexual. For the blacks, this behavior was flattering and fun, but for the whites, it was a serious business. To them, blacks took the place of males, and they needed the blacks to play this role in order for themselves to feel normal.[5]

These early studies are quite consistent with each other. They describe imprisoned females as having a strong tendency toward intimate affiliations in small groups rather than a total prisoner subculture. There is much emphasis on homosexual relations, but not necessarily overt physical acts. Two outstanding features are the pseudo-family system and the interracial aspects of the courtship process. As we look at more recent studies, one of the questions to keep in mind is whether or not there have been any changes in this subcultural pattern in the forty to sixty years since Otis, Ford, Selling, and Moreno did this research.

There were no studies at all of female prisons and reformatories in the 1940s, and only three in the 1950s. Jennings continued the studies at Hudson with an additional sociometric analysis and found that leaders and isolates among the institutionalized girls had largely the same characteristics as their counterparts in the free society.[6]

In the second study, Harper reported on the role of the "fringer" in a women's prison in the South.[7] Cross-cutting the usual prisoner status structures were two factions composed of both staff members and inmates. The "fringers" were found to be a small number of individuals who did not have stable relations with either of the two factions because they would or could not conform to the norms of either group. Harper divides the "fringers" into three groups: the betrayers, the disorganized personalities, and the newcomers. "Fringers" had three effects on the inmate population. They tended to reinforce the integration of the factions by violating faction norms, which thus threatened the solidarity of the groups. They also reinforced faction integration by emphasizing the need of avoiding those who broke faction rules. Finally, they lessened antagonism between factions by acting as "counterirritants."[8]

In the final study published in the 1950s, Kosofsky and Ellis examined a sample of a hundred of the inmates' illegally written "script" notes that had been confiscated by the administration at Burlington County Guidance Center in Mt. Holly, New Jersey, a state-operated juvenile center serving girls from eleven to eighteen years old.[9] The inmate population was half white and half black, had average I.Q. levels, and came from socioeconomic backgrounds ranging from the lowest class to the middle class. The "scripts" were illegally written communications between inmates, usually of the "love letter" variety. They utilized the pen names of inmates to mislead the prison authorities. Their tone was more romantic than sexual, with little overt sexuality mentioned. The pseudo-family units and the associated familial roles were often referred to in the notes, while discussions of real family experiences previous to prison life were rare. Inmates playing the masculine role were seen as dominant and emotionally strong and were referred to as "studs," while those inmates acting in traditionally feminine ways were seen as submissive and tolerant and were termed the "frails."

## Brief Studies of Attitudes and Adjustment

In contrast to earlier decades, the 1960s saw the publication of more than a dozen journal articles dealing with incarcerated females, plus the appearance of the first three full-scale studies of the subject. Novick reviewed the pseudo-family pattern in a casework paper delivered at the National Conference on Social Welfare and made recommendations for more inviting institutional group programs that would divert female prisoners from their pseudo-family involvements.[10] At a California institution for women, Cassel and Clayton found that some women had ideals that were even more immature than their actual self-images,[11] but since the study was conducted without adequate controls, this finding is of little consequence.

At the Wisconsin School for Girls, Halleck and Hersko found that the inmates' term for homosexual behavior was "girl stuff" and that their hierarchical social structure awarded the "butch" (playing the masculine role) girls higher status than the more feminine "femme" girls.[12] Sixty-nine percent of the girls admitted involvement in "girl stuff" to some degree, 5 percent admitted having been involved in direct genital stimulation, 9 percent indicated that they intended to remain in "girl stuff" after release from the institution, and 9 percent admitted being involved in "girl stuff" before incarceration. The researchers discovered an interesting phenomenon (which is in contrast to the earlier findings of Kosofsky and Ellis): Many of the girls who "went together" showed little differentiation into masculine or feminine roles and that the girls themselves defined "girl stuff" behavior as involving hand holding, kissing, and *imaginary* sexual involvement. The girls who were participants in more overt sexual acts were often considered outside of the familial "girl stuff" system.

Halleck and Hersko suggest that the girls' personality and psychological makeup offer an explanation for the homosexual relationships within the institution. Most of the girls had used heterosexual relationships on the outside as vehicles for obtaining love, status, and acceptance. The authors believe that the unpleasant experiences many of the girls had with men (incest, rape, and so forth) created a basic fear of men. The girls often equated the feminine role with degradation, vulnerability, and helplessness. The homosexual pattern was thus seen by the authors as "a thinly disguised parent-infant dyad" that was not at all motivated by the physio-sexual needs of the girls.[13]

Miller and Hannum were unable to find any psychological differences between known homosexual and other female prisoners,[14] and Hammer supported Halleck and Hersko's conclusion that female homosexual relationships in prison were more of the mother-daughter variety than cases of adult sexuality.[15] Although incarcerated women may need mothering because of inadequate nurturing experiences in childhood, they often have already become mothers themselves. Zalba found that more than half of the prisoners at the California Institution for Women had minor children living at home while they were incarcerated.[16]

Taylor found that homosexually tinged relationships along with friendships involving pseudo-homosexual role playing were called "darls" by inmates at the Arohata Borstal Institute for Girls in New Zealand.[17] There was a distinction between "darls" and "special darls," with the former involving moderate friendship feelings and the latter involving intensely emotional relationships. All "darl" relationships, special or otherwise, had specific and general expectations of behavior attached to them. The formal organization that kept inmate and staff members separated was reinforced by the use of inmate argot. The girls who had been socially rejected seemed to receive some feeling of personal worth through the argot and pet names. Taylor studied forty-six notes written between "darls" and "special darls" to try to determine the significance of the "darl" names. He found that the girls with many different "darl" names were socially popular and those who had the least names given them were withdrawn, independent, and suspicious.

In a later study at the same institution, Taylor found that two-thirds of the imprisoned girls were tattooed, generally by themselves while incarcerated.[18] This practice had resisted all administrative attempts at eradication. He found that tattooed girls had been incarcerated more, had more criminal attitudes, had been more isolated from their families, were more masculine in their behavior and sexual orientation, and showed higher levels of tension and anxiety than those girls who were not tattooed.

Adamek and Dager studied a Midwestern home for delinquent girls operated by the Sisters of the Good Shepherd.[19] By a combination of a caring attitude and harsh discipline, the sisters were able to foster considerable identification with the staff and the institutional program on the part of the delinquents and to eliminate any prisoner subculture that might inhibit their therapeutic aims. The rule of silence enforced twenty-two hours a day, constant planned activities, a demerit system, and a nightly confession-therapy group were some of the control elements that were used. The authors believe that male delinquents would have more actively resisted this program and developed a prisoner subculture despite all staff attempts to prevent it.

In the last brief report published in the 1960s, Bondeson analyzes argot knowledge as an index of criminal socialization in a Swedish state training school for girls.[20] Those prisoners who knew more argot terms were likely to have greater social influence and to have higher status in the prisoner social system. These leaders also expressed more antisocial values and had more extensive criminal experiences on their records. Bondeson argues effectively that training school is a place where girls are taught the criminal subculture, and the longer they stay, the more they learn.

Surveying the brief studies of the 1960s, we are struck by their unsystematic character. What we find is a series of largely unrelated pieces of research rather than a serious attempt to gain comprehensive knowledge about female prisoner subcultures. This kind of effort did not appear in print until the mid-1960s.

## The Mid-1960s: When It Rains, It Pours

After decades with little or no research on women's prisons, the results of five major studies on the topic were published in the late 1960s. Ward and Kassebaum wrote two articles and a book, *Women's Prison: Sex and Social Structure*, on one prison for women in 1965; Giallombardo did the same in *Society of Women: A Study of Women's Prisons* for another institution a year later; and Mitchell's doctoral dissertation "Informal Inmate Social Structure in Prisons for Women," comparing two women's prisons and perhaps the best of Tittle's articles on men and women in a narcotics hospital appeared in 1969.[21] Although Heffernan's book, *Making It in Prison: The Square, the Cool and the*

*Life,*[22] was not published until 1972, it can be included in this period because the dissertation on which it is based was completed in the 1960s.

Ward and Kassebaum did the field work for their articles and book at the California Institute for Women in Frontera, California, where they focused on sexual and familial bonding among the prisoners. Among the socio-sexual roles identified by the authors were the "true homosexual," the "jail house turnout," the "butch" and the "femme." The familial roles found in earlier studies of institutions for delinquent girls were not in evidence. New prisoners at Frontera were besieged with numerous anxieties and questions that ultimately forced them deeper into the inmate social system for consultation and advice. Ward and Kassebaum suggest that because Western culture enforces protective and restrictive controls over its female population, the feelings of fear and instability that the female inmate experiences are partially the result of the loss of emotional support and guidance previously provided by parent, brother, boyfriend, or husband. The women at Frontera seemed to be less well adapted to living with and trusting each other than male prisoners in other institutions. Perhaps for that reason, the stress on group solidarity and intergroup loyalty found in men's prisons appeared to be lacking at Frontera.

In *Women's Prison: Sex and Social Structure*, the various responses to imprisonment are examined, and the prison family structure is viewed in the light of the specific roles women are taught within the larger societal system. The sexual roles, practices, myths, and justifications are seen by the authors as mechanisms to avoid depersonalization rather than as directly tied to the inmates' physical needs or desires. Although the enculturation process was a relevant factor in understanding female inmate behavior, they found that an individual's personality and appearance played a significant role in determining whether an inmate would assume the "butch" or "femme" role. Many variables were causally related to inmates entering lesbian alliances, but evidence of innate homosexual tendencies or emotional illness was not discovered.[23]

The prison love affairs at Frontera seemed to be unstable, short lived, and explosive in nature, and they involved strict role differentiation between the "butch" and the "femme." The "butch" was expected to play a dominant male role, to pursue the "femme," and to always act strong, controlled, and independent. When a "butch" and a "femme" engaged in overt sexual behavior, the "butch" was expected to remain physically distant from the "femme" while sexually satisfying her (called "giving up the work"). Sexual reciprocity virtually never occurred because the "butch" feared appearing emotionally vulnerable or weak to the "femme."[24]

Using questionnaires, Ward and Kassebaum asked 220 inmates and 70 staff members what aspects of imprisonment were hardest for the inmates to adjust to. One of the choices was lack of sexual involvement with men, and a majority of the staff members chose that item, while only five of the inmates chose it. The authors conclude that the physical deprivation of heterosexual outlets or the attractiveness of another woman as a sexual object were less significant in explaining homosexuality at Frontera than an analysis of the social and psychological benefits that were gained by participants in these relationships.[25]

Rose Giallombardo's book, *Society of Women: A Study of a Women's Prison*, was published in 1966 on the basis of more than a year of study at the Federal Reformatory for Women at Alderson, West Virginia. Her major task was to compare her findings on female inmate cultures with the literature on the culture of the male prison in order to determine what was common and what was variable.

Giallombardo begins by hypothesizing that the direction and focus of the prisoner society at Alderson is largely determined by certain general features of American society that are imported into the institution. She examines the extent to which the responses made by women in the prison social structure are reflections of the cultural expectations of differential sex roles in the larger society and suggests that the female prisoners' lack of cohesion and loyalty can be seen as directly related to the reinforced pattern of competition between women within the external culture. Females in society almost always fulfill their ego and identity needs through tasks involving nurturing and affectional behavior and therefore respond distinctively to the prison setting.[26] In *Society of Women*, Giallombardo provides the first in-depth analysis of how sex roles in society impact the female prison system.

Giallombardo discusses the various conditions of imprisonment for female and male inmates and concludes (unlike Ward and Kassebaum) that there are impressive similarities between male and female prisons with regard to the basic conditions for survival. In both kinds of institutions there is an informal social structure that attempts to cope with the enforced deprivations that proceed out of prison living conditions. Although the prison structures are similar, their specific meanings for the inmates are different. The author argues that the womens' social system is aimed at establishing a substitute world in which the inmates can construct identity patterns that are relevant to life outside of the institution, whereas male inmates build their social system with the purpose of combatting the detrimental effects of the social and physical deprivations inherent in the prison setting.[27]

Giallombardo identified a number of different social roles within the Alderson prison. The "snitcher," a prisoner who tells prison officials tales concerning other inmates' misbehavior, was very much despised among the general inmate population, even though group solidarity was not as well defined or adhered to by the female inmates as by male inmates. The "square," a prisoner who was not considered really criminal and who did not engage in homosexual activities, was not hated, but was seen as gullible and a "fool." The other social types discovered by Giallombardo included the "jive bitch," "rap buddy," "honey," "femme," "stud broad," "cherry," and "punk." The general expectations and norms attached to the various role types show that the

Alderson prisoners lived under a different convict code than their counterparts in prisons for men.[28]

Individual self-interest and initiative were not looked down on by Alderson inmates, unlike the situation in male prisons, and the only real normative distinction made between sharing and selling concerned the family network, which was similar in structure and function to the pseudo-families described in earlier studies of female prisons. Close personal friends or lovers existing on the family plane were expected to aid each other through the distribution of material goods and services, but this comradeship seldom extended between groups or to individuals not directly identified as kin.[29]

Heffernan conducted the empirical research for *Making It in Prison* at the District of Columbia Women's Reformatory in Occoquan, Virginia, where a majority of the inmates were blacks from large urban centers. She started out to test Clemmer's and Wheeler's (see Chapter 1) findings concerning the social world of male prisoners. Clemmer had discovered a positive correlation between length of time imprisoned and prisonization (defined as inmate normative code adherence) and Wheeler found a U-shaped curve relating code adherence, social relationships, and prisonization. Heffernan, however, through questionnaire data at Occoquan, found essentially no relationship between conformity and the social structure of the inmate community. She had three goals for her study: (1) to establish whether an inmate social structure existed at Occoquan that acted through specific roles and norms to cohesively bind the inmates together; (2) to discover why those who rejected the normative structure were not isolated; and (3) to examine the roles of the "square," the "cool," and the "life" and their functions as adaptive structures within the prison environment.[30]

The "square," the "cool," and the "life" were terms the author found Occoquan prisoners using frequently. She considers them to be three major forms of orientation and adaptation to the inmate world that are indicative of attitudinal structures and orientations towards imprisonment. Four variables were found to be related to deviant-conventional reference group association in the prison: marital status, birth, occupation, and contact with convicted criminals. Heffernan suggests that various types of inmates bring different attitudes, norms, and values into the prison setting and that interaction is highest among inmates of similar attitudes and backgrounds.[31]

The inmate social system was found by Heffernan to be directly influenced by the three subsystems: the "square," the "cool," and the "life." The "square" subsystem was made up of those noncriminal inmates who accepted the normative attitudes and values of the larger conventional society, while the "cool" subsystem involved the professional criminals who went along with the inmate system unless their own plans for release from prison were threatened. In contrast, the "life" was a subsystem of political, economic, and familial ties within the prison that acted to protect the habitual criminal, who had been in and out of prison from an early age, from further societal rejection.[32]

The homosexual alliances at Occoquan were found to be essentially economic or social in nature, not sexual. While the prisoners supported the family system of "play" relationships, overt sexual activity was normatively restricted and ridiculed. The economic organization of the family members tended to coincide with personal relationships so as to avoid affronting the noninvolvement maxim of the inmate code, and therefore economic activity was not looked down on as were personal lesbian relationships.[33] In summary, Heffernan found that the inmate system involved power and status hierarchies and that the various deprivations associated with imprisonment were mitigated by the informal social system.

Since Tittle's work has been discussed earlier in this book, we will not repeat it here. Instead, we'll move on to a consideration of Mitchell's dissertation, "Informal Inmate Social Structure in Prisons for Women: A Comparative Study," which was completed under the direction of Barth at the University of Washington, but was influenced by both Schrag and Hayner. Mitchell administered questionnaires to more than three-quarters of the prisoners in two women's prisons, one of which was oriented primarily toward custody and the other toward treatment. These data were supplemented by informal observations plus interviews with most of the women in each institution.

Women incarcerated at the treatment-oriented institution were in general less negative toward staff than those imprisoned in the custody-oriented institution.[34] No consistent pattern of attitudes toward other prisoners was found in either institution.[35] Many of the differences between institutions were not statistically significant, which may have been due to the small prisoner populations involved. Just over fifty prisoners were surveyed at each prison.

Mitchell was interested in factors correlated with homosexual behavior in prison. She found that a higher proportion of women were involved in homosexuality at the treatment institution than at the custody institution and that the only factor significantly related to homosexuality in both institutions was previous participation in homosexuality outside the prison.[36] Unfortunately, her institutional difference is misleading, for as Propper has correctly pointed out, there was a large enough difference between institutions on the proportion of prisoners engaging in homosexuality outside the institution to explain away the difference in institutionalized homosexuality.[37] The treatment-oriented institution had higher rates of homosexuality because it contained more women with histories of previous homosexuality, not because of the treatment orientation of the institution. Propper also shows that Mitchell's use of the term "homosexual relationship" is ambiguous and that there is confusion between participation in homosexual acts and "true" homosexuality in her analysis.[38]

## Contemporary Research on Correctional Institutions for Females

The explosion of literature on men's prisons in the 1970s has not been matched by the research on female correctional institutions. Relatively few good studies of female prisoner subcultures have appeared, though there are a number of peripheral publications of considerable quality available in most large libraries. For example, there are literary reports by both Burkhart and Chandler and an outstanding technical data analysis by Glick and Neto.[39] Burkhart conducted in-depth interviews with approximately four hundred women in twenty-one correctional facilities and shows their suffering in detail. Chandler's interviews were limited to the California system, where she spent more time interviewing staff than prisoners, but in her report she includes tabular presentations of questionnaire responses from administrators at thirty of the thirty-four American prisons for adult women felons. The Glick and Neto study presents empirical data on incarcerated women and the characteristics of the institutions in which they are kept. None of these monographs qualify as scientific studies of female prison subcultures, but they are all useful sources for a more general examination of women's prisons.

Journal articles published in the 1970s illustrate biosocial, psychological, and sociological approaches to the study of prisoner subcultures in prisons for females. On the biosocial level, Cavior et al. found that physical attractiveness was related to institutional performance;[40] Climent et al. found that several medical variables were related to violent behavior in general;[41] and Ellis and Austin found that aggressive acts within the institution were related to the menstrual cycle.[42] Two psychological studies conducted at the Iowa State Women's Reformatory showed that chronic resistance to prison rules was related to a negative concept of the mother figure[43] and that it was the potential benefit rather than the possibility of censure that was significant in female prisoners' choice of unethical behavior in hypothetical situations.[44]

The sociological approach was represented by articles by both Carter and Foster, plus a paper by Jensen.[45] Carter's slight popularization in *Society* describes the usual pseudo-family and homosexual relationships in a reform school for girls. A special contribution by Carter is her delineation of two pseudo-family systems existing side by side. In addition to the pseudo-families as described in earlier publications, Carter found two macrofamily groupings that were institution wide,[46] much like the large ethnic gangs described by Jacobs.[47]

Foster shows that the proportion of female prisoners participating in pseudo-families varies from none in Ward and Kassebaum's study of the California Institution for Women to 48 percent in the Ohio Reformatory for Women, 63 percent at the Ohio Girls' School, and 71 percent at the New Jersey Girls' School. The data from these last three institutions were taken from unpublished M.A. theses by Le Shanna and Wentz that are otherwise unavailable in the literature.[48] Foster posits both positive and negative functions for the pseudo-family system, but feels that additional research is necessary to determine the full treatment implications of pseudo-families.[49]

Jensen administered questionnaires to a random sample of females at a prison for women located in the southeastern region of the United States. His findings for the women largely replicated many of the classic studies of male prisoner subcultures. He found that group contact with other prisoners was related to the adoption of the convict code. Women in the middle phase of imprisonment were more accepting of the code than those in the early or terminal phases. But importation variables such as age, education, urban origin, and felony status (as compared with misdemeanants housed in the same facility) were more strongly related to convict code acceptance than indigenous origin variables.[50]

Three major studies of subcultures in women's prisons have been published in the last few years. In 1974, Giallombardo's second book on female correctional institutions appeared. *The Social World of Imprisoned Girls*[51] examines prisoner social systems in three schools for girls, each of which is located in a different region of the United States and occupies a different position on the treatment-custody continuum. She expected to find additional evidence of the interrelationship of the prison subculture and the culture of the larger society, as well as informal kinship systems in each institution.[52] As with most scientific inquiries, she found what she was looking for, but her concentration on this topic caused her to ignore many other possibilities for analysis.

*The Social World of Imprisoned Girls* is a major work in every way. It has significant strengths, which make it necessary reading for all administrators and researchers in the field, but it also has significant weaknesses. Among its strengths are the fact that it examines three institutions instead of one, the detail of the field research (which used participant observations, interviews, and questionnaires), the sophistication of Giallombardo's theoretical orientation, and her pains to make the book relevant for policy development as well as theory building. Weaknesses include a vagueness about the relationship between homosexuality and the pseudo-family system, an incomplete development of the comparative aspect of the multi-institutional study, and an unwillingness to test theoretical possibilities that are alternatives to her own position. She amasses material in support of the idea that the social organization of girls in prison mirrors sex role structures in the larger society without taking advantage of the data at hand to see whether other importation variables or other characteristics of the prison setting (such as the attitudes of staff members) might be more important.

The kinship system had a different name in each of the three institutions studied, but whether called the "racket," the "sillies," or "chick business," it had the same structural characteristics. In all three institutions, family membership was pervasive: It embraced 84 percent of the girls at the eastern institution, 83 percent at the central, and 94 percent at the western.[53] These proportions are higher than those found in any of the studies cited by Foster.[54] The argot family roles making up these family systems were very similar to socially accepted sex roles in the larger society. Giallombardo believes that although the objective deprivations are similar in male and female prisons, they are experienced differently because of significant differences in the enculturated sexual identities of males and females outside the prison.[55] This finding is an extension of Giallombardo's earlier work in *Society of Women.*

A second comprehensive contemporary study of female prisoner subcultures is Simmons' unpublished doctoral dissertation, "Interaction and Leadership among Female Prisoners,"[56] completed at the University of Missouri at Columbia under Galliher. Because she wanted to ascertain the meaning of experiences for the prisoners themselves rather than to excessively impose scientific categories upon them, Simmons used informal interviews and participant observation as her main methodological techniques. The data were gathered at the State Industrial Farm for Women in Goochland, Virginia, where the author also gathered biographical and criminological data from the case files on every woman incarcerated at the institution during the research period in 1973.

Simmons examined three major variables: levels of interaction between prisoners, leadership, and homosexuality. In addition to studying the relationships between these variables, she related each of them to a selection of background variables. Women who interacted most frequently were young and black, with normal intelligence and high school educations and with extensive criminal histories, particularly including drug offenses and drug addiction.[57] Leaders were likely to be black, urban, not currently married, and recidivists.[58] Homosexuality was also related to a number of these variables, but most interestingly to variables indexing prisonization. Women reporting a physical homosexual affair in prison constituted only 14 percent of the first-timers, 21 percent of those with two to five felonies, 33 percent of those with six to ten felonies, and 36 percent of the women with eleven or more felonies. Only 5 percent of the women with less than a one-year current sentence admitted a physical homosexual involvement while imprisoned, as compared with 20 percent of those with one to five years and 26 percent of those with six or more years. Finally, only 13 percent of the women who had spent less than one year behind bars reported a physical homosexual affair, but 32 percent of those with one to five years and 33 percent with more than five years of prison experience admitted engaging in overt homosexual behavior.[59]

Those inmates who were higher in levels of interaction tended to be leaders and, to a lesser extent, homosexuals, but the relationship between leadership and homosexuality was more complex. Not all homosexual participants were likely to be leaders—just those playing the male "stud" role,[60] which would seem to indicate that even in women's prison, the "males" are dominant.

Simmons did not find the pseudo-family structures described by Giallombardo and other investigators of prisons for females.[61] Her findings much more closely resemble those of Ward and Kassebaum discussed earlier. Another way in which Simmons' results differ from Giallombardo's is in the high rate of fights at Goochland. She hypothesizes that the continual staff attempts to suppress homosexual relationships result in homosexual triads in which "studs" have more than one "femme." When the suspected partners are moved to different parts of the institution, the "stud" takes another "femme," thereby setting up the triangle and potential conflict.[62] This finding can be valuable for institutional administrators in that it illustrates how a "good" policy can lead to clearly negative results. The informal social controls exerted by the pseudo-family networks may be much more effective than formal controls enforced by staff members.

The last of the three contemporary studies of female prisoner subcultures is Propper's unpublished doctoral dissertation, "Importation and Deprivation Perspectives on Homosexuality in Correctional Institutions," which is summarized in a paper delivered at the 1976 meeting of the American Society of Criminology.[63] Under the guidance of David Street at the University of Michigan, Propper developed an add-on questionnaire that was appended to a larger questionnaire administered as part of the National Assessment of Juvenile Corrections project funded by the Law Enforcement Assistance Administration. Four female and three coeducational institutions were included in her analysis. Ninety-three percent of the girls at these institutions completed the add-on questionnaire, and a similar proportion of institutional staff members filled out comparable forms.

The seven youth institutions were scattered through the East, Midwest, and South. Five were public facilities and two were private Catholic institutions. The proportion of prisoners reporting homosexual behavior ranged from 6 percent to 29 percent, but this seemingly large range accounted for only 4 percent of the variance in the girls' homosexual behavior. Furthermore, Propper was unable to find systematic differences between the institutions that could explain the differences in homosexual participation.[64] Part of the problem was probably that the institutions were all relatively oriented toward treatment, so a meaningful treatment-custody comparison was not possible.

Propper abandoned the attempt to find interinstitutional factors and looked instead for variables that would explain the within-institution variation in homosexual behavior. The best predictor of homosexual participation during the present term of imprisonment was previous homosexuality, which accounted for 29 percent of the variance. Only 12 percent of the girls who were homosexual virgins at entering the institutions admitted engaging in homosexuality while incarcerated, as compared with 71 percent of those with previous homosexual experience.[65] Among those girls who were introduced to homosexuality on the current term of imprisonment, the only significant predictive variable was number of times in group or foster homes, and that relationship was so weak that it only explained 2 percent of the variance. Furthermore, the differences between institutions were largely explained away by controlling on previous homosexuality, so previous homosexuality was left as the only variable with any significant impact on institutional homosexuality in this study.[66]

Correcting Giallombardo's confusion between pseudo-family roles and homosexual behavior, Propper separates them and finds very little overlap between the two. She did find that husband and wife role occupants in all-female pseudo-families were more likely than other prisoners to engage in homosexuality, but most pseudo-family members adopted mother-daughter roles, and were less likely to participate in homosexual acts than other prisoners. In the coeducational institutions, boys took over the male roles, so the possibilities for female role choice were decreased.[67]

The significance of previous homosexual involvement in explaining institutional homosexuality gives some support to the importation theory of prisoner subcultures, but of the other fourteen importation variables tested, only one had any relationship with institutional homosexuality. The indigenous origin theory fared even worse, with none of the fourteen variables representing actual or perceived deprivations being significant in predicting institutional homosexuality.[68] In summary, Propper's methodology and analysis are among the best carried out on prisoner subcultures to date and hopefully will become generally available in book form.

*Comparisons between Males and Females in Prison*

How do male and female prisoners differ? Do these personality and background factors lead to differences in prisoner social organization? Many projects have studied one sex, but few have studied both sexes simultaneously with the intention of comparing them. Sutker and Moan found that females and males in four Louisiana institutions differed in various ways, the most significant of which was type of offense, in which females were more likely to be incarcerated for homicide, forgery and checks, and drug offenses.[69]

Using MMPI profiles of matched groups of North Carolina corrections admissions, Panton found that male prisoners were more pessimistic, irritable, emotionally immature, and complaining, while female prisoners were more generally deviant, withdrawn, and less confident about their ability to cope in the marketplace.[70] Males were more likely to experience authority conflict and females to feel isolated and insufficiently gratified in their social relationships.

Cochrane's study of value systems compared male and female prisoners from Michigan with matched control groups of respondents from a national probability sample.[71] In general, prisoners had a shorter time perspective and valued those things that had personal relevance in the near future. Female prisoners differed more from female controls than male prisoners did from their controls and were characterized by a more "masculine" value system, which thus suggests that sex role deviance may be related to female criminalization.

Toch's study of human breakdowns in New York prisons included material on female prisoners.[72] He found that more women than men had deliberately injured themselves. Among the females, young women, Latins, and those with a drug history were more likely than others to do so. Compared with men, women were more likely to experience crises about coping, self-linking, and self-release. About 80 percent of the women who experienced breakdowns reported a great release of pent-up emotions. Women self-injurers were more likely to recidivate in injuring themselves than male self-injurers.

Fox has contributed a descriptive chapter on women in crisis to Toch's book, in which he reports that women were more concerned about support from significant others in a crisis situation than men were.[73] He believes that the inability to play meaningful socially approved roles is more problematic for incarcerated women than the physical deprivations of imprisonment. In response to the deprivations of imprisonment, men are more dependent on their own resources, developed through the masculine role, but for women to deal with these problems, they require security and responsiveness in others. Because these conditions are in extremely short supply in prison, they are forced to regress to more immature behavior, which is often self-destructive.

In *Convicts, Codes and Contraband*,[74] Williams and Fish summarize the characteristics of the economic system in female prisoner subcultures in one chapter, and then go on to make a detailed comparison between male and female prisoner subcultures in a second chapter. This analysis points out that economic producers in male prisons are either craftsmen called "merchants" or cliques controlled by a "right guy" who largely recreates the structure of an organized crime family based on his experiences with it on the street. Women also do what they learned before incarceration, but in their case it is simple thievery. Although women breadwinners play male roles in pseudo-family organizations, they do not adopt male modes of economic production because their socialization experiences outside the prison have not prepared them to do so.[75]

## Conclusion

At the beginning of this chapter, we discussed the results of studies completed between 1913 and 1934 and asked whether these findings would still be applicable in the 1970s. The answer is yes. Carter's 1973 article, "Race, Sex, and Gangs," could, except for the style of presentation, be exchanged with any of the early articles by Otis, Ford, or Selling. The continuity in both form and content is striking and thus supports the generalization that similar deprivations stimulate the development of similar defensive social systems, but does not rule out Giallombardo's position that female prisoners import most of the characteristics of their social systems from the sex-linked roles they occupied on the streets. The condition of women in American society has not yet changed so much that it would greatly modify the role characteristics imported into female correctional institutions.

Two secondary points can also be made. First, there apparently are some institutions in which pseudo-families are not present, though only two are represented in the literature. Possibly, the prevalence and importance of pseudo-families is inversely proportional to the mean age of the prisoners. The second point is that, as with male correctional institutions, prison administrators can significantly impact the form and content of female prisoner subcultures by varying not only the availability of subcultural roles, but also the conditions under which those roles can be acted out. Adamek and Dager's data illustrate the almost complete suppression of subcultural phenomena, and Simmons' study shows how much administrative policies can alter the patterns of customary role enactment. Accordingly, viewing administrators as the pawns of prisoner leaders is probably incorrect—just the reverse seems to be nearer to the truth.

# 5 Institutions for Boys

In 1973, 794 publicly operated juvenile detention and correctional facilities existed in the United States, which is an increase of 10 percent since 1971. These institutions housed 45,694 youngsters, of which 35,057 were boys and 10,637 were girls.[1] This total is an underestimate for several reasons. First, it does not include many juveniles incarcerated in privately funded institutions. Even more important is the fact that it is a one-day census figure and thus does not account for the total number of youngsters experiencing incarceration at some time during the year. While many of the institutions for boys have better staff and more programs than comparable facilities for adults, some of the research discussed in this book suggests that prisoner subcultures among boys are more violent, antistaff, and exploitative than those among adults.

## Early Studies

Although many articles were written on juvenile delinquents before World War II and in the decade afterwards, the first empirical study of a prisoner subculture in an institution for boys was not published until 1958, when Weeks' *Youthful Offenders at Highfields* appeared.[2] Like earlier studies, such as "Two Approaches to the Cure of Delinquents,"[3] the Highfields study focuses on the evaluation of a program design rather than the characteristics of the adolescent prisoner subculture. Furthermore, the short term of stay and the community orientation of the program at Highfields make it an inappropriate example of a correctional institution for boys. By this same criterion, research at Silverlake, the Provo project and similar nontotal institutions has been excluded from consideration in this chapter.[4] A better time to start our analysis is 1959, in which two articles described prisoner subcultures in boys' institutions, one of which is in the United States and the other in England.

In the American article, Barker and Adams make some general comments on the subculture at the State Industrial School for Boys in Golden, Colorado.[5] They found two kinds of leaders at Golden. One held power largely by brute force, but the other ruled through charisma (and probably a high level of social skills, though Barker and Adams don't emphasize this). The subculture was found to have a negative effect on most of the boys, partially because they picked out and emphasized each others' weaknesses and problems in the unending battle for dominance, thus increasing the negative elements in their self-images.

At the North Sea Camp Borstal Institution in England, Rose analyzed leadership and social structure between 1952 and 1954.[6] His social strata included leaders, their lieutenants, leader aspirants, followers, independents, and the rejected. This structure is amazingly similar to the status system at an Ohio reformatory described by Bartollas and others in the 1970s.[7] Leaders at the North Sea Camp dominated in all aspects of institutional life. They went to the front of every line, had the best beds in the dormitories, and had other boys do their errands for them. Leaders set the fashion in dress as well as in the general demeanor of their groups.[8]

## Studies of the 1960s

### Hollymeade, The Triumph of a Delinquent Subculture

After eight months of participant observation at a private institution for juvenile delinquents, Howard Polsky wrote *Cottage Six*, an outstanding description of life in a therapeutic rather than a custodial institution.[9] With a high staff-inmate ratio and many professionals available to the boys, the institution should have been reasonably successful at breaking up the delinquent subculture, but it wasn't. The professionals confined their activities to interviews in their offices and left the control of the residence units to the cottage parents, who were evaluated partially by how well they kept peace. In order to keep things running smoothly, the cottage parents had to delegate much of their authority to the delinquent leaders, who used their power to exploit those under them. The prisoner social system had control over the socialization processes that occurred in the cottages, and so the boys reaffirmed each other's delinquency instead of being rehabilitated by their experience at Hollymeade.

Polsky's research focused on a single cottage in which twenty boys lived with the cottage parents. The basic social strata in Cottage Six were the leaders, their associates, "con-artists," "quiet types," "bushboys," and "scapegoats."[10] Boys were assigned into a stratum based on how tough they were. Five deviant processes were common in the cottage: ranking, scapegoating, aggression, threat-gestures, and deviant skills and activities. All these processes were used by high-status boys to keep lower-status boys in their places.[11] Life for those at the bottom of the status hierarchy was so devastating that instead of improving by the time of release, most of them ended up in mental hospitals.[12]

Aggression and exploitation are extensively detailed by Polsky, but there is only one mention of homosexuality and that talks about labels rather than actual behavior.[13] Since the absence of sexual exploitation seems rather unlikely in this highly exploitative society, either the boys kept such activities secret from him, or he refrained from mentioning them in his book for extrascientific reasons. Except for this omission, Polsky's book is a complete study of an adolescent prisoner subculture, which also includes extensive material on the technique of participant observation and the author's problems in trying to be a neutral observer in a criminal setting.[14]

## A Comparative Study of Juvenile Institutions

In research conducted from 1958 to 1960, Vinter, Janowitz, Perrow, Sarri, Street, and Zald analyzed the interrelationships between institutional orientation, staff, and clients in seven juvenile institutions. A project of great scope, this study produced two books, three doctoral dissertations, and a flock of journal articles.[15] The discussion below is derived from the monograph by Vinter and Janowitz, which is the first and least available of these reports.

The seven institutions studied were selected so as to vary in orientation: Two were oriented toward obedience (custody), two toward training, two toward treatment, and one was a mixed orientation type. The solitary opposition model, so typical of maximum security prisons for men, was found only at the most custodial of the seven institutions. When all seven were compared, that social relations between delinquents were more extensive at treatment institutions than elsewhere became evident. The lower level of institutional control over the boys' behavior in treatment organizations permitted them the freedom to develop more extensive social systems. Instead of being more negative, prisoner social systems were more positive in treatment institutions than in the other types of institutional organizations.[16]

In the treatment institutions, the boys had more positive attitudes toward the institution and perceived staff members as being more helpful and cooperative than the boys at custody institutions. Prisoner leaders in treatment organizations were more positive than their followers, while leaders in custody institutions were more negative than their followers.[17] The authors conclude that prisoner social organization reflects the realities of the organization in which it develops more than any imported factors.[18] The focus of this complex investigation is more on institutional structures than prisoner subcultures, but its comparative design permits the reader to see once again that administrative policies can have a significant impact on the development of the society of captives.

## Other Studies of the 1960s

The negative picture of life at Hollymeade was replicated by Fisher, who used observations, interviews, and sociometry to study Lodge G at Lomo, a small state institution for delinquent boys.[19] In Lodge G, the major interactional patterns were victimization and patronage. Agitation, exploitation, and physical attack were used by the stronger delinquents against boys who were weak and unskilled at self-defense. Staff members supported these activities by refusing to sympathize with the victims and calling them "cry babies." In essence, staff licensed some of the boys to victimize others, and in return for this and other kinds of patronage, the inmate leaders helped to maintain a semblance of order in the Lodge.[20]

The power of the cottage culture is further demonstrated in a study of agreement and reasons for agreement between youngsters and staff by Jones.[21] The type of institution, staff position involved, and the nature of the subject to be agreed upon were unrelated to agreement, but there were systematic differences between cottages. Commenting on this finding, Jones says that the inmate system at the cottage level may be the causal force in defining staff directions as either legitimate or illegitimate.

Additional support for this image of juvenile corrections comes from a study of a boys training school in the Washington, D.C. system by Rubenfeld and Stafford.[22] Their findings are similar to Polsky's. They characterize relations between delinquents at the training school as a sadomasochistic struggle for privilege, power, and material goods. Three passive homosexual roles were discovered: the "punk," "sweet boy," and "girl." Each was more passive and therefore more stigmatized than the one before it.

A number of other studies imply that juvenile correctional institutions are not so bad, or they challenge the accepted model of prisoner subcultures in other ways. Eynon and Simpson did not find deteriorating self-concepts in an Ohio training school, nor did they find a basic split between the boys and staff members.[23] At three British youth institutions, the boys had a more positive opinion of the institution's impact than the staff did.[24] At the Federal Youth Center in Englewood, Colorado, there was no relationship between length of incarceration and unfavorable definitions of the institution.[25] Finally, in an unpublished doctoral dissertation, Wellford found no direct relationship between prisoner clique membership and commitment to the convict code at Cedar Knoll School in Pennsylvania.[26] At this institution, there was no integrated oppositional subculture among the boys taken as a whole. Nearly one-third of the boys were socially isolated,[27] and the other boys in each cottage had a subcultural group of their own.[28]

## Recent Investigations of Boys' Prisons

In the 1970s, there was no rush to study total institutions for boys. Few empirical investigations were carried out, and many of those that were implemented were evaluation studies of therapeutic programs that paid little attention to the task of understanding prisoner subcultures. The emphasis on community corrections, diversion programs of various sorts, and treatment modalities has obscured the fact that many boys are still spending fairly long stretches of time in medium or maximum security facilities.

The 1970s began with an exceptionally fruitful doctoral research project by Schwartz.[29] He collected case file information and administered questionnaires to nearly all of the boys incarcerated at the Glen Mills School in Pennsylvania. In this study, he found that the cottage social structure exerted its influence on individuals through close friends where group cohesion was moderate or high, and directly on the individual where cohesion was low.[30] Prisoner perspectives at Glen Mills were divided into three dimensions: criminal value orientation, conformity to the inmate code, and peer identification. These were then taken as dependent variables and crosstabulated with an assortment of independent variables, some of which were preinstitutional and others situational. Among Schwartz's most important findings are the following:

1. Criminal value orientation was especially sensitive to indices of cultural deprivation.
2. Conformity to the inmate code was similarly influenced by measures of prior criminality.
3. Both cultural deprivation [a situational variable] and prior criminality [an importation variable] were significant factors in the level of peer identification.
4. Orientation toward staff was more important than integration into prison primary groups in its influence on the criminal value orientation and inmate code conformity of the boys, but they were equally influential on peer identification.
5. Length of confinement had a significant impact on only inmate code conformity.
6. In general, both preprison and situational variables must be taken into account in explaining the perspectives of imprisoned boys.[31]

Although Schwartz's dissertation has never been published, these and other results of his work are reported in journal articles published in *The Journal of Criminal Law, Criminology and Police Science* and *Criminology*.[32]

Many of the other studies published in the 1970s produced information on the effects of institutionalization. Hautaluoma and Scott found a decrease in socially desirable values as length of institutionalization increased.[33] Delinquents studied by Ray and Yarbrough showed the greatest acceptance of delinquent norms in the middle phase of imprisonment,[34] which supports Wheeler's U-shaped curve hypothesis (see Chapter 1). At the Indiana Boys' School, the self-concept of first offenders significantly declined with time spent in the institution. For those cases where self-concept improved, the boys had become increasingly delinquent.[35] An Israeli study showed that institutionalized delinquents had a poorer future time perspective than delinquents on probation, soldiers, or students in a vocational training school.[36] Among boys at the Chillicothe Reformatory, while parole information increased as the release date approached for those low in alienation, those high in alienation not only had lower levels of parole information at all stages of incarceration, but did not bother to learn more as their release date approached.[37]

A much more important study of the effects of institutionalization is reported in a series of articles by Zingraff and Thomas, based on a survey of 86 percent of the boys in a state-supported juvenile correctional institution located in the southeast.[38] These authors found that the occupancy of antisocial roles was strongly related to commitment to the convict code, and that both of these variables were related (though at a weaker level) to postprison expectations.[39] Feelings of powerlessness generated by institutional conditions were also related to postprison expectations and accounted for much of the association between prisonization and postprison expectations when analyzed by using partial correlation coefficients. This finding suggests that the structure of the institution reduces its potential for rehabilitating delinquents,[40] which is a conclusion similar to that reached for adult institutions in other studies by Thomas we have discussed earlier.

### Three Significant Dissertations

Not all doctoral dissertations make significant contributions to knowledge. For example, Caffrey's examination of violent behavior among adolescent homosexuals incarcerated at Rikers Island, New York City, does not adequately deal with either the homosexual or violent behavior of these boys.[41] On the other hand, three valuable dissertations were completed on juvenile institutions between 1973 and 1975 and are discussed in this section. The first two of these remain unpublished as of this date.

In conducting his doctoral research, Theis administered questionnaires to boys incarcerated at the Maumee Youth Camp and Fairfield School for Boys, both public institutions in the Ohio system.[42] At these institutions, race and age did not have significant differentiating effects on any of the variables studied.[43] Delinquent identification was positively related to prior police contacts, but not to the other labeling variables of court appearances or prior incarcerations. Self-esteem was slightly reduced by number of previous court appearances, but unaffected by the other labeling variables. Inmate solidarity and delinquent identification were strongly associated, with those high on delinquent identification being very likely to be high on solidarity with other prisoners. The higher the inmate solidarity, the lower the individual's self-esteem. Low self-esteem was also related to negative postprison expectations. Although there was some evidence of the negative effects of delinquent labeling, length of time incarcerated was unrelated to self-esteem.[44] Theis concludes that although institutionalization is not the crucial variable in the development of a delinquent label, it may change the basic nature of the delinquent identification the boys experience.[45]

In the second dissertation, Gold did a participant observation of one cottage in an institution for emotionally disturbed youngsters, in which her methodology largely followed Polsky's, as does her title, "Cottage Seven: Intended and Unintended Consequences of a Behavior Modification Program."[46] Although the boys at the cottage were not necessarily delinquent, they generally had participated in considerable delinquent behavior before becoming institutionalized. Gold found little evidence of a deviant subculture like Polsky's, and while this absence could be due to the young age of the boys or the treatment image of the institution, much more important factors would seem to be the favorable staff-inmate ratio, the policy of constant supervision, and the behavior modification techniques used (based on a token economy).[47] Dare we conclude that the behavior change technology now available is adequate for us to stifle prisoner subcultures and promote "therapeutic" changes, if only we are willing to spend the money necessary for adequate staffing?

Before leaving the Gold study, we would do well to repeat her observations of positive and negative consequences for the boys of the token economy behavioristic therapy program at Cottage Seven. The program provided a high level of external order and stability, and the status system always let the boys know where they were ranked and why. These factors permitted each boy to experience success as he met objectives and earned rewards. Unfortunately, the use of behavioral techniques depersonalized relations between staff and clients. Dependency, compliance, and manipulation tended to be reinforced at the expense of independence and autonomy. In addition, the amoral trading of rewards for behavior was not effective in inculcating human values and morals.[48] We may view these problems as being too great to be quickly dismissed on the basis of the positive effects of the program, and the candy-coated behaviorism of William Glasser's "Reality Therapy"[49] may offer a better balance of manipulation and the encouragement of independence and autonomy.

**A Comprehensive Study of Victimization.** The third doctoral research project on juvenile institutions to be discussed in this section is one of the most significant ever conducted on the topic and is the basis of Clemens Bartollas' dissertation, "Runaways at Training Institution, Central Ohio."[50] The project that produced this dissertation also led to a number of papers, articles and chapters[51] that have been summarized in *Juvenile Victimization: The Institutional Paradox,*[52] which is a book no youth corrections administrator can afford to ignore.

Written by the research team of Bartollas, Miller, and Dinitz, this volume proceeds from the assumption that no formal structure can prevent a prisoner subculture from emerging[53] (which is a very different point from Gold's). The institution studied is in downtown Columbus and houses a maximum of 192 boys, with 24 in each of 8 cottages. Each cottage is staffed with one social worker and six youth leaders. The complex methodology of the investigation included extensive participant observation, interviews, demographic, criminal history and physical data abstracted from official records, and the administration of a battery of psychological tests.

The exposition begins where it should—that is, with the intake orientation procedures and the processing of new inmates by their older, or at least more experienced, fellow prisoners. The reputation of the institution was such that new admittees were too fearful to listen to the orientation lectures by staff members, and once they were in the intake cottage, the other boys immediately subjected them to tests designed to ascertain whether they could be exploited for food, clothes, cigarettes, and sex. Sexual exploitation was found to be severe, with blacks pressuring whites in most of the encounters. If the new boy looked and acted tough, exploitation was minimized; if any weaknesses were shown, he was immediately misused by the others. The reputation earned in three weeks of residence at the intake cottage largely determined each boy's fate when he was moved to a permanent cottage.[54]

Nearly all of the most seriously exploited boys were white, and most of the most serious exploiters were black. As in many adult prisons, the whites were disorganized and the blacks stuck together. Boys were acquainted with the local version of the convict code shortly after arrival. This code had standards for all prisoners, but also some that were specific to blacks or Caucasians. The general code items were "exploit whomever you can," "don't kiss ass," "don't rat on your peers," "don't give up your ass," "be cool," "don't get involved in another inmate's affairs," "don't steal squares" (cigarettes), and "don't buy the mind-f--king." Additional norms for blacks were "exploit whites," "no forcing sex on blacks," "defend your brother," and "staff favor whites." For whites, the additional norms were "don't trust anyone" and "everybody for himself."[55]

Dominant boys exploited submissive boys in every way possible. The forms of exploitation were hierarchically arranged, with a boy's status largely determined by (and inverse to) the level of exploitation suffered. Bartollas et al. identified thirteen levels of exploitation, beginning with the taking of the victim's institutional dessert, followed by institutional favorite foods, canteen pop and candy, parents' pop and candy, institutional clothing, toilet articles, cigarettes, personal clothing, radios, physical beating, anal sodomy, masturbation of others, and oral sodomy. Sexual exploiters and victims did not differ on age, weight, intelligence, height, number of previous commitments, or number of previous offenses, but victims were more likely to be white, middle class, and not good at impression management in interpersonal interaction.[56]

Labeling was part of the victimization gestalt. Staff applied both formal and informal labels to the boys. An "R" suffix was given to boys considered dangerous, and an "E" suffix to those judged to be mentally disturbed. By this official system, boys given both "R" and "E" suffixes should have been the most mentally unhealthy, but the Gough Adjective Checklist showed them to be the healthiest of all the boys. Staff also used a number of informal labels, including "punk," "sickie," and "pussy." They often made open bets on a boy's future adjustment after release in front of him. Even worse, they sometimes used labels to pass on a boy's sexually exploitable status to the other prisoners, thereby inadvertently setting up a sexual attack. Another of their labels, the "booty bandit," referred to habitual sexual exploiters. The boys' labels for each other were similar to the staff labels, though which came first was not clear. Nevertheless, the label helped to assure that a boy's exploitability and personal weaknesses would be known to all and could not be escaped.[57]

In the institution, 19 percent of the boys were exploiters who were never themselves exploited, 34 percent were both exploiters and victims at different times, 10 percent were independents who never participated in exploitation in either role, 21 percent were occasionally victims and never exploiters, and 17 percent were victims all the time.[58] The social roles in the status hierarchy were in general similar to those found by Polsky at Cottage Six and by Rose at the North Sea Camp Borstal Institution, as discussed in an earlier section of this chapter. Ranked from highest to lowest, these roles included the "heavy," his "lieutenants," the "slick" (who was an independent), the "boys who profit" (from their time in the institution), the "booty bandit," the "peddlar," "messup," "thief," "queen," and "scapegoat." Instead of helping boys who were low on the status hierarchy, staff members abandoned them to their fate as victims of exploitation, and even discriminated against them themselves.[59] Some of the boys become so disorganized through these experiences that they mutilated themselves or attempted suicide.[60]

Total institutions have a staff subculture as well as an inmate subculture, which is usually ignored in prison studies. Bartollas et al. were able to discern a staff code that was an analogue of the convict code. Its main tenets were "only blacks 'make it' here," "unless you have been here, you don't know what it's like," "be secure" (custody orientation), "there is a certain way to inform on staff," "don't take no s--t," "be suspicious," "be loyal to the team," "take care of yourself," "stay cool, man," "the administration will screw you," "don't listen to social workers," and "don't do more than you get paid for." Negligence and inappropriate exchange transactions between staff and boys occurred regularly, much as described by Sykes in *The Society of Captives*.[61] But while Sykes paid little attention to staff exploitation of prisoners, Bartollas et al. list five forms: deception, physical brutality, encouraging inmate victimization, aiding escapes, and sexual exploitation of inmates.[62]

Limitations of space preclude a full review of the analysis contained in *Juvenile Victimization*. Readers interested in more information about psychological testing, the ecological analysis of indefensible space, and other topics will have to consult the full text of the book. The authors' conclusion stands well for the conclusion to all the studies carried out to date on correctional institutions for juveniles: "It is now all too obvious that not even a dedicated staff, a low resident-staff ratio, an excellent physical plant, and a client-centered orientation are sufficient to offset prior experience and the general anti-therapeutic effects of coercive treatment."[63]

# 6

## Recent Developments in Prisoner Subcultures

For many decades, changes in both the outward appearance of American prisons and the pattern of social relations between the prisoners within have been small in magnitude and slow in developing. Then, starting in the middle of the 1960s, prisons began to change. Since then, not only has there been an increased amount of change, but the speed of the change has continually accelerated and has left prison administrators confused and in a state of shock. In this chapter, we will briefly discuss some of the changes and issues that have affected prisoner subcultures. In addition, we will make some modest predictions for the future of corrections.

### Changes of Scale

There has been a rapid rise in the number of incarcerated felons in the state and federal prison systems in the past few years. Efforts at diverting convicted felons from incarceration in the late 1960s and early 1970s reduced prison populations until about 1972. By 1974, this pattern had turned around, and prison populations were increasing all over the country. The Wisconsin system increased from about 2,100 inmates in 1973 to over 3,000 inmates by late 1975. The Texas system added 2,000 inmates to its 1972 population of 15,700 in two and a half years. The proportion of convicted felons being placed on probation had leveled off, so that continued increases in felons fed into the institutional and noninstitutional populations at approximately equal rates.[1]

Between 1974 and 1975, only California decreased its commitments per 100,000 residents, according to a survey by the National Clearinghouse for Criminal Justice Planning and Architecture.[2] The states with the highest number of inmates per 100,000 state residents were North Carolina (238), Georgia (210), South Carolina (186), Florida (167), and Maryland (163). In contrast, North Dakota had only 27 prisoners per 100,000 state residents, followed by Minnesota at 35, Hawaii at 39, Maine at 46, and Rhode Island and South Dakota at 47. *Corrections Magazine* did its own survey of prison populations as of January 1, 1976, and found an increase of nearly 24,000 prisoners in just one year.[3] Again, California was the only state system without an increase, and that was due largely to the adoption of new guidelines. The states suffering the largest increases in prisoners (and therefore the greatest strains on their systems) were Wyoming (73 percent), Florida and South Carolina (38 percent), and South

Dakota (34 percent). The high percentage rises in Wyoming and South Dakota are misleading because those two states had a small base population as of January 1, 1975, but Florida and South Carolina added 38 percent increases on top of what were already two of the largest prison systems in the country. California's prison population actually decreased 20 percent. The smallest increases were recorded by Louisiana (0.3 percent), Indiana (1 percent), and Vermont (2 percent). The federal prisons, near capacity at 21,000 in 1971, exceeded 26,000 (22 percent above rated capacity) by March 1976.[4]

Severe overcrowding is being experienced by prison systems in the Southeast, but also elsewhere, such as New Mexico and Oklahoma. In Georgia, there are over 500 women in a prison designed not too many years ago to hold 240. The men's facilities are so overcrowded that one year is being cut from the sentences of nonviolent offenders to make room for convicted felons waiting in the county jails. In four weeks after an October 1975 order, Georgia released 423 offenders without parole restrictions. The Florida prison system was so overwhelmed by the addition of 3,000 inmates in a year that they were being housed in warehouses and tents and being calmed by tranquilizers when necessary.[5] The cost of the correctional component of the criminal justice system is similarly rising. A recent government report shows an 18 percent budget increase from 1973 to 1974—to a total expenditure of over three billion dollars. The three-year rise from 1971 to 1974 was 39 percent. In this same period, correctional employment rose 18 percent and correctional salary expenditures rose 44 percent.[6]

Overcrowding is likely to produce increased levels of violence and other social problems in prisoner populations. In a study conducted at the Federal Correctional Institution in Texarkana, Texas, Paulus et al. found that crowding produced both lower tolerance of crowding (a negative cycle) and an increase in negative attitudes.[7] However, social density rather than spatial density (square footage per prisoner) was found to be the major variable producing this effect.

In interviews conducted by this author with prison administrators around the country, the connection between overcrowding and prison problems (particularly violence) came up again and again, thereby indicating one situation about which administrators and researchers seem to agree.

There is research evidence to suggest that violent prisoners have larger body-buffer zones than nonviolent prisoners.[8] If this is true, then what may be happening is that as institutional crowding increases, prisoners are forced so close together that many of them cannot avoid violating the body-buffer zones of the violent prisoners, who become increasingly edgy as more and more fellow prisoners approach them too closely. Finally, some of them strike out and the rate of assaults and murders within the institution increases.

What are the prospects for the future? Many humanists will continue to offer strong opposition to the building of new institutions. Some states will be able to increase the proportion on probation, but that is only a short-term solution. The public will continue to demand that at least the "dangerous" felons be incarcerated for long periods of time. The population at risk will continue to increase for some years to come—until the World War II "baby boom" children move out of the criminogenic ages of the teens and twenties.[9]

The one bright spot is that the latest victimization study shows no statistically significant increase in the violent crimes of robbery, rape, and assault from 1973 to 1974. The crimes that did increase were nonviolent, such as commercial burglary and household larceny.[10] Another indication of this trend is found in the January-June 1976 *Uniform Crime Reports*, which shows that violent crime was down 6 percent in the first six months of 1975.[11] If this trend continues, and we believe that it will, the future will see a lower proportion of convicted felons in prison even though the total volume of crime will continue to rise. Eventually, as the American population ages due to lowered birth rates, the pressure on penal institutions will be further reduced.

## Prisoners' Rights

Israel Drapkin holds that prisoners are denied far more human rights than those specified by law.[12] The stability of the prison system before the mid-1960s was upheld by the ability of prison administrators to keep their charges from filing court cases and by the unwillingness of the courts to consider prisoners' rights when an occasional case did slip through and come to their attention. Once these factors changed, the courts began to require that prisoners lose no more human rights than those clearly specified by law or demonstrably necessary for human safety.

The beginning of serious court intervention into prison conditions was *Jackson* v. *Bishop* 404F. 2nd 571 (1968), in which whipping was declared to be illegal under the 8th Amendment (cruel and unusual punishment) by a federal court. Sol Rubin argued in 1974 that most courts still ignored prison conditions and that even where decisions favoring prisoners were handed down, prison administrators were largely able to avoid implementing these decisions fully.[13] Sullivan and Tifft agreed and concluded that administrative noncompliance could not be explained away as being due to ignorance, excessive focus on efficiency, or the complexities of legal decisions. Noncompliance was due more to a managerial style in which even prison officers were not accorded their legal rights.[14]

These arguments were forcefully set aside by the action of U.S. District Court Judge Frank M. Johnson, Jr., who on January 13, 1976, handed down a detailed order against the continuation of conditions in the Alabama prison system that he judged to be barbaric and inhumane.[15] The order contained forty-four major standards covering overcrowding, segregation and isolation, classification, mental health care, protection from violence, living conditions, food service, correspondence and visitation, educational, vocational, work and recreational opportunities, staff, and physical facilities. For example, confinement in an isolation cell for punishment was limited to twenty-one days and had to be decided upon in such a way as to meet due process requirements. If a prisoner voluntarily requested being placed in isolation, he or she had to be released upon request. Administrative segregation could not be for more than seven days without a formal review to document good cause for a longer segregation period.[16] The staff of the prison system was required to be raised from 383 to 692 positions.[17]

The order required these standards to be monitored by a Human Rights Committee composed of 39 citizens. In the first year, the budget for the correctional system was projected to rise from 20 to 55 million dollars,[18] with a total price tag of 200 million to modernize the system.[19] Doubts about Judge Johnson's willingness to put teeth into his orders were dispelled in August 1975 when he cut off all new admissions to the Alabama prisons because of the overcrowding. At that time, there were 5,100 inmates in the system, which had a rated capacity of 2,600. By March 1976 the population was down to 4,000, with newly sentenced felons waiting in county jails for eventual transfer to a state facility.[20]

Although juveniles and women have not been in the spotlight of court-ordered prison reforms as often as men, court decisions about men's prisons apply to them fully. In the case of juveniles, they are entitled not only to all the rights of adult prisoners, but also to those held by nonconfined children. The only limitation on these rights apply to instances where imposing restrictions can be shown to be necessary for safe confinement or treatment.[21]

An interesting twist in this situation is that participation in legal action, or at least contact with a legal services project, may have a more prosocial influence upon prisoners than many so-called rehabilitative programs. A study of prisoners admitted to the Washington State prison system in June, July, and August 1974 and followed up in 1975 found that exposure to the legal services project had a positive effect on attitudes toward the police, lawyers, the law, and the judicial system.[22] None of the six control variables used could explain away these relationships, and participation in the legal aid program was associated with decreased prisonization between the 1974 and 1975 testings. In fact, participation in the legal aid program was a better predictor of 1975 prisonization scores than 1974 prisonization scores.

## Politicization of Prisoners

Prisoners have always been political. In the past, at least the leaders if not most prisoners understood the political aspects of their relationships with administrators and acted accordingly. The difference is that modern prisoners are now often political in their orientation toward the outside world, of which prison administrators are but a small part. In a series of interviews conducted by this author at one institution, all ten prisoners claimed to be political prisoners rather than professional criminals, and there was much talk of the amount of revolutionary literature coming into the facility.

At another prison, informants indicated that while most incoming prisoners are socially inadequate, personally insecure, low in intelligence and poorly educated, a smaller number exhibit radically different characteristics. These individuals are socially skilled, communicate well, are at least average in intelligence, personally secure and educated either formally or by self-study. They have a good grasp of the weaknesses of both the criminal justice system and the larger capitalist society. Under no circumstances do they want to be a part of the American social system as now constituted.

When did political prisoners become part of the American prison scene? If we ignore the American Revolution itself, then the first political prisoners probably originated in the Whiskey Rebellion. The Rebellion produced seventeen prisoners in 1794-95, all of whom received presidential pardons after serving sentences of less than a year. There have been many other groups of political prisoners down through the years, but the event that ushered in the modern period in America was the imprisonment of Ms. Rosa Parks at the beginning of the Montgomery bus boycott in 1955.[23] Aside from civil rights prisoners, we can place the expansion of American political criminals as prisoners in the mid-1960s with the proliferation of the Black Muslims in American prisons. The role of the political prisoner began with young blacks but quickly spread to other segments of the prisoner population.[24]

Another input into the development of the role of the political prisoner was the incarceration of groups of war resisters in the late 1960s. While these men may have been only morally radical when they entered the prison, evidence indicates their experience of prison conditions, including many instances of mistreatment far in excess of the legal pains of imprisonment, turned them into political radicals. Gaylin gives many examples of their extreme, though non-violent resistance to prison authorities.[25] This kind of behavior must have opened the eyes of many fellow prisoners to the advantages of adopting the role of the political prisoner.

Civil rights workers, war resisters, and the Black Muslims all influenced the growth of the political prisoner role from within the prison, but there were also influences from outside—influences that increased as prisons became more permeable. The eroding legitimacy of the state and the politicizing of many segments of the population that were previously powerless and apolitical (college students, the poor, and racial or cultural minorities) have had a huge impact upon the prisons. These groups influence each other in a spiral of increasing politicization of areas of life previously thought to be beyond the realm of political analysis and action.[26] When an activist from one of these groups is incarcerated, he will be able to interpret penal conditions, both oppressive and otherwise, to other prisoners in such a way as to make them ready for revolution. Prisons also feed back activists into the general society, where their intimate knowledge of the system can make them more effective as reformers or radicals.[27]

Interestingly, prisons are the one place in America where leaders from scattered radical movements and widely differing institutional bases rub shoulders with one another and exchange insights and ideologies as they do commissary items. Men from ghettos that currently experience the same levels of unemployment, business failure, family dislocation, and so on as America did in the 1930s depression cross-fertilize with radical college students who have never seen poverty outside of books, but who have much to teach about the theory of revolutions. A fair statement may be that our prisons have replaced the college campuses as the major developing-ground for radicalism.[28]

Erik Olin Wright sees the process of radicalization in prisons as arising when prisoners first challenge the administration. When they resist, the liberal legitimacy of the prison dissolves into repression, thereby revealing a liberal totalitarianism that rests on force alone and polarizes the prisoner-staff split still further.[29] At this point, considerable prisoner support is likely to be forthcoming from reformers and radicals outside the prison.

Even "rehabilitation" programs are split into proadministration and proprisoner camps. The proadministration programs hope to produce passive, unambitious, conforming, industrious citizens, while the proprisoner programs aim at self-actualization, social awareness and involvement, and an active stance toward societal and institutional change as well as personal development.[30] In the isolated institution, active programs can be suppressed by the administration, but with strong support from outside the institution (sometimes including correctional administrators at the state or federal levels), they can become a major force in radicalizing the prisoner population.

From the viewpoint of administrators, political prisoners are practically impossible to rehabilitate. The political prisoner role serves the prisoner's ego-defense needs of projection and rationalization so well that the appeal of criminal or sick models of prisoner behavior, both less antirehabilitation, is greatly reduced.[31] Liberal criminologists advise administrators to cut the progression from politicization to riots and other prison disturbances by providing legitimate political opportunities such as self-government of one kind or another,[32] but there is little chance that sophisticated radicals will be bought off so easily.

Perhaps the best tack for those who control prisons is to siphon off as much moderate prisoner support as possible by a combination of self-government and innovative rehabilitation-reform programs, while waiting for a trend away from politicization to develop in the outside society. For radicals within and outside prisons, the aim will be to foster incidents (such as Attica) and revelations (such as Murton's at the Cummins State Prison Farm) that will further undermine the already tenuous legitimacy that prisons have in modern societies. Unless America changes, the future seems likely to contain many victories for radical forces and little more than a series of administrative rearguard actions limited by inadequate funding and decreasing public support.

## Race and Ethnic Group Relations

The first major prison race relations riot was in 1962.[33] Since then, dozens of major disturbances have been at least attributed to, if not caused by, racial conflicts. Part of this upheaval has been due to a change in the racial composition of prison populations. In all the institutions examined by this author, officials reported rises in both the absolute number of minority prisoners and the sense of identity in each minority group. Official statistics show that 47 percent of all prisoners in state correctional facilities in 1974 were black. Although whites were listed as 51 percent (2 percent were from other racial groups), this figure included ethnic minorities such as Chicanos who do not identify themselves with Anglos.[34]

General statistics obscure the variation between institutions. Prisons drawing from urban populations usually have a majority of blacks (occasionally Chicanos) while those serving rural states often still have more whites than all other minorities combined. Racial conflict on an individual or group basis is limited so long as white prisoners clearly control the institution. When a minority becomes large enough to challenge that control, mass racial violence often breaks out between groups. Once a minority group has become dominant, group violence decreases but racially motivated violence between individuals stays high. Perhaps the best example is the prevalence in many prisons of gang rapes by blacks on young white prisoners.

In interviews conducted by this author, prison officials made much of the increase in violence due to minority groups, but there was never any mention of the fact that ethnic groups are often a stabilizing force within the prison. Jacobs found that the leaders of the Stateville Penitentiary (Illinois) chapters of four major Chicago gangs all did what they could to avoid violence between gangs.[35] The description by Davidson of the operation of Familia in *Chicago Prisoners, The Key to San Quentin* makes clear that ethnic solidarity can promote a smooth-running prison as well as destroy it.[36] When ethnic groups become self-help groups, as they have in Washington State, they may concentrate on ethnic identity and personal growth rather than conflict with other prisoners.[37] Of course, there is always the possibility that reading ethnic classics such as *Soul On Ice, The Autobiography of Malcolm X,* and *Soledad Brothers: The Prison Letters of George Jackson* will radicalize ethnic self-help groups.[38]

Nationally, the major prisoner groups organized around race and ethnicity include the Mexican Mafia, Nuestra Familia (both Chicano), the Black Guerrilla Family, the Black Muslims, the Black Panthers (all black), the Young Lords (Puerto Rican) and the Aryan Brotherhood (white).[39] Many other local groups could be named, but they differ little from those mentioned here. Although there is constant conflict whenever an institution contains two or more of these groups, the only really sustained violence has been between the Mexican Mafia and Nuestra Familia in California. At Folsom, the headquarters of the Mexican Mafia in the California prison system, Mafia agents will kill any Familia member who comes into the institution. Prison officials try to keep the two opposing groups in separate institutions, but it is not always possible to accurately ascertain the group membership of every incoming prisoner.

Looking to the future, we see that our prisons will become less and less white. For the most part, they will continue to be located in all-white rural areas and staffed largely by local residents. Judicial and administrative decisions have tended to slightly reduce the ethnic and racial differences between staff and prisoners,[40] but the long-term impact of these decisions is likely to be small for structural reasons. One of the strongest arguments in favor of community corrections (actually dispersed prisons) is that the new institutions will be located close to the cities from which the prisoners came, thereby making it easier to recruit minority staff. The stabilizing influence of a staff in which minority group members are well represented will no longer be ignored by those in power.

## Prisoner Drug Use

Prisoners have always used drugs whenever they could obtain them. The harshness of prison conditions makes the relief provided by drug use difficult to resist. Traditionally, alcohol (in "pruno"), tobacco, and caffeine (in coffee) have been major commodities in the informal prisoner system of exchange. Today, these continue in importance, but they have been extensively supplemented with powerful stimulants, depressants, and hallucinogens. Prisoners find an ounce of marijuana or a few pills much easier to stash than a gallon of fermenting orange juice.

Roffman and Froland cite statistics from various studies suggesting that from 20 to 50 percent of incarcerated felons have major problems related to drug use (including alcohol).[41] A high percentage of prisoners were using drugs at the time they committed their most recent crime. An even higher percentage use drugs in the institution when they can get them.

Officials and knowledgeable older prisoners interviewed by this author were unanimous in emphasizing the strong drug orientation of prisoners incarcerated within the last decade. These prisoners were generally younger than prisoners had been in the past and were characterized as having no loyalty to anyone or anything. They were often linked to violence within the institution. Institutions serving rural states seemed to have less problems related to prisoner drug use than institutions located in urban states, but all were impacted to some degree.

There are two ways in which drug use can lead to violence in prisons. The first way is because of the psychopharmacology of the drugs. This view is the most common, but it is greatly overemphasized since of all the drugs, only amphetamines and other strong stimulants have the effect of increasing the probability of violence in users. Most depressants and hallucinogens actually decrease the probability of violence. Alcohol, though technically a depressant, releases inhibitions in such a way as to favor violence in individuals who have a predisposition in that direction.

Most drug-related prison violence develops as a result of irregularities in the economic and political transactions that surround the flow of drugs into the institution and from prisoner to prisoner. Someone can't pay a debt incurred in a drug purchase. Another prisoner doesn't have enough pills to supply all his customers. A third steals his drugs from someone in an adjoining cell. These and dozens of other irregular situations occur constantly in the prison drug trade. Each time, violence is a possible outcome. Since there is some evidence that the more custody-oriented the institution, the higher the drug use,[42] the maximum security state and federal institutions can be expected to have more drug-related violence than other institutions.

As long as institutions increase their permeability, they are not going to be successful in keeping drugs from entering the prison compound. As new drugs are developed and become popular on the streets, they will inevitably filter into the institution. In the past, drugs have been used to keep troublesome prisoners sedated. There are reports that this is still a common practice in some institutions. Both self-administration and institutionally forced use of drugs are likely to continue into the future. The most innovative, though hardly the most humanistic proposal was made by Irizarry in 1971.[43] He predicted that in the future, the institution will use forced doses of drug antagonists to block the action of any recreational drugs prisoners might use. Medical monitoring will identify any drug users that slip through the system.

## Economic Exploitation of Prisoners

In mid-1972, the total labor income potential of incarcerated Americans was about $7,000 per person, which comes to between two and three billion dollars for the nation. Estimates are that approximately half this amount is wasted every year due to the inefficiency of prison industries and the fact that many prisoners have no jobs at all.[44] If prisoners work at half their potential, one additional reason is probably that they are paid even less. In New York, which is one of the better states, prisoners are initially paid eight cents an hour. If their sentence is long enough, they may eventually work up to the maximum of 28 cents per hour.[45] At that rate, if a prisoner worked eight hours a day without taking any vacations or holidays during the year, he could earn a grand total of $728. Beginning prisoners working that hard would earn only $208 per year, if they were lucky enough not to be injured due to the dangerous conditions that exist in many prison sweat shops.

What union would tolerate such conditions for its workers? Obviously, none. For that reason, prison administrators have been quick to crush any attempts to unionize American prisons. In Ohio, the prisoners' union went on an eleven day "wildcat" strike, after which administrative action practically wiped out the organization. An alternative is to base the union outside rather than inside the prison, which is the technique used by the San Francisco-based Prisoners' Union (cofounded by John Irwin). The membership is national rather than local and has risen to over 25,000.[46]

Prisoners' unions are a new thing on the world scene. The first known prisoners' union was KRUM (The Association for the Humanizing of the Penal System), which was organized in Sweden in 1966. KRUM has been very vocal in favor of prison reforms in Sweden and has not been without impact on the penal system there. In recent years, it has come to favor broad societal change rather than limited prison-related goals. It now opposes all forms of imprisonment and the class society itself.[47] Whether or not American prisoners' unions will develop in this direction remains to be seen.

Because prisoners are so poorly paid (many prisoners are paid nothing at all for their work), they are easy prey for another form of economic exploitation: medical experiments, particularly drug testing. The first recorded medical experiment on prisoners was done by Colonel R.P. Strong in a 1904 study of the plague.[48] Over the years, the literature has generally been favorable to using prisoners for medical experiments and drug research.[49] Only recently has this practice been carefully and objectively evaluated.

The best of the contemporary evaluations is *Drug Experiments on Prisoners: Ethical, Economic, or Exploitive?* by Peter B. Meyer.[50] Participation in drug testing is dangerous, but it promises income, decreased boredom, and a bit more freedom from administration control. Because these commodities are in very short supply in prisons, prisoners are willing to endanger their lives to obtain them when "street people" would never do so. Meyer shows that these experiments have a regressive impact on the distribution of income, which means that they tend to take money from the poor to give to the rich. The poorest of the poor are the prisoners themselves. According to Meyer, among the groups that benefit the most are the shareholders in the drug companies, who share in the huge profits made possible, in part, by cheap drug testing; the middle and upper classes, who are the only people with enough buying power to buy drugs, even at the slightly lower prices made possible by prison drug testing; and a small number of physicians who are able to test an average of fifty drugs every three years because of the lack of strict standards for institutional testing.

The economic exploitation of prisoners is likely to diminish in coming years. Prisoners' pay is certain to increase, though not up to the free society level, and mandatory deductions for room, board, and family support will reduce their paychecks to not much more than their current salaries. Medical and drug experimentation will be either very strictly controlled or outlawed completely. Enacted law, court decisions, and administrative regulations are already moving in this direction. The Mexican system in which private enterprise is not only allowed but encouraged inside of prisons may be adopted in some states.[51] After all, training in free enterprise and the necessity of working to earn all but the barest necessities is congruent with what we take to be good citizenship in a capitalist society.

## Self-Government

The idea that prisoner self-government is a new reform, perhaps innovated at the Washington State Penitentiary in the early 1970s, is patently false. It was preceded by dozens of earlier self-government experiments. The earliest of these was in 1793 at the Walnut Street Jail in Philadelphia. For a full history of inmate self-government, the interested reader should consult J.E. Baker's *The Right to Participate, Inmate Involvement in Prison Administration.*[52]

At the Washington State Penitentiary, administrators were hampered by a combination of directives from the state office and a desire to have the Resident Government Council attain legitimacy in the eyes of the prisoners. After all, the major administrative advantage of prisoner self-government is its potential to replace what prisoners define as illegitimate administrative power with legitimate (and therefore stabilizing) power produced by a combination of administration and self-government actions.[53] When prisoners insisted on electing the most antisocial rather than prosocial candidates, the administration found it difficult to stop them without undermining what little legitimacy the resident government had built up among them. As a result, the quality of the council deteriorated every six months when elections were held. Members of the council often took advantage of their positions to reap large profits in the prison contraband distribution system. After a few years, the Resident Government Council was declared to be a failure and was replaced by a more traditional structure.

Despite its weaknesses, the Resident Government Council was instrumental in motivating at least a few of its members to give up crime. In the first two or three of the six-month terms, the council may have been the most effective rehabilitation program in the prison, as well as lending enough stability to the prisoner population to avoid several potential riots. Other administrators must be finding the prisoner councils to be useful, for 56 percent of the correctional institutions responding to a recent national survey indicated that they had inmate councils of some sort.[54] There is no reason to think that this percentage will not rise to at least 90 percent in coming years.

## Violence

Not all violence in prisons is precipitated by prisoners, but it is prisoner-generated violence that is the focus of this section. This subject was of concern to every administrator interviewed in the field by this author as well as to older prisoners who were more at home in the traditional system of the 1950s and before. Some pointed to the increase in the size of prison minorities, others to the rise of drug user as a prison type, and a few to the general decline of morality in American society. All these reasons have some truth in them (except perhaps the last), but an even more important point is that there has been a fundamental change in the distribution of offenders in the prison community.

In the 1950s, a much higher proportion of convicted felons went to prison than is true today. Most of them were property offenders, and this was a stabilizing force among prisoners. In this decade, diversion at various levels of the criminal justice system has steadily increased the proportion of violent offenders in the prisons. By 1974, 52 percent of all offenders in state prisons had been convicted of one of five violent crimes: homicide, kidnapping, sexual assault, robbery, and assault.[55] People who committed these crimes outside the prison would seem likely to commit them again under the pressure-cooker conditions that exist in nearly all prisons.

Hans Mattick has analyzed prison violence for the period 1930 to 1970.[56] He found that from 1930 to 1960, reported violence was largely a matter of self-mutilations or prisoner fighting against prisoner. After 1960, suicides, ambiguous deaths, and violence directed toward correctional officers increased. In earlier times, the violence was largely confined to southern prisons, but it is now found everywhere. At one time, violence was usually the result of a major realignment of power-sharing factions among administrators and prisoners. Now, the white professional criminals with whom administrators dealt easily are no longer in control of the prison.

A few administrators have begun to work well with dominant ethnic groups, but for the rest, the prison seems strangely out of control. According to Fogel, the maximum security unit at Rhode Island's state penitentiary has little violence now because the administration has shared power with aggressive black and syndicate prisoners, but the medium security unit, where this has not happened, has a very high level of violence.[57]

Although self-mutilation is no longer common in American prisons, it continues to be found in other parts of the world. H.H.A. Cooper spent fourteen months observing prisoners at the Luringancho prison near Lima, Peru.[58] Of 1,500 prisoners observed, about 400 had visible scars from one or more self-mutilations in the past. These were often inflicted while being held by the police rather than in Luringancho. If self-mutilations are an index of the barbarism of a prison system, we may conclude that humanitarian reforms have made more progress in America than in many other non-European countries.

One of the most important questions about any riot is who participates and who doesn't. Careful research has answered this question for the ghetto riots of the 1960s. Straus and Sherwin have done a similar analysis of the August 1968 riot at the Lebanon Correctional Institution, an Ohio medium security institution serving young offenders on their first felony conviction.[59] They compared riot leaders and riot participants with a random sample of the general prisoner population and found that blacks and younger prisoners were overrepresented among the rioters. The youngest prisoners were likely to be followers, while riot leaders were likely to be from the intermediate age group. Married men, participants in treatment programs, and those with no recorded institutional rule infractions were less likely to have participated in the riot. While there were some methodological problems with this study, its results gain additional validity from the fact that they correspond closely with the informal observations of prison administrators and well-informed older prisoners all over the country.

If loose security causes an increase in prison violence, perhaps increased security can decrease it. This question was carefully evaluated when the California prisons implemented stricter security measures in 1973.[60] Data on prisoner assaults and stabbings were collected for six-month periods before and after the new security measures. The study findings show that tighter security decreased violence immediately, but that it steadily rose thereafter. Total stabbings decreased, but there was no significant difference in the rate of fatal stabbings or assaults on staff. Stabbings perpetrated by cliques and those with a racial basis showed significant decline, but stabbings due to personal conflicts increased. By and large, this study shows the limitations on any attempt to solve prison problems by merely changing administrative and custody procedures.

As we implied in the discussion of overcrowding, the short-term prospects for an improvement in this situation are not good, but there is some hope that there will be some decrease in prison violence over a longer time period.

## Family Relations and Homosexuality

In a study of seventy-three presently or previously married prisoners at the Washington State Penitentiary, Butenhoff and Knight found that twenty-seven had been divorced during incarceration.[61] Of these, ten felt that their marital stability declined due to the effects of incarceration. Among the forty-six who were still married, sixteen reported a decline in marital stability due to incarceration. Fourteen indicated that their marriages had actually improved while they were in prison.

At about the same time, Brodsky was doing a much more elaborate study at the Illinois State Penitentiary in Menard.[62] In this study, changes in prisoners' relationships with family and friends were evaluated clinically as well as by self-reports. In the clinical assessments, 39 percent of the prisoners and 22 percent of the relationships deteriorated, while 11 percent of the prisoners and 6 percent of the relationships improved. The rest were stable. In the self-evaluations, prisoners were relatively optimistic about family relationships, but less so for friendships. Parents were generally loyal, spouses either became closer or more distant, and relationships with female friends were very likely to deteriorate.

The 1974 survey[63] of prisoners in state prisons found that nearly half of the sentenced prisoners had never been married, and one-fourth were either divorced or separated. Less than a quarter of the prisoners were currently married, as compared with approximately three-quarters of the adult males in the United States. Approximately 10 percent had lost their spouses during the present prison term due to divorce, separation, or death. Most prisoners received visits by family or friends less than once a month, though nearly two-thirds received at least one letter or telephone call per week.

Everyone is concerned about the deterioration of prisoners' families, but little is being done about it. Visiting conditions have been improved in many prisons, and furloughs are granted to selected prisoners in some states. Few prison systems have any staff assigned to work with prisoners' spouses in an attempt to keep families together. Conjugal visits have been widely discussed but rarely implemented in American prisons. Hopper's book, *Sex in Prison*, describes the most famous American conjugal visitation program.[64] Despite a very positive evaluation by Hopper, the practice has not spread. Bolivia, Brazil, Columbia, and many other Latin American countries have permitted conjugal visits for a long time.[65] Conjugal visitations at La Mesa Penitenciaria in Mexico have been briefly described by John Price.[66]

This author's field visits included one Canadian institution that had an on-going program of conjugal visits. The prison had a series of trailers parked outside the security area. Married prisoners with security clearance could spend a weekend with their families there every so often, though there were not enough trailers to make visits as common as they should be. Prisoners appeared happy to have this opportunity, and administrators seemed delighted to have this technique available to increase their social control over the institution.

One of the best ways of dealing with heterosexual deprivation in prison is to engage in homosexual behavior. Sexual behavior in prison was ignored in most of the studies completed before 1970, but is being looked at more realistically today. Consensual homosexuality is tolerated in many prisons as a means of control,[67] but other prisons try to minimize it on the theory that homosexual triangles are conducive to violence.

Prison rape, though perhaps less common than consensual homosexuality, is a major feature of all American prisons. Exposure to the possibility of rape, often by gangs of fellow prisoners, must be counted as one of the pains of imprisonment, though this form of punishment by the state is certainly unconstitutional. Scacco's *Rape in Prison*[68] is the first book to be written on the topic. While it is sensationalistic at times and has other deficiencies as well, the book gives the reader a generally accurate picture of the situation.

The next several decades will see increased attempts to keep prisoners and their families together in recognition of the fact that an intact family to return to is one of the most important factors in prisoners' successful adaptation to the free world after release. There will be more conjugal visit programs, but these will not be found everywhere. The courts and public sentiment will force administrators to do more to control prison rapes, though there will always be a certain amount of this activity. Other types of the victimization of prisoners by prisoners, including physical assaults and murders, burglary, and robbery, will also be minimized. Prisons will be less terrifying for the weak and less gratifying for the strong.

## Social Science Research

This book documents the scarcity of social (or behavioral) science studies of prison communities before 1960, the gradual increase between 1960 and 1970, and the flood of studies completed since 1970. There would doubtless have been many more research projects except for the opposition to research that is shown by many prison administrators. The name of the game in prison administration is control, and control requires power. Knowledge is power, so the distribution of knowledge in the institution is controlled as much as possible by the staff. The fundamental characteristic of social science, as for all science, is that it democratizes knowledge. What people take to be true can be based on objective facts obtained in a fashion that can be duplicated by the powerless as well as the powerful, not merely on the definitions and pronouncements of those in positions of authority.

Social scientists can be useful to administrators if they limit their interests to discovering better ways of controlling prisoners, but dangerous if they make that knowledge equally available to everyone or, even worse, if their discoveries help prisoners to resist administrators more successfully. A recent survey of fifty-three adult and twenty-one youth correctional agencies showed that both types allocated less than one-half of one percent of their budgets to research.[69] In-house researchers were preferred to outside researchers (no doubt for reasons outlined above), and when asked to cite the research studies they found useful, administrators mentioned technical control-oriented publications. Almost none of the studies they praised were theoretical in any way.

We have pointed out that medical studies of prisoners have often victimized their subjects by paying them inadequately and asking them to volunteer in situations where they were not entirely free to refuse. In addition, ethical considerations are involved in these studies in that the procedures may have been damaging to prisoners' physical or mental health because of lack of available safeguards or because the dangers were not fully explained to prisoners when they volunteered. In contrast, social science research has almost never been damaging to prisoners. Quite to the contrary, it has probably been the major factor in the improvements that have been made in prison conditions over the past few decades.

Looking into the future, there will be an increase in social science prisoner research at the same time that there will be a decrease in the use of prisoners for medical experimentation. Administrators and captives of the criminal justice system such as the Law Enforcement Assistance Administration will scramble to try to find more effective and efficient ways of dealing with prisoners and the public, but there will continue to be a large volume of purely academic research that promises to be more supportive of prisoners as human beings. A small, but growing portion of academic research will also begin to reveal to the scientific community and the general public the impossible difficulties and dilemmas inherent in the roles of prison officer and prison warden.

## Deinstitutionalization

In recent years, many researchers and reformers have come to believe that the best prison is no prison at all, or at least as little as possible. In this section, we will briefly treat the supports for deinstitutionalization, examples of deinstitutionalization, and the limits of this process.

### Research Support for Deinstitutionalization

Dozens of studies discussed in earlier chapters have documented the negative effects of institutionalization on prisoners' commitment to prosocial norms, values, and beliefs. A typical finding is that the acceptance of criminal norms is particularly intense during the middle phase of incarceration,[70] though the negative effects extend right up to and past the time of release from the institution.

Some will argue that these negative effects are a price worth paying for exposure to the positive effects of rehabilitation programs. In the past, this argument may have cast a shadow. Today, the work of Martinson[71] and others has summarized all we have been able to prove about the positive effects of rehabilitation. After examining all the adequately designed research studies ever completed on the topic, Martinson was forced to conclude that no one method of treatment seemed to be effective. In general, he found no reason to think that penology had found any reasonably sure way of even reducing, let alone eliminating recidivism.

What is it about prisons that is so destructive? The common answer is that rubbing shoulders with many other criminals turns first-time prisoners into hardened criminals, so that prisons are, in essence, schools of crime. There is some truth in this position, but not as much as people would like to think. Both psychologists and sociologists have tried to show that the most destructive aspects of prison life are due to structural (and largely unchangeable) aspects of the prison itself. For example, Sargent argues that the enforced passivity of prison life produces ego regression to an infantile level (which is an observation that has repeatedly been made about Nazi concentration camps).[72] This regression leads to such a severe separation anxiety that many prisoners deliberately do something to set back their release date every time they "get short." Sargent finds that if we examine the demands of rioting prisoners, such as the recent Attica and Tombs (New York City) riots, they will show a strong attempt to resist the ego regression that is a consequence of enrolled passivity.

Social psychology offers another answer that developed from the famous Zimbardo experiment at Stanford.[73] In that experiment, a sample of volunteer male college students were clinically evaluated as "normal" and randomly assigned to role-play either guards or prisoners. There was no training, but the structure of the experiment was designed so as to imitate the psychosocial texture of interpersonal relations as they occur in prison. Within a few days, the prisoners became helpless, passive, depressed, and dependent, while the guards became more oriented toward power and status. Some prisoners became so emotionally disturbed within a matter of days that the experiment had to be prematurely terminated. At least one-third of the guards became excessively dehumanizing and aggressive toward the prisoners.

Both these studies suggest that what makes prisons so destructive is not due to staff inadequacies or even poor administrators. Instead, it is due to the basic and largely unchangeable structural characteristics of the prison as an institution. Since no reforms or retraining and upgrading of staff will change these structural relations, the implication is that the only way to make prisons better is to eliminate them. The exceptionally careful analysis of data from a quasi-experimental study of the effects of imprisonment in Connecticut by Andrew Hopkins gives us perhaps the best evidence to date that imprisonment is worse or at least no better than noninstitutional treatment.[74] Since institutionalization is much more expensive than noninstitutional treatment, there is no reason to use it if it is no more effective. The one exception is that there are certain violent offenders who must be incapacitated to protect the public, whatever the cost and however worthless the treatment.

David Shichor has analyzed the difference between people-changing and people-processing organizations.[75] Prisons basically are not set up as people-changing organizations. He sees a future in which people processing into new statuses, which are degraded, will continue to be the major focus of the prison. Should society decide that helping rather than degrading offenders should be the major orientation of corrections, prisons will probably not be the setting chosen for this change in function.

A final argument in favor of deinstitutionalization is that the public is much more willing to consider it than has previously been true. In a recent survey of a representative sample of Washington State residents, Rose and Riley found that 73 percent of the citizens gave rehabilitation high priority as a prison goal.[76] Deterrence received the least support, with punishment and protection falling in between. Considerable support was expressed for a wide variety of modern rehabilitation-oriented programs, including increased vocational training (94 percent for, 2 percent against), prisoner self-government (60 percent for, 29 percent against), conjugal visits (53 percent for, 35 percent against), and increased use of community corrections (68 percent for, 19 percent against). While supporting a program in theory is not the same as supporting the funding necessary to implement that program, this study's evidence undermines the argument that prisons are the way they are because the public demands it.

## Deinstitutionalization in Practice

Community corrections may or may not be a serious attempt at deinstitutionalization. Many of the community corrections centers that have been proposed are nothing more than miniature maximum security institutions. They offer better staff recruiting, easier visits by family and friends, and superior opportunities for training and work release. By breaking up the prisoner population, they may undermine the prisoner subculture, and they will definitely weaken the power position of prisoners in their battles with staff.

The Board of Directors of the National Council on Crime and Delinquency has decided that confinement is not appropriate for any offenders except for the dangerous few.[77] Seen in this perspective, community corrections loses much of its importance. A much more direct approach to the problem of decentralization was taken by Vermont, which simply closed its maximum security prison at Windsor in the summer of 1975: The Vermont State Prison will now be turned into a housing complex for the elderly.[78]

Vermont was the first state to close its maximum security prison, but the first deinstitutionalization was carried out in Massachusetts. Dr. Jerome Miller became head of the Massachusetts Department of Youth Services in late 1969. After having his attempts at reforms within existing institutions undermined for two years, he began to close facilities in the winter of 1971-72. The large reformatories were replaced by 80 nonresidential programs, 120 residential programs, and 200 foster homes.[79] As of August 1975, 1,864 youngsters were sentenced to the Department of Youth Services. Of these, 105 were in secure programs, 214 in group care facilities, 167 in foster care, 565 in nonresidential programs, and 813 living at home with minimum supervision.[80]

## The Limits of Deinstitutionalization

When we look at the large number of manifest and latent functions served by prisons,[81] believing that most of these monoliths will be closed is difficult.

Prisons are an expression of our society. They are unlikely to be greatly changed unless there is a corresponding change in the larger society.

One change that will not occur in the near future is the public's becoming "soft on crime." Americans may favor many prison reforms, but they also favor long sentences for serious offenders, and there has to be some place to house these felons. In a public opinion survey conducted in an urban area in the southeast, there was a very high consensus on the relative seriousness of crimes against persons, crimes against property, and crimes without victims.[82] The more serious crimes were assigned very long sentences by the respondents. The average sentence length for murder was thirty-eight years, twenty-six years for rape, sixteen for selling illegal drugs to minors, and fourteen years for armed robbery. In general, males, upper-income respondents, and those with higher occupational prestige and more education favored shorter sentences, but differences were small.

In addition, deinstitutionalization will not be very helpful if prisoners receive little acceptance in their local communities. A recent study completed in Florida compared the attitudes of prisoners on work release with those of men who stayed in prison until it was time for parole.[83] This study found that work release did not have effects different from continued institutionalization in the areas of perceptions of the availability of jobs, expectation of avoiding future troubles with the law, achievement motivation, or commitment to middle-class norms. Work release actually harmed self-esteem more than staying in the institutions. The scientists who conducted the study hypothesized that work release did not have the positive effects expected because prisoners working in the community encountered negative reactions from their fellow citizens. According to these findings, there is little point in facilitating prisoner contacts with the outside world if this is to be the end result.

## Women's Issues

Because women are only 3 to 4 percent of all the prisoners in an adult correctional system, they are ignored in the planning of the total system. Their institutions are small, usually between fifty and three hundred prisoners.[84] There are a few exceptional institutions scattered across the nation, such as the one at Purdy in the State of Washington. Purdy looks more like a college campus than a prison, and under the administration of Edna Goodrich, it reached new heights of institutional concern and functioning on behalf of prisoners instead of against them. Most women's prisons, on the other hand, have poor physical plants, and are too starved for funds to provide meaningful or useful programs.

Granted that male prisoners have become more violent and will continue in this direction for some time to come, the question is whether or not this trend also represents changes in female prisoner populations. Freda Adler, author of *Sisters in Crime,*[85] believes that female prisoners are less and less willing to accept the overcrowding and inadequate staffing that are typical in women's prisons. Female criminals are becoming more violent and highly politicized. They now participate in prison riots the same as men do: in 1971 at Alderson Federal Reformatory for Women and in 1973 at the Philadelphia House of Corrections.

Adler's thesis is supported by a study of changes in prisoner characteristics at the Iowa Women's Reformatory from 1960 to 1970.[86] Staff there felt that the more recent prisoners were more difficult to handle and more emotionally disturbed than earlier prisoners. Clinical testing did show significantly higher scores on the M.M.P.I. depression and schizophrenia scales, but the only other statistically significant difference was that newer prisoners had fewer previous incarcerations. Nonsignificant trends were toward shorter sentences, lower ages, more drug offenses, and more unmarried prisoners.

Just the opposite position is taken by Joann Morton, who sees few changes in female prisoner populations over the years.[87] Since most female offenders are lower class, they have not been moved by the women's liberation movement. The movement has been largely peopled by and oriented toward white upper- and middle-class women who are college educated.

There is abundant evidence that women's prisons differ from men's prisons and that female prisoners differ from male prisoners. Female crimes will continue to increase in number and seriousness. A decline in sexism in the criminal justice system will mean more women incarcerated, not less. Determining whether women experience a greater or lesser degree of the pains of imprisonment than men is difficult. Showing that external physical conditions differ does not mean that the sexes subjectively experience them differently. Research to date does not clearly illuminate the complex interaction between the changing characteristics of female prisoners, conditions in women's prisons, their subjective experience of these conditions, and their actual or potential violence while incarcerated. Nevertheless, we might reasonably expect to see an increase of riots and other forms of violence in the near future.

## Conclusion

If the prison scene was a football game and 1976 was halftime, the score would be prisoners 21 and staff 7. The large number of staff injuries and the fact that the referees sometimes seem to be prejudiced in favor of the prisoners assure us that the score will be even more one-sided in the second half. Strangely enough, a prisoner victory will be averted not through the efforts of the opposing team, but rather because prisoners are ceasing to exist as anything like a unified body with a consistent (convict) code of behavior. The dissolving of the opposing team structure of modern corrections will not be mourned by anyone of good faith.

# 7 Conclusions and Policy Recommendations

Pure scientific research, without any application now or in the future is an ideal type that does not exist. All properly conceived and executed research profits humankind in one way or another. The only question is whether the benefits are immediate or long term. In this chapter, we will make some theoretical generalizations based on the review of research that has dominated our discussion up to this point.

1. Prisoner subcultures can be controlled by administrators to the extent that they have control over the reward system of the prison, through which they can control access to prisoner roles, both prosocial and antisocial. In some prisons, administrators have had their control diminished by government officials and corrections system bureaucrats at the state or national levels. With these exceptions, administrators have more than enough power to control prisoner subcultures directly. The more successful wardens have always done so through the "con boss" system, wherein they exchanged information and other favors for the basic support of the high status prisoners.

This route can still be followed in some prisons, but where minority groups are powerful, coopting prisoner leaders may be more difficult. In this situation, wardens will find a helpful practice is to integrate officials with a minority heritage into the prison administration as well as line staff. They will also be wise to give the fullest possible support to minority activities of a politically moderate or conservative nature in order to cut the middle ground out from under radical and violence-prone minority leaders.

The principle of administrative control points to the fact that a warden's allowing the prisoner subculture to run his prison for him is his own fault. He is either unaware of how to deal effectively with the prisoner subculture or unwilling to put out the effort necessary to do an adequate job. In the first case, sociological retraining is appropriate. In the second case, he should be immediately removed from his post.

2. Many of the most negative effects of imprisonment derive from the structure of the prison, the attitude that society and its representatives take toward prisoners, and similar factors that are beyond the control of administrators or prisoners. The more punitive the attitude of the society at large toward prisoners, the more negative the effects of prison life will become. When we talk of changing prisoners for the better, the prison is its own worst enemy. For this reason, the average administrator, who heads a poorly funded and poorly staffed facility, should not be expected to rehabilitate most of his charges.

123

One thing seems clear, and that is that the *vast* majority of prisoners will never be made into law-abiding citizens by imprisonment simply because they are prisoners, with all that implies. The social structures and subcultures that grow up in prison settings are interpersonal disasters. Some people will improve themselves anywhere, *even* in prison. The realistic administrator should try to make conditions conducive to personal growth for those prisoners who triumph over their misfortunes well enough to desire it. Rehabilitation programs should be available, but will not reach most prisoners if participation is mandatory instead of voluntary.

3. The prisoner subculture is a force in the creation of antisocial attitudes in custody-oriented institutions. The greater the power of subcultural leaders in this setting, the more negative and antisocial the prison will become. Mastering the art of sociological analysis formally or informally is the only way to control the subculture. By controlling it, one could expect to (1) decrease general negativism and criminal influences in the prison, (2) make it less unpopular for individual prisoners to make prosocial changes, and (3) at least prevent the deterioration of most prisoners. More positive goals are unrealistic in the maximum security setting, through they are possible in alternative settings such as a therapeutic community.

4. We know that prisoner subcultures develop both as responses to the pains of imprisonment and because of norms, values and beliefs that most prisoners import into the prison with them from their criminal and/or poverty class backgrounds. The more we skim off the less severe felons through diversionary programs, the greater will be the proportion of the remaining prisoners who will import antisocial cultural elements into the prison setting. There will be many possibilities for therapeutic programs in the diversionary programs, community corrections, and so forth, but very limited possibilities for those who are left in the "max-max" units.

5. Prison riots usually result from administrative actions that redistribute power among prisoners. The more the hegemony of prisoner leaders is threatened by administrative actions, the less they will be coopted by the system. They will then throw their weight behind a program of agitation that usually does not have a riot as its specific goal, but once the prisoner population gets excited enough, the situation sometimes gets out of control and a riot results. Again, a careful sociological analysis of the internal political effects of administrative actions is the way to avoid difficulty.

6. The prisoners who are the most healthy psychologically are the least likely to be successful in custody-oriented prisons. To avoid the most antisocial offenders' rising to the top, they should be classified out of the general population. In fact, each level of psychosocial criminality should have its own classification niche, with completely separate facilities from the other levels of prisoners.

7. The prisoner population is highly differentiated, not only with respect to

status and role, but in level of integration into the prisoner subculture, degree of antisocial orientation, and so forth. The greater the level of prisoner differentiation, the greater the extent to which classification into isolated units is a desirable penological technique. Through the measurement of differentiating characteristics, classification techniques can become objective and scientific.

A series of mini-prisons or isolated units within a large facility should be classified by type of offender, based on psychosocial rather than legal criteria. Those types of offenders most willing to give up the convict code and to participate fully in a therapeutic community should be housed together. At the other end of the continuum, there will be mini-prisons filled with felons who are so resistant to change that there is almost no chance of resocializing them. These people should be segregated out from the more treatable cases simply to prevent infection—not in the hope of helping them. Through a constant skimming process, we can reduce the number of serious cases, but we can never eliminate them completely. The price for this skimming process is that those remaining in the "max-max" unit will be increasingly hard to control, as mentioned in point four.

8. There are stringent limitations on treatment strategies based on court decisions, legislative funding, social science knowledge, and morals that are part of the Christian tradition. The greater these limitations, the harder planning effective behavior change techniques becomes. Three examples of these limitations are listed below.

1.  If prisoners are not permitted to communicate with one another, they cannot develop a negative prisoner subculture. Complete physical isolation would accomplish this goal, but sensory deprivation studies and the biographies of totally isolated men give strong testimony that this produces insanity, not rehabilitation. In anything less than total isolation, prisoners will find ingenious ways to communicate. Such semi-total isolation would be fairly effective at reducing inmate exploitation, but it would also almost certainly be cruel and unusual punishment under the constitution.

2.  There is some evidence that radical behavior therapy coupled with ever-present supervision would greatly decrease the impact of prisoner subcultures. The problem is that in order to be really effective, the behavior therapy has to be so harsh that we may not wish to institute such a program for ethical reasons. In addition, it is beyond the funding limits of almost all contemporary corrections systems.

3.  Another possibility is to restrict the number of prisoners who can congregate together. Mini-prisons will do this, but research shows that cottages with sixteen prisoners are large enough to produce subcultures strong enough to neutralize any therapeutic program that might be present. To be successful, a mini-prison would have to be set up as a therapeutic community, with heavy staffing at the start but reduced staffing as the

community solidified its commitment to therapeutic norms, values and beliefs. Again, current funding levels do not permit this kind of program development.

9. There is an extensive literature on the creation and maintenance of therapeutic communities. Except for those items mentioned in previous chapters, we will not refer to this literature in this book.[1] Instead, let us spend a moment talking about staffing these programs. In the first place, prison experience should not be a criterion for hiring. Staff should be trained after hiring, not be expected to come pretrained. Although desirable, a college education should not be a requirement. If education, training, and prior experience are not the major criteria for selecting staff in a therapeutic community for felons, what will we use?

Since therapeutic communities are helping communities, staff employed there should be competent at helping others, and no other criterion should take precedence over a helping capability. The higher the helping capabilities of staff, the greater the effectiveness of any rehabilitative program. In his seminal two-volume work on the helping process, Carkhuff summarizes all the research on effective helpers and finds that people who are good at helping always have a higher level of personal functioning than their clients.[2] No training, experience, or status can take the place of a high level of personal functioning, and this can be measured through direct observations in problem settings as well as paper and pencil psychological tests. According to Carkhuff, characteristics definitely associated with successful helpers are genuineness, specificity, concreteness, willingness to be confronting when necessary, and ability at interpretation. Characteristics associated with successful helpers for which the research evidence is not strong enough to be certain of their value include self-disclosure, openness and flexibility, commitment, and confidence.[3]

10. The goodness of fit of theoretical models to institutional conditions varies with the characteristics of the institution studied. No model or theory is universal. The competition between the importation and indigenous origin theories of prisoner subcultures is thus misguided. Neither could possibly win. Each explains some of the variance in prisoner subcultures, with the relative importance of each theory varying with the institution examined. In general, the more custody-oriented the institution, the greater the objective deprivations suffered by prisoners; the greater the objective deprivations, the greater the subjective deprivations felt by prisoners; and the higher the level of felt deprivations, the more adequate the indigenous origin model will be in explaining the characteristics of the resulting prisoner subculture.

11. Although the imagery of a monolithic prisoner subculture is a handy description, there are fewer institutions each year in which this picture is reasonably accurate. In surveying the literature on prisoner subcultures, we find that the more contemporary the study, the less likely the unitary subculture

model is to be consistent with the data collected. Wherever minority groups begin to gain numbers, multiple subcultures arise. Many prisoners are isolates in all custody-oriented institutions. Among female prisoners, small groups, often with a pseudo-family morphology, take precedence over any all-encompassing prisoner subculture. In prisoner groups of all ages and sexes, the more masculine the role, the higher the status associated with playing that role.

12. Prisons place too much emphasis on punishments as a social control mechanism. The greater the punishments, the greater the deprivations that are part of incarceration, and the greater the strength of the prisoner subculture. We need to find creative ways of rewarding prisoners. Rewards should never become rights. Instead, prisoners should earn them. Through this process, administrators can gain control of the prisoner subculture. The evidence examined in this book suggests that conjugal visits would be useful as one of the new rewards, but would not be a panacea. The token economy model shows us how to convert many more common rights back into earned rewards. Of course, basic human rights should never have to be earned, but there are many privileges that have come to be taken as rights by today's prisoner, and this should be reversed.

13. Finally, a philosophical point: Rehabilitators are in the business of reconstructing meaning. All people need to be immersed in a compelling symbol system that interprets life's experiences so as to make them subjectively meaningful. The higher the subjective meaningfulness of a rehabilitative program, the more it will succeed in reconstructing the web of meaning for its participants and therefore in rehabilitating them in the most basic meaning of the term. The lower the subjective meaningfulness of a program, the more prisoners will fill the moral void with antisocial norms, values, beliefs, and definitions of the situation.

In an age in which religion, patriotism, and communism are relatively unsuccessful in the ideological battle for the American consciousness, we cannot expect therapy programs with inadequate staffing to succeed where all others have failed. Different webs of meaning will be attractive to different kinds of people. When creating new programs, planners should first use Weber's *verstehen* to put themselves in the skins of their projected clients and then ask themselves whether the programs they contemplate will provide a compelling source of meaning for these clients to incorporate into their personal motivational systems as a guide for future conduct.

# Notes

# Notes

## Chapter 1
## Pioneering Studies of Prisons for Men

1. Joseph Fulling Fishman, *Sex in Prison* (New York: National Library Press, 1934).

2. James Hargan, "The Psychology of Prison Language," *Journal of Abnormal and Social Psychology* 30 (October-December 1935): 359-65.

3. Hans Reimer, "Socialization in the Prison Community," *Proceedings of the American Prison Association* (1937): 151-55.

4. Henry H. Goddard, *The Kallikak Family* (New York: Macmillan, 1931); Richard L. Dugdale, *The Jukes* (New York: G.P. Putnam's Sons, 1910).

5. Andrew W. Brown and A.A. Hartman, "A Survey of the Intelligence of Illinois Prisoners," *Journal of Criminal Law and Criminology* 28 (January-February 1938): 707-19.

6. Simon H. Tulchin, *Intelligence and Crime, A Study of Penitentiary and Reformatory Offenders* (Chicago: University of Chicago Press, 1939).

7. Fred Otto Erbe, "A Study of the Social Backgrounds of Life Inmates at Fort Madison Penitentiary," *Journal of Criminal Law and Criminology* 31 (July-August 1940): 166-74.

8. Ruth Sherman Tolman, "Some Differences in Attitudes Between Groups of Repeating Criminals and of First Offenders," *Journal of Criminal Law and Criminology* 30 (July-August 1939): 196-203.

9. L.M. Hanks, Jr., "Preliminary Study of Problems of Discipline in Prisons," *Journal of Criminal Law and Criminology* 30 (March-April 1940): 879-87.

10. Donald Rasmussen, "Prisoner Opinions About Parole," *American Sociological Review* 5 (August 1940): 584-95.

11. Norman Hayner and Ellis Ash, "The Prisoner Community as a Social Group," *American Sociological Review* 4 (June 1939): 362-69.

12. Norman Hayner and Ellis Ash, "The Prison as a Community," *American Sociological Review* 5 (August 1940): 577-83.

13. Hayner and Ash, "The Prisoner Community," pp. 364-67.

14. Ibid., pp. 367-68.

15. Norman Hayner, "Washington State Correctional Institutions as Communities," *Social Forces* 21 (March 1943): 317.

16. Ibid., pp. 320, 321.

17. Donald Clemmer, "Leadership Phenomena in a Prison Community," *Journal of Criminal Law and Criminology* 28 (March-April 1938): 861-72.

18. Donald Clemmer, *The Prison Community* (New York: Holt, Rinehart & Winston, 1940).

19. Ibid., p. 83.

20. Ibid., pp. 114-15, 321-29.

21. Ibid., p. 89.

22. Ibid., pp. 105, 117-23, 130-33; George Simmel, *Sociologie* (Leipzig: Dunker and Humblat, 1908).

23. Ibid., pp. 294-96.

24. Ibid., pp. 257-58.

25. Ibid., 256, 263

26. Ibid., p. 299.

27. Harold Garfinkel, "Conditions of Successful Degradation Ceremonies," *American Journal of Sociology* 61 (March 1956): 420-24.

28. Clemmer, *The Prison Community*, pp. 300-02.

29. Ibid., p. 313.

30. Donald Clemmer, "Observations on Imprisonment as a Source of Criminality," *Journal of Criminal Law and Criminology* 41 (September-October 1950): 311-19.

31. Donald Clemmer, "Some Aspects of Sexual Behavior in the Prison Community," *Proceedings of the 88th Annual Congress of Correction of the American Correctional Association* (1958): 381-84.

32. Donald Clemmer, "The Prisoner's Pre-Release Expectations in the Free Community," *Proceedings of the American Correctional Association* (1959).

33. S. Kirson Weinberg, "Aspects of the Prison Social Structure," *American Journal of Sociology* 47 (March 1942): 722.

34. Jerome Gerald Sacks, "Troublemaking in Prison: A Study of Resistant Behavior as an Administrative Problem in a Medium Security Penal Institution," unpublished Ph.D. dissertation, The Catholic University of America, Washington, D.C., 1942, pp. 129-131.

35. Norman Polansky, "The Prison as an Autocracy," *Journal of Criminal Law and Criminology* 33 (May-June 1942): 16-22.

36. Marshall C. Greco and James C. Wright, "The Correctional Institution in the Etiology of Chronic Homosexuality," *American Journal of Orthopsychiatry* 14 (1944): 304-05.

37. George Devereux and Malcolm C. Moos, "The Social Structure of Prisons, and the Organic Tensions." *Journal of Criminal Psychopathology* 4 (October 1942): 311-17.

38. T. Veblen, *The Theory of the Leisure Class* (New York: Vangard Press, 1928).

39. Devereux and Moos, "The Social Structure," pp. 316-21.

40. Ibid., pp. 317-18.

41. Maurice L. Farber, "Suffering and the Time Perspective of the Prisoner," *University of Iowa Studies in Child Welfare* 20 (1944): 177-78.

42. Ibid., pp. 187-93, 208.

43. Clarence Schrag, "Social Types in a Prison Community," unpublished M.A. thesis, University of Washington, Seattle, 1944, and Clarence Schrag, "Crimeville: A Sociometric Study of a Prison Community," unpublished Ph.D. dissertation, University of Washington, Seattle, 1950.

44. See Donald L. Garrity, "Effect of Length of Incarceration Upon Parole Adjustment and Estimation of Optimum Sentence," unpublished Ph.D. dissertation, University of Washington, Seattle, 1958; Stanton Wheeler, "Social Organization in a Correctional Community," unpublished Ph.D. dissertation, University of Washington, Seattle, 1958; John W. Kinch, "Certain Social-Psychological Aspects of Types of Juvenile Delinquents," unpublished Ph.D. dissertation, University of Washington, Seattle, 1959; Peter G. Garabedian, "Western Penitentiary: A Study in Social Organization," unpublished Ph.D. dissertation, University of Washington, Seattle, 1959; George Sherman Rothbart, "Social Conflict in Prison Organization," unpublished Ph.D. dissertation, University of Washington, Seattle, 1964; Arlene Edith Mitchell, "Informal Inmate Social Structure in Prisons for Women: A Comparative Study," unpublished Ph.D. dissertation, University of Washington, Seattle, 1969; and Werner Gruninger, "Criminalization, Prison Roles and Normative Alienation: A Cross-Cultural Study," unpublished Ph.D. dissertation, University of Washington, Seattle, 1974.

45. Rothbart, "Social Conflict," p. iii.

46. Clarence Schrag, "Leadership Among Prison Inmates," *American Sociological Review* 19 (February 1954): 37-42.

47. Clarence Schrag, *Crime and Justice: American Style* (Washington D.C.: Government Printing Office, 1971).

48. Clarence Schrag, "A Preliminary Criminal Typology," *Pacific Sociological Review* 4 (Spring 1961): 11-16.

49. Ibid., pp. 14-15.

50. Clarence Schrag, "Some Foundations for a Theory of Correction," in Donald R. Cressey, ed., *The Prison: Studies in Institutional Organization and Change* (New York: Holt, Rinehart and Winston, 1961).

51. Ibid., p. 356.

52. Clarence Schrag, "Social Role, Social Position, and Prison Social Structure," *Proceedings of the American Correctional Association* (1959): 185-86.

53. Schrag, "Social Types."

54. Schrag, "Social Role," pp. 183, 186.

55. Schrag, *Crime and Justice*, pp. 208-12.

56. See Walter A. Lunden, "Antagonism and Altruism Among Prisoners," in P.A. Sorokin, ed., *Forms and Techniques of Altruistic and Spiritual Growth* (Boston: Beacon Press, 1954), pp. 447-60; John James, "The Application of the Small Group Concept to the Study of the Prison Community," *British Journal of Delinquency* 5 (April 1955): 296-80; Harvey Powelson and Reinhard Bendix, "Psychiatry in Prison," *Psychiatry* 14 (February 1951): 73-86; and F.E. Haynes, "The Sociological Study of the Prison Community," *Journal of Criminal Law and Criminology* 29 (November-December 1948): 432-40.

57. Alfred C. Schnur, "Prison Conduct and Recidivism," *Journal of Criminal Law and Criminology* 40 (May-June 1949): 36-42.

58. Lloyd W. McCorkle and Richard Korn, "Resocialization Within Walls," *The Annals of the American Academy of Political and Social Science* 293 (May 1954): 88-91.

59. Ibid., pp. 88-91.

60. Raymond J. Corsini, "A Study of Certain Attitudes of Prison Inmates," *Journal of Criminal Law and Criminology* 37 (July-August 1946): 132-40.

61. Raymond Corsini and Kenwood Bartkeme, "Attitudes of San Quentin Prisoners," *Journal of Correctional Education* 4 (October 1952): 43-46.

62. William R. Morrow, "Criminality and Antidemocratic Trends: A Study of Prison Inmates," in T.W. Adorno, ed., *The Authoritarian Personality* (New York: Harper & Row, 1950), pp. 817-90.

63. Vernon Fox, "The Effect of Counseling on Adjustment in Prison," *Social Forces* 32 (March 1954): 285-89.

64. Patrick J. Driscoll, *Readings in Criminology and Penology* (New York: Columbia University Press, 1964), 595.

65. The more valuable articles include the following: Charles E. Smith, "The Homosexual Federal Offender," *Journal of Criminal Law, Criminology and Police Science* 44 (January-February 1954): 582-91; Benjamin Karpman, "Sex Life in Prison," *Journal of Criminal Law and Criminology* 37 (January-February 1948): 275-86; Herbert A. Bloch, "Social Pressures of Confinement Toward Sexual Deviation," *Journal of Social Therapy* 1 (April 1955): 112-25; Donald Webster Cory, "Homosexuality in Prison," *Journal of Social Therapy* 1 (April 1955): 137-40; George J. Train, "Unrest in the Penitentiary," *Journal of Criminal Law, Criminology and Police Science* 44 (September-October 1953): 277-95; and Robert M. Lindner, "Sex in Prison," *Complex* 6 (Fall 1951): 5-20.

66. Karpman, "Sex Life in Prison," pp. 480-83.

67. Lindner, "Sex in Prison," p. 12.

68. Smith, "The Homosexual Federal Offender," pp. 584-85.

69. Bloch, "Social Pressures," pp. 120-21.

70. See Ronald L. Akers, Norman Hayner, and Werner Gruninger, "Homosexual and Drug Behavior in Different Types of Prisons," paper presented to the

Second Inter-American Congress of Criminology, Caracas, Venezuela, 1972, and "Homosexual and Drug Behavior in Prison: A Test of the Functional and Importation Models of the Inmate System," *Social Problems* 21 (Winter 1974): 410-22.

71. Gresham Sykes, "Men, Merchants, and Toughs: A Study of Reactions to Imprisonment," *Social Problems* 4 (October 1956): 130-38, and "The Corruption of Authority and Rehabilitation," *Social Forces* 34 (March 1956): 257-62. See also Gresham Sykes and Sheldon L. Messinger, "The Inmate Social System," in R. Cloward, ed., *Theoretical Studies in the Social Organization of the Prison* (New York: Social Science Research Council, 1960), pp. 5-19.

72. Gresham Sykes, *The Society of Captives* (New York: Atheneum, 1966).

73. Ibid., pp. 18-39.

74. Ibid., pp. 84-102.

75. Ibid., pp. 91-104.

76. Sykes, "Men, Merchants, and Toughs," p. 133.

77. Sykes and Messinger, "The Inmate Social System," pp. 6-8.

78. Sykes 1966, pp. 47-61, and "The Corruption of Authority and Rehabilitation," pp. 257-62.

79. I once witnessed an incident in which a veteran officer committed a severe breach of custody for which he could have lost his job. Approximately fifteen prisoners were present, but when an official investigation was launched, none of them reported having seen a thing. Since that time, I've often wondered how much contraband was smuggled into the prison or how many deviant acts were permitted in payment for the prisoners' covering up of the incident. There was probably quite a bit, for within a year the prison administration moved the officer to another part of the institution.

80. Sykes, 1966, p. 107.

81. Ibid., pp. 110-11, 120-28. Precisely the same theory appeared in print at the same time in an article by Frank Hartung and Maurice Floch, "A Social Psychological Analysis of Prison Riots: An Hypothesis," *Journal of Criminal Law, Criminology and Police Science* 47 (May-June 1956): 51-57.

82. Charles L. Hulin and Brendan A. Maher, "Changes in Attitudes Toward Law Concomitant with Imprisonment," *Journal of Criminal Law, Criminology and Police Science* 50 (September-October 1959): 247.

83. Michael Morello, "A Study of the Adjustive Behavior of Prison Inmates to Incarceration," unpublished Ph.D. dissertation, Temple University, Philadelphia, 1958, pp. 63, 68.

84. Ibid., p. 75.

85. Ruth S. Cavan and Eugene S. Zemans, "Marital Relationships of Prisoners in Twenty-Eight Countries," *Journal of Criminal Law, Criminology and Police Science* 49 (July-August 1958): 133-39.

86. Ibid., pp. 138-39.

87. Donald P. Jewell, "Mexico Tres Marias Penal Colony," *Journal of Criminal Law, Criminology and Police Science* 48 (November-December 1957): 410-13.

88. Johan Galtung, "The Social Functions of a Prison," *Social Problems* 6 (Fall 1958): 127-40. See also Johan Galtung, "Prison: The Organization of Dilemma," in Cressey, ed., *The Prison: Studies in Institutional Organization and Change*, pp. 107-45.

89. Richard H. McCleery, *Policy Change in Prison Management* (East Lansing: Michigan State University Press, 1957). See also Richard H. McCleery, "Communication Patterns as Bases of Systems of Authority and Power," in Cloward, *Theoretical Studies in the Social Organization of the Prison*, pp. 56-77.

90. Ibid., pp. 28-34.

91. Richard H. McCleery, "The Governmental Process and Informal Social Control," in Cressey, ed., *The Prison: Studies in Institutional Organization and Change*, pp. 149-88.

92. Donald Cressey, "Achievement of an Unstated Organizational Goal," *Pacific Sociological Review* 1 (Fall 1958): 43-49.

93. Donald Cressey, "Contradictory Directives in Complex Organizations: The Case of the Prison," *Administrative Science Quarterly* 4 (June 1959): 1-19.

94. Oscar Grusky, "Organizational Goals and the Behavior of Informal Leaders," *American Journal of Sociology* 65 (March 1968): 59-67.

95. Oscar Grusky, "Role Conflict in Organization: A Study of Prison Camp Officials," *Administrative Science Quarterly* 3 (July 1959): 452-72.

96. Donald Cressey and Witold Krassowski, "Inmate Organization and Anomie in American Prisons and Soviet Labor Camps," *Social Problems* (Winter 1957).

97. Harold Garfinkel, "Conditions of Successful Degradation Ceremonies," pp. 420-24.

98. Alexander I. Solzhenitsyn, *The Gulag Archipelago* (New York: Harper & Row, 1974-75).

99. Stanton Wheeler, "Socialization in Correctional Communities," *American Sociological Review* 26 (October 1961): 697-706. See also Stanton Wheeler, "Social Organization and Inmate Values in Correctional Communities," *Proceedings of the American Correctional Association* (1959): 189-98.

100. Wheeler, "Socialization," pp. 705-11.

101. Stanton Wheeler, "Role Conflict in Correctional Communities," in Cressey, ed., *The Prison: Studies in Institutional Organization and Change*, pp. 229-59.

102. Richard Cloward and Lloyd Ohlin, *Delinquency and Opportunity: A Theory of Delinquent Gangs* (Chicago: Free Press, 1966).

103. Richard A. Cloward, "Social Control and Anomie: A Study of a Prison Community," unpublished Ph.D. dissertation, Columbia University, New York, 1959, p. 95.

104. Emile Durkheim, *Suicide: A Study in Sociology* (London: Routledge and Kegan Paul, 1952); R.K. Merton, "Social Structure and Anomie," *American Sociological Review* 3 (1938): 672-82; and Albert Cohen, Alfred Lindesouth, and Karl Schuessler (eds.), *The Sutherland Papers* (Bloomington: University of Indiana Press, 1956).

105. This argument is presented in less detail but greater availability in his "Social Control in the Prison," in Cloward, ed., *Theoretical Studies in the Social Organization of the Prison*, pp. 20-48.

106. Cloward, "Social Control and Anomie," pp. 216-18.


**Chapter 2**
**A Period of Maturation in Institutional Studies**

1. Irving Goffman, *Asylums* (Garden City, New York: Doubleday, 1961).

2. Harold Garfinkel, "Conditions of Successful Degradation Ceremonies," *American Journal of Sociology* 61 (March 1965): 420-24.

3. Goffman, *Asylums*, pp. 24-37.

4. Ibid., pp. 61-63.

5. Ibid., pp. 67-73. As an example of this point, I once took a long-termer out of the Washington State Penitentiary for a day trip, and he was terrified by the speed at which I was driving. I stayed under twenty-five miles an hour all the way, but this super-tough, "right guy" prisoner trembled the whole time, for he had experienced no movement more rapid than running for eight long years.

6. Ibid., p. 82.

7. Ibid., pp. 117-19.

8. N. Perry, "The Two Cultures and the Total Institution," *British Journal of Sociology* 25 (September 1974): 345-55.

9. George A. Hillery, Jr., "Villages, Cities, and Total Institutions," *American Sociological Review* 28 (October 1963): 785-90.

10. Ira Rosenblatt, "The Effect of Punitive Measures on Attitudes of Prison Inmates Toward Authority," unpublished Ph.D. dissertation, New York University, New York, 1961, p. 90.

11. Arthur V. Huffman, "Sex Deviation in a Prison Community," *Journal of Social Therapy* 6 (1960): 179.

12. Arthur V. Huffman, "Problems Precipitated by Homosexual Approaches on Youthful Offenders," *Journal of Social Therapy* 4 (1961): 220-21.

13. William Edward Mann, "Socialization in a Medium-Security Reformatory," *Canadian Review of Sociology and Anthropology* 1 (1964): 146-47.

138

14. Columbus B. Hopper, "The Conjugal Visit at Mississippi State Penitentiary," *Journal of Criminal Law Criminology and Police Science* 53 (June 1962): 340-43.

15. Columbus B. Hopper, *Sex in Prison* (Baton Rouge: Louisiana State University Press, 1969).

16. Norman S. Hayner, "Characteristics of Five Offender Types," *American Sociological Review* 26 (February 1961): 97-98.

17. Ibid., pp. 98-102.

18. Elmer Johnson, "Sociology of Confinement, Assimilation and the Prison 'rat'," *Journal of Criminal Law, Criminology and Police Science* 51 (January-February 1961): 528-33. For information about the role of the rat in another prison setting, see Harry Wilmer, "The Role of the 'Rat' in the Prison," *Federal Probation* 29 (March 1965): 44-49.

19. Joseph C. Mouledous, "Organizational Goals and Structural Change: A Study of the Organization of a Prison Social System," *Social Forces* 16 (March 1963): 284-87. For an in-depth study of the role of the trusty, see W.L. McWhorter, "Trusty—A Sociological Analysis of an Inmate Elite," unpublished Ph.D. dissertation, Southern Illinois University, Carbondale, 1972.

20. Mouledous, pp. 287-90.

21. John Cleveland Watkins, "The Modification of the Subculture in a Correctional Institution," paper presented at the 94th Congress of Correction, Kansas City, Missouri, 1964, pp. 12-17.

22. John Irwin and Donald R. Cressey, "Thieves, Convicts and the Inmate Culture," *Social Problems* 10 (Fall 1962): 145-47.

23. Ibid., pp. 145-55.

24. Julian Roebuck, "A Critique of 'Thieves, Convicts and the Inmate Culture'," *Social Problems* 11 (Fall 1963): 193-201.

25. Charles R. Tittle and Drollene Tittle, "Social Organization of Prisoners: An Empirical Test," *Social Forces* 43 (December 1964): 216-21.

26. Charles R. Tittle and Drollene Tittle, "Structural Handicaps to Therapeutic Participations: A Case Study," *Social Problems* 13 (Summer 1965): 81.

27. Peter Garabedian, "Western Penitentiary: A Study in Social Organization," unpublished Ph.D. dissertation, University of Washington, Seattle, 1959.

28. Peter Garabedian, "Social Roles and Processes of Socialization in the Prison Community," *Social Problems* 11 (Fall 1963): 140-41.

29. Ibid., pp. 144-45.

30. Peter Garabedian, "Social Roles in a Correctional Community," *Journal of Criminal Law, Criminology and Police Science* 55 (September 1964): 341-45.

31. Ibid., p. 346.

32. Peter Garabedian, "Legitimate and Illegitimate Alternatives in the Prison Community," *Sociological Inquiry* 32 (1962): 180-81.

33. Garabedian, "Social Roles and Processes," pp. 142-52. See Peter Garabedian, "The Natural History of an Inmate Community in a Maximum Security Prison," *Journal of Criminal Law, Criminology and Police Science* 61 (March 1970): 78-85, for a brief report on Garabedian's most recent work on prisoner subcultures at the Washington State Penitentiary.

34. Terence Morris and Pauline Morris, *Pentonville, A Study of an English Prison* (London: Routledge and Kegan Paul, 1963). Their research at Pentonville is also reported in Terence Morris and Pauline Morris, "The Experience of Imprisonment," *British Journal of Criminology* 2 (1962): 337-60.

35. Morris and Morris, *Pentonville*, pp. 222-23.

36. Ibid., pp. 231-37.

37. Ibid., pp. 243-45.

38. Alvin Rudoff, "Prison Inmates: A Involuntary Association," unpublished Ph.D. dissertation, University of California, Berkeley, 1964, pp. 76-82, 137.

39. Ibid., Table V, pp. 77-79.

40. Ibid., pp. 146-52.

41. Ibid., pp. 177-84.

42. Elliot Studt, Sheldon Messinger, and Thomas P. Wilson, *C-Unit: Search for Community in Prison* (New York: Russell Sage Foundation, 1968), p. 279.

43. Thomas P. Wilson, "Patterns of Management and Adaptations to Organizational Roles: A Study of Prison Inmates," *American Journal of Sociology* 74 (September 1968): 146-57.

44. George Sherman Rothbart, "Social Conflict in Prison Organization," unpublished Ph.D. dissertation, University of Washington, Seattle, 1964 (reprinted by R & E Research Associates, Palo Alto, 1974).

45. Daniel Glaser, *The Effectiveness of a Prison and Parole System* (Indianapolis: Bobbs-Merrill, 1964).

46. Ibid., p. 98.

47. Richard A. Cloward, "Social Control and Anomie: A Study of a Prison Community," unpublished Ph.D. dissertation, Columbia University, New York, 1959.

48. Glaser, *The Effectiveness of a Prison*, pp. 100-16.

50. Ibid., pp. 563-73.

51. Ibid., pp. 578-83.

52. Thomas Mathieson, "A Functional Equivalent to Inmate Cohesion," *Human Organization* 27 (Winter 1968): 117-24.

53. Thomas Mathieson, *The Defenses of the Weak* (London: Tavistock, 1965), pp. 221-25.

54. Hugh F. Cline, "The Determinants of Normative Patterns in Correctional Institutions," in N. Christie, ed., *Scandinavian Studies in Criminology*, Vol. II (Oslo: Scandinavian University Books, 1968).

55. Ibid., pp. 173-81.

56. Ibid., pp. 178-83.

57. See Mann, "Socialization in a Medium-Security Reformatory," which was discussed earlier in this chapter.

58. William Edward Mann, *Society Behind Bars: A Sociological Scrutiny of Guelph Reformatory* (Toronto: Social Science Publishers, 1967), pp. 57-65.

59. Ibid., pp. 60-61, 88.

60. Ibid., pp. 65-73.

61. Ibid., p. 11.

62. Ibid., pp. 102-20.

63. Roland Wulbert, "Inmate Pride in Total Institutions," *American Journal of Sociology* 71 (July 1965): 1-9; Robert Martinson, *Social Interaction Under Close Confinement* (Berkeley: University of California Institute for Social Science, 1966; Norman Denzin, "Collective Behavior in Total Institutions: The Case of the Mental Hospital and the Prison," *Social Problems* 15 (Winter 1968): 353-65; and Bernard Berk, "Organizational Goals and Inmate Organization," *American Journal of Sociology* 71 (March 1966): 522-34.

64. Wulbert, "Inmate Pride," pp. 3-8.

65. Ralph H. Turner and Lewis M. Killian, *Collective Behavior* (Englewood Cliffs: Prentice-Hall, 1957).

66. Denzin, "Collective Behavior," pp. 356-64.

67. Oscar Grusky, "Organizational Goals and the Behavior of Informal Leaders," *American Journal of Sociology* 65 (March 1968): 59-67.

68. Berk, "Organizational Goals," pp. 524-29.

69. Ibid., pp. 530-34.

70. Martinson, *Social Interaction*, pp. 1-19.

71. Ibid., pp. 19-36.

72. Alan J. Davis, "Sexual Assaults in the Philadelphia Prison System and Sheriff's Vans," *Transaction* 6 (December 1968): 9.

73. Ibid., pp. 10-16.

74. John H. Gagnon and William Simon, "The Social Meaning of Prison Homosexuality," *Federal Probation* 32 (March 1968): 23-29.

75. Clyde B. Vedder and Patricia King, *Problems of Homosexuality in Corrections* (Springfield, Ill.: Charles C. Thomas, 1967).

76. Alfred C. Kinsey, W.B. Pomeroy, and C.E. Martin, *Sexual Behavior in the Human Male* (Philadelphia, W.B. Saunders, 1948).

77. James R. Claghorn and Dan R. Beto, "Self-mutilation in a Prison Mental Hospital," *Psychiatry and Journal of Social Therapy* 13 (May 1967): 131-33.

78. Robert Wallace, "Ecological Implications of a Custody Institution," *Issues in Criminology* 2 (Spring 1966): 47-60.

79. Robert E. Park, Ernest W. Burgess, and R.D. McKenzie, *The City* (Chicago: University of Chicago Press, 1925).

80. Judson W.R. Landis, "Moral Value Structure of Laborers and Penitentiary Inmates: A Research Note," *Social Forces* 46 (December 1967): 269-74.

81. E.H. Johnson, "Pilot Study: Age, Race and Recidivism As Factors in Prisoner Infractions," *Canadian Journal of Corrections* 8 (1966): 268-83.

82. John R. Stratton, "The Measurement of Inmate Change During Imprisonment," unpublished Ph.D. Dissertation, University of Illinois, Champaign, 1963; Glaser, *The Effectiveness of a Prison*; and Albert Cohen, Alfred Lindesmith and Karl Schoessler (eds.), *The Sutherland Papers* (Bloomington: Indiana University Press, 1956).

83. Stratton, "The Measurement of Inmate Change During Imprisonment," pp. 256-62. See also Appendix E in Glasser, *The Effectiveness of a Prison*.

84. Robert C. Atchley and Patrick M. McCabe, "Socialization in Correctional Communities: A Replication," *American Sociological Review* 33 (October 1968): 774-85.

85. Charles Wellford, "Factors Associated With Adoption of an Inmate Code: A Study of Normative Socialization," *Journal of Criminal Law, Criminology and Police Science* 58 (June 1967): 197-203.

## Chapter 3
## Contemporary Approaches to the Study of Prisoner Subcultures

1. Will Charles Kennedy, "Prisonization and Self Conception: A Study of a Medium Security Prison," unpublished Ph.D. dissertation, University of California, Los Angeles, 1970.

2. Daniel Glaser, *The Effectiveness of a Prison and Parole System* (Indianapolis: Bobbs Merrill, 1964); Gene Kassebaum, David A. Ward, and Daniel M. Wilner, *Prison Treatment and Parole Survival: An Empirical Assessment* (New York: Wiley Press, 1971).

3. Kennedy, "Prisonization and Self Conception," p. 48.

4. Ibid., pp. 72-76.

5. Ibid., p. 103.

6. Ibid., pp. 121-27.

7. Ibid., pp. 194-204.

8. Columbus Benjamin Ellis, "The Prison Social System: An Analysis of Consensus and Normative Structures," unpublished Ph.D. dissertation, Louisiana State University and Agricultural and Mechanical College, Baton Rouge, 1970, pp. 123-33.

9. Anthony L. Guenther, "Alienation, Inmate Roles, and Release Ideology in a Penitentiary Setting," unpublished Ph.D. dissertation, Purdue University, Lafayette, Ind., 1972.

10. Ibid., p. 111.

11. Ibid., pp. 108-109.

12. Ibid., p. 85.

13. Ibid., pp. 132-33.

14. Ibid., p. 137.

15. See ibid., pp. 22-25 and 31-37.

16. Werner Gruninger, "Criminalization, Prison Roles, and Normative Alienation: A Cross-Cultural Study," unpublished Ph.D. dissertation, University of Washington, Seattle, 1974.

17. Ibid., pp. 89-92.

18. Ibid., pp. 100-102.

19. Ibid., pp. 91-92.

20. Ibid., p. 113.

21. Richard A. Cloward, "Social Control and Anomie: A Study of a Prison Community," unpublished Ph.D. dissertation, Columbia University, New York (1959).

22. Gruninger, "Criminalization," p. 145.

23. Ibid., pp. 234-37, 241.

24. Ibid., pp. 240, 249.

25. Ibid., pp. 240-41.

26. Gordon P. Waldo, "The Criminality Level of Incarcerated Murderers and Nonmurderers," *Journal of Criminal Law, Criminology and Police Science* 61 (March 1970): 60-70.

27. Joseph W. Rogers and Elizabeth S. Alexander, "The Penal Press: Opportunities for Correctional Research," *Journal of Research in Crime and Delinquency* (January 1970): 1-10.

28. John M. Wilson and John D. Snodgrass, "The Prison Code in a Therapeutic Community," *Journal of Criminal Law, Criminology and Police Science* 60 (December 1969): 472-78.

29. R.N. Nagasawa and E.H. Pfuhl, "Pains of Imprisonment and the Female Social System," unpublished manuscript, Arizona State University, Tempe, 1971.

30. J.R. Faine, "A Self-Consistency Approach to Prisonization," *Sociological Quarterly* 14 (Autumn 1973): 576-88.

31. Lee H. Bowker, "Prisoner Perceptions of Activities Relevant to Parole Board Action," *Volunteers in Corrections Newsletter*, May 1975.

32. Ibid., pp. 12-14.

33. Ibid., pp. 14, 18.

34. Charles W. Thomas, "Toward a More Inclusive Model of the Inmate Contra-Culture," *Criminology* 8 (November 1970): 251-62.

35. Charles W. Thomas and Samuel C. Foster, "Prisonization in the Inmate Contraculture," *Social Problems* 20 (Fall 1972): 237. See also Charles W. Thomas and Eric C. Poole, "The Consequences of Incompatible Goal Structures in Correctional Settings," *International Journal of Criminology and Penology* 3 (1975): 35, and Charles W. Thomas and Samuel C. Foster, "On the Measurement of Social Roles Adaptation in the Prison Community," *Criminal Justice Review* 1 (Spring 1976): 16-17.

36. Thomas and Foster, "Prisonization," pp. 235-37.

37. Charles W. Thomas, "Conflicting Processes of Socialization in the Prison Community," *Georgia Journal of Corrections* 1 (April 1972): 41. See also Charles W. Thomas and Samuel C. Foster, "The Importation Model of Inmate Social Roles: An Empirical Test," *Sociological Quarterly* 14 (Spring 1973): 230-33, and Charles W. Thomas, "Prisonization or Resocialization? A Study of External Factors Associated With the Impact of Imprisonment," *Journal of Research in Crime and Delinquency* 10 (January 1973): 18-20.

38. Charles W. Thomas and Michael J. Miller, "Adult Resocialization in Coercive Organizations," paper presented to the Annual Meeting of the Eastern Sociological Society, New York, 1971, p. 31.

39. Ibid., p. 25.

40. Ibid., p. 31. See also Thomas, "The Importation Model," p. 231; "Conflicting Processes," p. 40; and "Prisonization or Resocialization?" p. 19.

41. Charles W. Thomas, "Theoretical Perspectives on Alienation in the Prison Society," *Pacific Sociological Review* 18 (October 1975): 483-99.

42. Charles W. Thomas, "Prisonization and Its Consequences, An Examination of Socialization in a Coercive Setting," *Sociological Focus* (forthcoming).

43. L.A. Bennett, "The Application of Self-Esteem Measures in a Correctional Setting: II. Changes in Self-Esteem During Incarceration," *Journal of Research in Crime and Delinquency* 11 (January 1974): 9-15.

44. Lee H. Bowker, Robert Brodey, and David Kenyon, "A Comparison of Views of the Decision-Making Process in the Washington State Correctional System by Residents, Institutional Staff, and Parole Board Members," paper presented at Symposium of the American Justice Institute, Coeur D'Alene, Idaho, 1973.

45. Ibid., pp. 15-16.

46. Ibid., p. 15.

47. Ibid., pp. 16, 24.

48. John F. Galliher, "Change in a Correctional Institution, A Case Study of the Tightening-Up Process," *Crime and Delinquency* 18 (July 1972): 263-70.

49. Charles W. Thomas, "The Importation and Deprivation Model Perspectives on Prisonization, A Comparison of Their Relative Importance," paper presented at the Annual Meeting of the Society for the Study of Social Problems, San Francisco, 1975.

50. Charles W. Thomas and Robin J. Cage, "Correlates of Prison Drug Use, An Evaluation of Two Conceptual Models," *Criminology* (forthcoming).

51. Ronald L. Akers, Norman Hayner, and Werner Gruninger, "Homosexual and Drug Behavior in Prison: A Test of the Functional and Importation Models of the Inmate System," *Social Problems* 21 (Winter 1974): 410-22.

52. Thomas and Cage, "Correlates of Prison Drug Use," (Footnote 42), 14.

53. John Hepburn and John R. Stratton, "Total Institutions and Inmate Self-Esteem: Inmates in a Federal Correction Center," *British Journal of Criminology* (in press).

54. Arthur G. Neal, Eldon E. Snyder, and Joseph K. Balogh, "Changing Alienations as Consequences of Imprisonment," paper presented at the 1974 Annual Meeting of the Society for the Study of Social Problems, Montreal, 1974.

55. John R. Faine and Edward Bohlander, Jr., "Prisoner Radicalization and Incipient Violence," paper presented at the Annual Meeting of the American Society of Criminology, Tucson, 1976.

56. See Lincoln J. Fry, "The Impact of Formal Inmate Structure on Opposition to Staff and Treatment Goals," *British Journal of Criminology* 16 (April 1976): 126-41; B.S. Brown, "Impact of Institutionalization on Recidivists and First Offenders," unpublished paper, Department of Corrections, District of Columbia, 1969; James J. Lembo, "The Relationship of Institutional Disciplinary Infractions and the Inmate's Personal Contact with the Outside Community," *Criminologica* 7 (January 1969); N.R. Curcione, "Social Relations Among Inmate Addicts," *Journal of Research in Crime and Delinquency* 12 (January 1975): 61-71; Stanley L. Brodsky and Norman E. Eggleston, *The Military Prison—Theory, Research and Practice* (Carbondale: Southern Illinois University Press, 1970), p. 131-44; and David Duffee, *Correctional Policy and Prison Organization* (New York: Halsted Press, 1975), pp. 75-125.

57. Kassebaum, Ward, and Wilner, *Prison Treatment and Parole Survival*, p. 147.

58. Robert Leger, "Socialization Patterns in the Correctional Community: A Replication and a Critique," paper presented at the Annual Meeting of the American Sociological Association, New York, 1976.

59. Mark V. Hansel, "The Measurement and Dimensionality of Inmate Social Roles in a Custodially Oriented Prison: An Ethnographic-Psychometric Study," unpublished Ph.D. dissertation, University of Iowa, Iowa City, 1974.

60. Ibid., pp. 254-64.

61. Irving Goffman, *Asylums* (Garden City, N.Y.: Doubleday, 1961).

62. See Y. Hasenfield, "People Processing Organizations, An Exchange Approach," *American Sociological Review* 37 (June 1972): 256-63, and David Shichor, "People-Changing-People-Processing Organizations," paper presented at the Pacific Sociological Meeting, San Diego, 1976.

63. Henry Burns, Jr., "A Miniature Totalitarian State: Maximum Security Prison," *Canadian Journal of Corrections* 9 (July 1969): 153-64; Madeline Karmel, "Total Institution and Self-Mortification," *Journal of Health and Social Behavior* 10 (June 1969): 134-41; Andrew C. Twaddle, "Utilization of Medical Services by a Captive Population: An Analysis of Sick Call in a State Prison," *Journal of Health and Social Behavior* 17 (September 1976): 236-48; and Charles R. Tittle, *Society of Subordinates: Inmate Organization in a Narcotic Hospital* (Bloomington: Indiana University Press, 1972), "Institutional Living and Rehabilitation," *Journal of Health and Social Behavior* 13 (September 1972): 263-75, "Institutional Living and Self-Esteem," *Social Problems* 20 (Summer 1972): 65-77, and "Inmate Organization: Sex Differentiation and the Influence of Criminal Subcultures," *American Sociological Review* 34 (August 1969): 492-505.

64. Burns, "A Miniature Totalitarian State," pp. 154-62.

65. Twaddle, "Utilization," pp. 240-47.

66. Karmel, "Total Institution," pp. 140-41.

67. Tittle, "Institutional Living and Self-Esteem," p. 66.

68. Tittle, "Institutional Living and Rehabilitation," pp. 273-74.

69. Tittle, "Institutional Living and Self-Esteem," pp. 70-71.

70. Ibid., pp. 75-76.

71. Tittle, "Inmate Organization," pp. 500-01.

72. Thomas F. Tabasz, *Toward An Economics of Prisons* (Lexington, Mass.: Lexington Books, 1975).

73. See Heather Strange and Joseph McCrory, "Bulls and Bears on the Cell Block," *Society* 11 (July-August 1974): 51-59; Anthony L. Guenther, "Compensations in a Total Institution: The Forms and Functions of Contraband," *Crime and Delinquency* 21 (July 1975): 243-54; and Virginia L. Williams and Mary Fish, *Convicts, Codes and Contraband: The Prison Life of Men and Women* (Cambridge, Mass.: Ballinger, 1974).

74. Ronald C. Huff, "Prisoners' Union: A Challenge for State Corrections," *State Government* 48 (Summer 1975): 145-49, "Unionization Behind the Walls," *Criminology* 12 (August 1974): 175-93, and "Unionization Behind the Walls: An Analytic Study of the Ohio Prisoners' Labor Union Movement," unpublished Ph.D. dissertation, Ohio State University, Columbus, 1975.

75. Strange and McCrory, "Bulls and Bears," pp. 57-59.

76. Guenther, "Compensations," pp. 252-53.

77. Williams and Fish, *Convicts*, pp. 140-53.

78. Huff, "Prisoners' Union," p. 145.

79. Huff, "Unionization Behind the Walls," pp. 183-86.

80. This story is most fully told in Huff, "Unionization Behind the Walls: An Analytic Study."

81. John Irwin, "The Trouble With Rehabilitation," paper presented at the Annual Meeting of the American Sociological Association, New York, 1973.

82. Jerry Reeves Sparger, "A Behavioral Analysis of Inmate Leaders in Prison Society," unpublished Ph.D. dissertation, University of Tennessee, Knoxville, 1973.

83. Ibid., p. 60.

84. Mordechai Rotenberg, "Relevant Audience and Organismic Involvement as Interacting Variables with Self-Identity: The Social Types in Prison," unpublished D.S.W. dissertation, University of California, Berkeley, 1969.

85. Ibid., pp. 82-84.

86. Phillip G. Zimbardo, "Pathology of Imprisonment," *Society* 9 (1972): 4, 6, 8.

87. Ernst A. Wenk and Rudolf H. Moos, "Prison Environment: The Social Ecology of Correctional Institutions," *Crime and Delinquency Literature* 4, no. 4 (1972): 591-621.

88. W.T. Austin and F.L. Bates, "Ethological Indicators of Dominance and Territory in a Human Captive Population," *Social Forces* 52, no. 4 (1974): 447-55.

89. Lauren Roth, "Territoriality and Homosexuality in a Male Prison," *American Journal of Orthopsychiatry* 41 (1971): 510-13.

90. Warren B. Miller, "Adaptation of Young Men to Prison," *Correctional and Social Psychiatry and Journal of Applied Behavior Therapy* 19, no. 4 (1973): 15-26; Robert Ellis Heise, *Prison Games* (Fort Worth, Tex.: privately published, 1976); John Irwin, *The Felon* (Englewood Cliffs, N.J.: Prentice-Hall, 1970); and Anthony J. Manocchio and Jimmy Dunn, *The Time Game: Two Views of a Prison* (New York: Dell Publishing, 1970).

91. Irwin, *The Felon*, pp. 68-79.

92. George D. Muedeking, "Negotiating Identities in the Prison Visiting Room," paper presented at the Annual Meeting of the Pacific Sociological Association, San Diego, 1976.

93. Lawrence D. Wieder, *Language and Social Reality: The Case of Telling the Convict Code* (The Hague: Mouton Press, 1974).

94. See for example, Azmy Ishak Ibrahim, "Deviant Sexual Behavior in Men's Prisons," *Crime and Delinquency* 20 (January 1974): 38-44.

95. Columbus B. Hopper, *Sex in Prison* (Baton Rouge: Louisiana State University Press, 1969), pp. 92, 102, 146-47.

96. Ibid., pp. 122-36.

97. Ibid., pp. 103-04, 146-47.

98. Leo Carroll, "Race and Sexual Assault in a Prison," paper presented at the Annual Meeting of the Society for the Study of Social Problems, Montreal, 1974.

99. For a summary of these actions through 1972, see "Sexual Assaults and Forced Homosexual Relationships in Prison: Cruel and Unusual Punishment," *Albany Law Review* 36, no. 2 (1972): 428-38.

100. Ronald L. Akers, Norman S. Hayner, and Werner Gruninger, "Homosexual and Drug Behavior in Prison: A Test of the Functional and Importation Models of the Inmate System," *Social Problems* 21 (Winter 1974): 410-22.

101. Howard K. Porter, "Prison Homosexuality: Locus of Control and Femininity," unpublished Ph.D. dissertation, Michigan State University, East Lansing, 1969.

102. Peter C. Buffum, *Homosexuality in Prisons* (Washington, D.C.: Government Printing Office, 1972); George L. Kirkham, "Homosexuality in Prison," in J. Henslin, ed., *Studies in the Sociology of Sex* (New York: Appleton-Century-Crofts, 1971); Edwin Johnson, "The Homosexual in Prison," in J. Susman, ed., *Crime and Justice, 1971-1972* (New York: AMS Press, 1974); Gene Kassebaum, "Sex in Prison," *Sexual Behavior* 2 (January 1972): 39-45.

103. For example, see Milton Burdman, "Ethnic Self-help Groups in Prison and on Parole," *Crime and Delinquency* 20 (April 1974): 107-18.

104. Some of the treatments of this topic are, Ross K. Baker, "Inmate Self-Government," *Journal of Criminal Law, Criminology and Police Science* 55 (1964): 39-47; Charles E. Reasons, "The Politicizing of Crime, The Criminal and the Criminologist," *Journal of Criminal Law and Criminology* 64 (March 1973): 471-77; and Stuart A. Brody, "The Political Prisoner Syndrome," *Crime and Delinquency* 20 (April 1974): 97-118.

105. N. Kantrowitz, "The Vocabulary of Race Relations in a Prison," *Publication of the American Dialect Society* 51 (1969): 23-34.

106. James B. Jacobs, "Participant Observation in Prison," *Urban Life and Culture* 3 (1974): 221-40.

107. James B. Jacobs, "Street Gangs Behind Bars," *Social Problems* 21 (1974): 395-411.

108. James B. Jacobs, "Stratification and Conflict Among Prison Inmates," *Journal of Criminal Law and Criminology* 66 (December 1976): 476-82.

109. Anthony R. Harris, "Imprisonment and the Expected Value of Criminal Choice, A Specification and Test of Aspects of the Labeling Perspective," *American Sociological Review* 40 (1975): 71-87.

110. Anthony R. Harris, "Race, Commitment to Deviance, and Spoiled Identity," *American Sociological Review* 41 (1976): 432-42.

111. Theodore R. Davidson, *Chicano Prisoners, The Key to San Quentin*

(New York: Holt, Rinehart and Winston, 1974). For the summary of this book, see Susan Stocking, "Family Secrets," *Human Behavior* (November 1974): 56-59.

112. Davidson, ibid., pp. 194-95.

113. Leo Carroll, *Hacks, Blacks and Cons: Race Relations in a Maximum Security Prison* (Lexington, Mass.: D.C. Heath and Co., 1974).

114. Leo Carroll, "Race and Three Forms of Prisoner Power: Confrontation, Censoriousness and the Corruption of Authority," paper presented at the Annual Meeting of the American Society of Criminology, Tucson, 1976.

115. Ibid., pp. 6-8.

116. Ibid., pp. 10-13.

117. Cornelius J. Lammers, "Strikes and Mutinies: A Comparative Study of Organizational Conflicts Between Rulers and Ruled," *Administrative Science Quarterly* 14 (December 1969): 558-72.

118. Elizabeth Edith Flynn, "Sources of Collective Violence in Correctional Institutions," in National Council on Crime and Delinquency, *Prevention of Violence in Correctional Institutions* (Washington, D.C.: Government Printing Office, 1973).

119. Richard W. Wilsnack, "Explaining Collective Violence in Prisons: Problems and Possibilities," in A.K. Cohen et al., eds., *Prison Violence* (Lexington, Mass.: D.C. Heath and Co., 1976), pp. 61-78.

120. Benjamin Beit-Hallahmi, "Aggressive and Sexual Fantasies in Violent and Non-Violent Prison Inmates," unpublished Ph.D. dissertation, Michigan State University, East Lansing, 1970, p. 55.

121. Edwin I. Megargee, "Population Density and Disruptive Behavior in a Prison Setting," in Cohen et al., eds., *Prison Violence*, pp. 140-41.

122. James Jacobs, "Prison Violence and Formal Organization," in Cohen et al., eds., *Prison Violence*, pp. 81-84.

123. Desmond Ellis, Harold G. Crasmick, and Bernard Gilman, "Violence in Prisons: A Sociological Analysis," *American Journal of Sociology* 80 (1974): 16-43.

124. Sawyer F. Sylvester, Jr., Christine Holden, David O. Nelson, John H. Reed, and Wendy J. Wolfson, "Homicide in Prisons," unpublished staff report, National Institute of Law Enforcement and Criminal Justice, Washington, D.C., 1974, pp. 78-92.

125. Elmer H. Johnson, *Correlates of Felon Self-Mutilations* (Carbondale, Ill.: Center for the Study of Crime, Delinquency, and Corrections, 1969).

126. Ibid., p. 13.

127. Ibid., p. 26.

128. Ibid., p. 62.

149

129. Ibid., pp. 116-18.

130. Hans Toch, *Men in Crisis* (Chicago: Aldine Publishing Co., 1975).

131. Ibid., p. 24.

132. Ibid., pp. 127-29.

133. Ibid., pp. 324-25.

134. Robert Johnson, *Culture and Crisis in Confinement* (Lexington, Mass.: Lexington Books, 1976).

135. Ibid., pp. 51-52.

136. Ibid., pp. 71-132.

137. See Tony Parker, *The Frying-Pan, A Prison and Its Prisoners* (New York: Harper & Row, 1970), and Stanley Cohen and Laurie Taylor, *Psychological Survival, The Experience of Long-Term Imprisonment* (New York: Random House, 1972).

138. John A. Price, "Private Enterprise in a Prison, The Free Market Economy of La Mesa Penitenciaria," *Crime and Delinquency* 19 (April 1973): 218-27.

139. Ross L. Hindman, "Research and Methodology: Inmate Interaction as a Determinant of Response to Incarceration," *British Journal of Criminology* 11 (October 1971): 382-90. The earlier article on this data is by Cline (as discussed in Chapter 2) and is summarized in Stanton Wheeler, "Socialization in Correctional Institutions," in D. Coslin, ed., *Handbook of Socialization Theory and Research* (Chicago: Rand McNally, 1969), pp. 1010-15.

140. Barry G. Morris, "Irrational Beliefs of Prison Inmates," *Canadian Journal of Criminology and Corrections* 16 (1974): 53-59.

141. D.F. Cousineau, "An Analysis and Pilot Study of Some Aspects of Argot," *Canadian Journal of Corrections* 6 (July 1964): 331-45.

142. E.S. Shihadeh and A.N. Nedd, "Inmate Evaluation of a Penitentiary Incentive Program," *Canadian Journal of Criminology and Corrections* 15 (April 1973): 229-38.

143. Joseph G. Troyer and Dean E. Frease, "Attitude Change in a Western Canadian Penitentiary," *Canadian Journal of Criminology and Corrections* 17 (July 1975): 258-59.

144. Lois James, *Prisoners' Perceptions of Parole–A Survey of the National Parole System Conducted in the Penitentiaries of Ontario, Canada* (Toronto: University of Toronto's Centre of Criminology, 1971).

145. Lois James, *Influence in the Prison Environment* (Toronto: University of Toronto's Centre of Criminology, 1974).

146. Ibid., p. 31.

147. Ibid., p. 102.

148. Ibid., pp. 49-50.

Chapter 4
Subcultures in Women's Prisons

1. Margaret Otis, "A Perversion Not Commonly Noted," *Journal of Abnormal Psychology* 8 (June-July 1913): 113-16.

2. Charles A. Ford, "Homosexual Practices of Institutionalized Females," *Journal of Abnormal and Social Psychology* 23 (January-March 1929): 442-48.

3. Lowell S. Selling, "The Pseudo-Family," *American Journal of Sociology* 37 (September 1931): 247-53.

4. J.L. Moreno, *Who Shall Survive* (Washington, D.C.: Nervous and Mental Disease Publishing Co., 1934).

5. Ibid., pp. 229-32.

6. Helen Jennings, *Leadership and Isolation* (New York: Longmans, Green and Co., 1943).

7. Ida Harper, "The Role of the 'Fringer' in a State Prison for Women," *Social Forces* 31 (October 1952): 53-60.

8. Ibid., p. 60.

9. Sidney Kosofsky and Albert Ellis, "Illegal Communication Among Institutionalized Female Delinquents," *Journal of Social Psychiatry* 48 (August 1958): 155-60.

10. Abraham G. Novick, "The Make-Believe Family: Informal Group Structure Among Institutionalized Delinquent Girls," in *Casework Papers from the National Conference on Social Welfare* (New York: Family Service Association of America, 1960), pp. 44-59.

11. R.N. Cassel and J. Clayton, "A Preliminary Analysis of Certain Social Self-Concepts of Women in a Correctional Institution," *Sociology and Social Research* 5 (1961): 316-19.

12. Seymour Halleck and Marvin Hersko, "Homosexual Behavior in a Correctional Institution for Adolescent Girls," *American Journal of Orthopsychiatry* 32 (October 1962): 911-17.

13. Ibid., pp. 915-16.

14. W.G. Miller and T.E. Hannum, "Characteristics of Homosexually Involved Incarcerated Females," *Journal of Consulting Psychology* 27 (1963): 277.

15. M. Hammer, "Homosexuality in a Women's Reformatory," *Corrective Psychiatry and Journal of Social Therapy* 11 (1965): 168-69. Also see Hammer's treatment of female hypersexuality in prison in "Hypersexuality in Reformatory Women," *Corrective Psychiatry and Journal of Social Therapy* 15 (1969): 20-26.

16. S. Zalba, *Women Prisoners and Their Families* (Los Angeles: Delmar, 1964), p. 53.

17. A.J.W. Taylor, "The Significance of 'Darls' or 'Special Relationships' for Borstal Girls," *British Journal of Criminology* 5 (October 1965): 406-18.

18. A.J. Taylor, "A Search Among Borstal Girls for the Psychological and Special Significance of their Tattoos," *British Journal of Criminology* 8 (1968): 170-85.

19. Raymond J. Adamek and Edward Z. Dager, "Social Structure Identification and Change in a Treatment-Oriented Institution," *American Journal of Sociology* 33 (1968): 931-44.

20. Ulla Bondeson, "Argot Knowledge as an Indicator of Criminal Socialization," in N. Christie, ed., *Scandinavian Studies in Criminology*, Vol. II (Oslo: Scandinavian University Books, 1968), pp. 173-84.

21. David Ward and Gene G. Kassebaum, *Women's Prison: Sex and Social Structure* (Chicago: Aldine, 1965), and "Homosexuality: A Mode of Adaptation in a Prison for Women," *Social Problems* 12 (Fall 1964): 159-77; Gene G. Kassebaum, David Ward, D.M. Wilner, and W.C. Kennedy, "Job Related Differences in Staff Attitudes Toward Treatment in a Women's Prison," *Pacific Sociological Review* 5 (Fall 1962): 83-88; Rose Mary Giallombardo, *Society of Women: A Study of a Women's Prison* (New York: John Wiley and Sons, 1966), "Social Roles in a Prison for Women," *Social Problems* 13 (Winter 1966): 268-88, and "Interviewing in the Prison Community," *Journal of Criminal Law, Criminology and Police Science* 57 (1966): 318-24; Arlene Edith Mitchell, "Informal Inmate Social Structure in Prisons for Women: A Comparative Study," unpublished Ph.D. dissertation, University of Washington, Seattle, 1969 (reprinted by R & E Research Associates, Palo Alto, California, 1975); and Charles R. Tittle, "Inmate Organization: Sex Differentiation and the Influence of Criminal Subcultures," *American Sociological Review* 34 (August 1969): 492-505.

22. Esther Heffernan, *Making It In Prison, The Square, The Cool and The Life* (New York: Wiley and Sons, 1972).

23. Ward and Kassebaum, *Women's Prison*, pp. 102-40.

24. Ibid., pp. 141-201.

25. Ibid., p. 153.

26. Giallombardo, *Society of Women*, pp. 14-17.

27. Ibid., pp. 102-04.

28. Ibid., pp. 105-32.

29. Ibid., pp. 125-27, 148-51.

30. Heffernan, *Making It In Prison*, pp. 10-17.

31. Ibid., pp. 25-40.

32. Ibid., pp. 41-43.

33. Ibid., pp. 87-104.

34. Mitchell, "Informal Inmate Social Structure," p. 17.

35. Ibid., p. 27.

36. Ibid., pp. 36-41.

37. Alice M.L. Propper, "Importation and Deprivation Perspective on Homosexuality In Correctional Institutions: An Empirical Test of Their Relative Efficacy," unpublished Ph.D. dissertation, University of Washington, Seattle, 1976.

38. Ibid., pp. 221-22, 232-33.

39. Kathryn W. Burkhart, *Women in Prison* (New York: Doubleday, 1973); Edna Walker Chandler, *Women in Prison* (Indianapolis, Indiana: Bobbs-Merrill, 1973); Ruth M. Glick and Virginia V. Neto, *National Study of Women's Correctional Programs* (Sacramento: California Youth Authority, 1976).

40. Helene Enid Cavior, Steven C. Hayes, and Norman Cavior, "Physical Attractiveness of Female Offenders: Effects on Institutional Performance," *Criminal Justice and Behavior* 4 (December 1974): 321-31.

41. Carlos E. Climent, Ann Rollins, Frank R. Ervin, and Robert Plutchik, "Epidemiological Studies of Women Prisoners, I.: Medical and Psychiatric Variables Related to Violent Behavior," *American Journal of Psychiatry* 130 (September 1973): 985-90.

42. Desmond P. Ellis and Penelope Austin, "Menstruation and Aggressive Behavior in a Correctional Center for Women," *Journal of Criminal Law, Criminology and Police Science* 62 (March 1971): 388-95.

43. J.R. Snortum, T.E. Hannum, and D.H. Mills, "The Relationship of Self Concept and Parent Image to Rule Violations in a Women's Prison," *Journal of Clinical Psychology* 26 (1970): 284-87.

44. J.P. Stefanowicz and T.E. Hannum, "Ethical Risk-Taking and Sociopathy in Incarcerated Females," *Correctional Psychologist* 4 (1971): 138-52.

45. Barbara Carter, "Race, Sex and Gangs," *Society* 11 (November-December 1973): 38-43; Thomas W. Foster, "Make-Believe Families: A Response of Women and Girls to the Deprivations of Imprisonment," *International Journal of Criminology and Penology* 3 (1975): 71-78; and Gary F. Jensen, "Perspectives on Inmate Culture: A Study of Women in Prison," paper presented to the Annual Meeting of the Society for the Study of Social Problems, Montreal, 1974.

46. Carter, "Race, Sex and Gangs," p. 42.

47. James B. Jacobs, "Street Gangs Behind Bars," *Social Problems* 21 (1974): 395-411.

48. L.L. Le Shanna, "Family Participation: Functional Response of Incarcerated Females," unpublished M.A. thesis, Bowling Green State University, Bowling Green, O., 1969, and D.J. Wentz, "The Role of Incarcerated Female Juvenile Delinquents' Self-Acceptance and Their Participation in the Sillies and the Make-Believe Family," unpublished M.A. thesis, Bowling Green State University, Bowling Green, O., 1965.

49. Foster, "Make-Believe Families," p. 77.

50. Jensen, "Perspectives on Inmate Culture," pp. 8-10, 15-16.

51. Rose Mary Giallombardo, *The Social World of Imprisoned Girls* (New York: John Wiley and Sons, 1974).

52. Ibid., p. 11-12.

53. Ibid., p. 248.

54. Foster, "Make-Believe Families," pp. 71-78.

55. Ibid., pp. 3-4. Also see pp. 240-46.

56. Imogene L. Simmons, "Interaction and Leadership Among Female Prisoners," unpublished Ph.D. dissertation, University of Missouri, Columbia, 1975.

57. Ibid., p. 100.

58. Ibid., pp. 125-27.

59. Ibid., pp. 153-55.

60. Ibid., pp. 165, 190.

61. Ibid., p. 132.

62. Ibid., pp. 192-93.

63. For a summary of Propper, "Importation and Deprivation Perspective," see Alice M. Propper, "Homosexuality in Female and Coed Correctional Institutions," paper presented at the Annual Meeting of the American Society of Criminology, Tucson, 1976.

64. Propper, "Importation and Deprivation Perspective," pp. 107, 137-39.

65. Ibid., pp. 153-54.

66. Ibid., pp. 157-60.

67. Ibid., pp. 200-01.

68. Propper, "Homosexuality in Female and Coed Correctional Institutions," pp. 8-9.

69. P.B. Sutker and C.E. Moan, "A Psychosocial Description of Penitentiary Inmates," *Archives of General Psychiatry* 29 (November 1973): 663-67.

70. James H. Panton, "Personality Differences Between Male and Female Prison Inmates Measured by the MMPI," *Criminal Justice and Behavior* 4 (December 1974): 332-39.

71. R. Cochrane, "The Structure of Value Systems in Male and Female Prisoners," *British Journal of Criminology* 11 (1971): 73-79.

72. Hans Toch, *Men in Crisis* (Chicago: Aldine Publishing Co., 1975), pp. 128-41.

73. James G. Fox, "Women in Crisis," in Toch, *Men in Crisis*, pp. 193-203.

74. Virginia L. Williams and Mary Fish, *Convicts, Codes and Contraband: The Prison Life of Men and Women* (Cambridge, Mass.: Ballinger, 1974).

75. Ibid., pp. 126-34.

## Chapter 5
## Institutions for Boys

1. National Criminal Justice Information and Statistics Service, *Children in Custody, Advance Report on the Juvenile Detention and Correctional Facility Census of 1972-73* (Washington, D.C.: Government Printing Office, 1975), pp. 1, 11.

2. Ashley Weeks, *Youthful Offenders at Highfields* (Ann Arbor: University of Michigan Press, 1958).

3. W. McCord and J. McCord, "Two Approaches to the Cure of Delinquents," *Journal of Criminal Law, Criminology and Police Science* 44 (1944): 442-67.

4. La Mar T. Empey and Steven G. Lubeck, *The Silverlake Experiment* (Chicago: Aldine, 1971); La Mar T. Empey and Jerome Rabow, "The Provo Experiment in Delinquency Rehabilitation," *American Sociological Review* 26 (1961): 679-696.

5. Gordon H. Barker and W. Thomas Adams, "The Social Structure of a Correctional Institution," *Journal of Criminal Law, Criminology and Police Science* 49 (1959): 417-99.

6. Gordon Rose, "Status and Grouping in a Borstal," *British Journal of Delinquency* 9 (1959): 258-73.

7. See Clemens Bartollas, Stuart J. Miller, and Simon Dinitz, *Juvenile Victimization: The Institutional Paradox* (New York: Halsted Press, 1976), as the most comprehensive report of this project.

8. Rose, "Status and Grouping in a Borstal," pp. 261-62.

9. Howard W. Polsky, *Cottage Six* (New York: Wiley and Sons, 1962), pp. 148-49.

10. Ibid., pp. 69-87.

11. Ibid., pp. 55-65.

12. Ibid., p. 185.

13. Ibid., pp. 63-64.

14. Ibid., pp. 44-54, 109-21.

15. The monographs are Robert D. Vinter and Morris Janowitz, *The Comparative Study of Juvenile Correctional Institutions: A Research Report* (Ann Arbor: School of Social Work, University of Michigan, 1961), and David Street, Robert D. Vinter, and Charles Perrow, *Organization for Treatment* (New York: Free Press, 1966). The unpublished doctoral dissertations are Rosemary Sarri, "Organizational Patterns and Client Perspectives in Juvenile Correctional Institutions: A Comparative Study" (University of Michigan, 1960); David Street, "Inmate Social Organization: A Comparative Study of Juvenile Correctional Institutions" (Ann Arbor: University of Michigan, 1960); and Mayer N.

Zald, "Multiple Goals and Staff Structure: A Comparative Study of Correctional Institutions for Juvenile Delinquents" (Ann Arbor: University of Michigan, 1960). The journal articles include David Street, "The Inmate Group in Custodial and Treatment Settings," *American Sociological Review* 30 (1965): 40-55; Mayer N. Zald and David Street, "Custody and Treatment in Juvenile Institutions: An Organizational Analysis," *Crime and Delinquency* 10 (1964): 249-56; Mayer N. Zald, "Organizational Control Structure in Five Correctional Institutions," *American Journal of Sociology* 68 (1962): 335-45, "Power Balance and Staff Conflict in Correctional Institutions," *Administrative Science Quarterly* 6 (1962): 22-49, and "The Correctional Institution for Juvenile Offenders: An Analysis of Organizational Character," *Social Problems* 8 (1960): 57-67; and R. Sarri and R.D. Vinter, "Group Treatment Strategies in Juvenile Correctional Institutions," *Crime and Delinquency* 11 (1965): 326-40.

16. Vinter and Janowitz, *The Comparative Study*, pp. 460-61.

17. Ibid., pp. 651-54.

18. Ibid., p. 665. A similar point was made in relation to runaway behavior by Lubeck and Empey in S.G. Lubeck and L.T. Empey, "Mediatory vs. Total Institutions: The Case of the Runaway," *Social Problems* 16 (1968): 242-60, and in relation to self-concept by Cohen and Vener in Bruce J. Cohen and Arthur M. Vener, "Self Concept Modification and Total Correctional Institutions," *Journal of Correctional Education* 20 (1968): 8-11.

19. Sethard Fisher, "Social Organization in a Correctional Residence," *Pacific Sociological Review* 4 (1961): 87-93.

20. Sethard Fisher, "Informal Organization in a Correctional Setting," *Social Problems* 13 (1965): 214-22.

21. J. Jones, "The Nature of Compliance in Correctional Institutions for Juvenile Offenders," *Journal of Research in Crime and Delinquency* 1 (1964): 83-95.

22. Seymour Rubenfeld and John W. Stafford, "An Adolescent Inmate Social System—A Psychological Account," *Psychiatry* 26 (1963): 241-56.

23. Thomas G. Eynon and Jon E. Simpson, "The Boy's Perception of Himself in a State Training School for Delinquents," *Social Service Review* 39 (1965): 31-37. See also Jon E. Simpson, Thomas G. Eynon, and Walter C. Reckless, "Institutionalization as Perceived by the Juvenile Offender," *Sociology and Social Research* 48 (1963): 13-23, and Thomas G. Eynon, Harry E. Allen, and Walter C. Reckless, "Measuring Impact of a Juvenile Correctional Institution by Perceptions of Inmates and Staff," *Journal of Research in Crime and Delinquency* 8, no. 1 (1971): 93-107. In K.L. Sindwanit and Walter Reckless, "Prisoner's Perceptions of the Impact of Institutional Stay," *Criminology* 10 (1973): 461-71, the boy's perceptions were found to be just a bit more positive than those of adult felons in a maximum security prison.

24. Walter C. Reckless, Thomas G. Eynon, and Jon E. Simpson, "Gauging

the Impact of Institutions on Delinquent Youth," *British Journal of Criminology* 4 (1963): 7-23.

25. B. Wood, G. Wilson, R. Jessor, and J. Bogan, "Troublemaking Behavior in a Correctional Institution: Relationship to Inmates' Definition of Their Situation," *American Journal of Orthopsychiatry* 36 (1966): 795-802.

26. Charles Wellford, "A Sociometric Analysis of a Correctional Community," unpublished Ph.D. dissertation, University of Pennsylvania, Philadelphia, 1969.

27. Ibid., pp. 130, 147.

28. Charles Wellford, "Contact and Commitment in a Correctional Community," *British Journal of Criminology* 13 (1973): 118.

29. Barry Schwartz, "The Influence Structure of a Correctional Community," unpublished Ph.D. dissertation, University of Pennsylvania, Philadelphia, 1970.

30. Ibid., p. 292.

31. Barry Schwartz, "Pre-Institutional vs. Situational Influence in a Correctional Community," *Journal of Criminal Law, Criminology and Police Science* 63 (1971): 532-43.

32. Ibid., pp. 532-43, and Barry Schwartz, "Peer versus Authority Effects in a Correctional Community," *Criminology* 11 (1973): 233-57.

33. J.E. Hautaluoma and W.A. Scott, "Values and Sociometric Choices of Incarcerated Juveniles," *Journal of Social Psychology* 91 (1973): 229-37.

34. John R. Ray and V.E. Yarbrough, "Effects of Institutionalization on Juvenile Delinquents," *American Journal of Correction* 36 (1974): 24, 28.

35. Robert S. Culbertson, "The Effect of Institutionalization on the Delinquent Inmate's Self-Concept," *Journal of Criminal Law and Criminology* 66 (1975): 88-93.

36. S.F. Landau, "Future Time Perspective of Delinquents and Non-Delinquents: The Effect of Institutionalization," *Criminal Justice and Behavior* 2 (1975): 22-36.

37. Melvin Seeman, "Alienation and Social Learning in a Reformatory," *American Journal of Sociology* 69 (1963): 270-84.

38. See Matthew T. Zingraff, "Conflicting Process of Socialization Among Juveniles in the Prison Community," *Georgia Journal of Corrections* 2 (1973): 63-70, and "Prisonization as an Inhibitor of Effective Resocialization," *Criminology* 13 (1975): 366-88; Charles W. Thomas and Matthew T. Zingraff, "Organizational Structure as a Determinant of Prisonization," *Pacific Sociological Review* 19 (1976): 98-116; and Charles W. Thomas, L. Thomas Winfree, and Jeffrey Hyman, "Consequences of Confinement for Juvenile Offenders," paper presented at the Annual Meeting of the Midwest Sociological Society, St. Louis, 1976.

39. Zingraff, "Conflicting Processes."

40. Thomas and Zingraff, "Organizational Structure."

41. Thomas Anthony Caffrey, "Assaultive and Troublesome Behavior Among Adolescent Homosexual Prison Inmates," unpublished Ph.D. dissertation, The City University of New York, 1974.

42. Harold E. Theis, "Factors Related to Delinquent Identification and Self Esteem of Incarcerated Male Delinquents," unpublished Ph.D. dissertation, Bowling Green State University, Bowling Green, O., 1975.

43. Ibid., p. 47.

44. Ibid., pp. 123-27.

45. Ibid., pp. 128-30.

46. Margaret Gold, "Cottage Seven: Intended and Unintended Consequences of a Behavioral Modification Program," unpublished Ph.D. dissertation, Case Western Reserve University, Cleveland, 1975. See also Gold, "Cottage Seven: Behavior Modification and the Fate of the Deviant Subculture," unpublished paper, The University of Akron, 1976.

47. Gold, "Cottage Seven: Intended and Unintended Consequences," p. 106.

48. Ibid., 142-44.

49. William Glasser, *Reality Therapy, A New Approach to Psychiatry* (New York: Harper & Row, 1965).

50. Clemens Bartollas, "Runaways at Training Institution, Central Ohio," unpublished Ph.D. dissertation, Ohio State University, Columbus, 1975.

51. See for example Clemens Bartollas, Stuart J. Miller, and Simon Dinitz, "The Boy Who Profits: The Limits of Institutional Success," paper presented at the Annual Meeting of the American Criminological Society, Chicago, 1974; Stuart J. Miller, Clemens Bartollas, James Roberts, and Simon Dinitz, "Victimization and Indefensible Spaces in a Juvenile Institution," paper presented to the American Society of Criminology, Toronto, 1975; Simon Dinitz, Stuart J. Miller, and Clemens Bartollas, "Staff Exploitation of Inmates: The Paradox of Institutional Control," in E. Viano and I. Drapkin, eds., *Exploiters and Exploited: The Dynamics of Victimization* (Lexington, Mass.: Lexington Books, 1975): 157-68; Clemens Bartollas, Stuart J. Miller, and Simon Dinitz, "The Informal Code in a Juvenile Institution," *Journal of Southern Criminal Justice* 1 (1975): 33-52; Clemens Bartollas, Stuart J. Miller, Simon Dinitz, and James Roberts, "Emotional Disturbance and Victimization in an End-of-the-Line Juvenile Institution," unpublished paper, Ohio State University, 1975; Stuart J. Miller, Clemens Bartollas, and Simon Dinitz, "The Heavy and Social Control in a Juvenile Institution," paper presented to the Alpha Kappa Delta Sociological Research Symposium, Virginia Commonwealth University, Richmond, 1974; Clemens Bartollas, Stuart J. Miller, and Simon Dinitz, "Becoming a Scapegoat:

Study of a Deviant Career," paper presented to the Alpha Kappa Delta Sociological Research Symposium, Virginia Commonwealth University, Richmond, 1974; Clemens Bartollas and Stuart J. Miller, "The White Victim in a Black Society," paper presented at the Annual Meeting of the American Society of Criminology, New York City, 1973; Clemens Bartollas, Stuart J. Miller, and Simon Dinitz, "The 'Booty Bandit': A Social Role in a Juvenile Institution," *Journal of Homosexuality* 1 (1974): 203-12; and, Clemens Bartollas, "Runaways at the Training Institution, Central Ohio," *Canadian Journal of Criminology and Corrections* (July 1975): 221-35.

52. Clemens Bartollas, Stuart J. Miller, and Simon Dinitz, *Juvenile Victimization: The Institutional Paradox* (New York: Halsted Press, 1976).

53. Ibid., p. xiv.

54. Ibid., pp. 53-60.

55. Ibid., pp. 62-67.

56. Ibid., pp. 75-81.

57. Ibid., pp. 31, 92-101.

58. Ibid., p. 134.

59. Ibid., pp. 106-25.

60. Ibid., pp. 164-66.

61. Gresham Sykes, *The Society of Captives* (New York: Atheneum, 1966).

62. Bartollas et al., *Juvenile Victimization*, pp. 200-14.

63. Ibid., p. 261.

## Chapter 6
## Recent Developments in Prisoner Subcultures

1. John J. Flanagan, "Imminent Crisis in Prison Populations," *American Journal of Correction* 37 (November-December 1975): 20-21.

2. National Clearinghouse for Criminal Justice Planning and Architecture, *United States Incarceration and Commitment Rates* (Champaign: University of Illinois at Urbana, 1975).

3. "U.S. Prison Population Hits All-Time High," *Corrections Magazine* 2 (March 1976): 9-10.

4. "It Has Come To Our Attention," *Federal Probation* 40 (June 1976): 87-88.

5. "Florida is Putting Prisoners Into Tents," *Corrections Magazine* 2 (November-December 1975): 56-67.

6. National Criminal Justice Information and Statistics Service, *Trends in Expenditure and Employment Data for the Criminal Justice System, 1971-1974* (Washington, D.C.: Government Printing Office, 1976).

7. P. Paulus, V. Cox, G. McCain, and J. Chandler, "Some Effects of Crowding in a Prison Environment," *Journal of Applied Social Psychology* 5 (1975): 90-91.

8. A.F. Kinzel, "Body Buffer Zone in Violent Prisoners," *American Journal of Psychiatry* 127 (July 1970): 59-64.

9. Flanagan, "Imminent Crisis," p. 20.

10. Richard W. Dodge, *Criminal Victimization in the United States: A Comparison of 1973 and 1974 Findings* (Washington, D.C.: Law Enforcement Assistance Aministration, 1976).

11. Federal Bureau of Investigation, *Uniform Crime Reports*, January-June, 1976 (Washington, D.C.: United States Department of Justice, 1976).

12. Israel Drapkin, "Prison Inmates as Victims," *Victimology, An International Journal* 1 (Spring 1976): 98-106.

13. Sol Rubin, "The Impact of Court Decisions on the Correctional Process," *Crime and Delinquency* 20 (April 1974): 129.

14. D.C. Sullivan and L.L. Tifft, "Court Intervention in Correction-roots of Resistance and Problems of Compliance," *Crime and Delinquency* 21 (July 1975): 213-22.

15. Charles S. Prigmore and Richard T. Crow, "Is the Court Remaking the American Prison System?" *Federal Probation* 40 (June 1976): 5-7.

16. "Alabama Prisons," *Criminal Justice Bulletin* (March 1976): 1-3.

17. "U.S. Prison Population Hits All-Time High," p. 18.

18. Prigmore and Crow, "Is the Court Remaking the American Prison System?" p. 8.

19. "U.S. Prison Population Hits All-Time High," p. 18.

20. Ibid., p. 18.

21. James D. Silbert and Alan Sussman, "Rights of Juveniles Confined in Training Schools," *Crime and Delinquency* 20 (October 1974): 373.

22. Geoffrey P. Alpert, John M. Finney, and James F. Short, Jr., "Legal Services, Prisoners' Attitudes and 'Rehabilitation'," paper presented at the annual meeting of the American Sociological Association, New York City, 1976.

23. Charles Goodell, *Political Prisoners in America* (New York: Random House, 1973).

24. Stuart A. Brody, "The Political Prisoner Syndrome, Latest Problem of the American Penal System," *Crime and Delinquency* 20 (April 1974): 102.

25. Willard Gaylin, *In Service of Their Country/War Resisters in Prison* (New York: Viking, 1970).

26. Charles E. Reasons, "The Politicizing of Crime, the Criminal and the Criminologist," *Journal of Criminal Law and Criminology* 64 (March 1973): 471-77.

27. Thomas Murton, *The Dilemma of Prison Reform* (New York: Holt, Rinehart and Winston, 1976).

28. Ross K. Baker, "Politics Goes to Prison," in J. Susman *Crime and Justice, 1971-1974* (New York: AMS Press, 1974).

29. Erik Olin Wright, *The Politics of Punishment, A Critical Analysis of Prisons in America* (New York: Harper & Row, 1973).

30. John Irwin, "The Trouble With Rehabilitation," paper presented at the 1973 meeting of the American Sociological Association, New York City, 1973, pp. 1, 2, 11.

31. Brody, "The Political Prisoner Syndrome," pp. 100, 105.

32. Daniel Glaser, "Politicalization of Prisoners: A New Challenge to American Penology," *American Journal of Correction* 33 (November-December 1971): 8.

33. Vernon Fox, "Analysis of Prison Disciplinary Problems," *Journal of Criminal Law, Criminology and Police Science* 49 (November-December 1972): 14.

34. James J. Stephen, *Survey of Inmates of State Correctional Facilities, 1974*, Advance Report (Washington, D.C.: National Criminal Justice Information and Statistics Service, 1976).

35. James B. Jacobs, "Participant Observation in Prison," *Urban Life and Culture* 3 (July 1974): 404.

36. Theodore R. Davidson, *Chicano Prisoners, The Key to San Quentin* (New York: Holt, Rinehart and Winston, 1974).

37. Milton Burdman, "Ethnic Self-Help Groups in Prison and on Parole," *Crime and Delinquency* 20 (April 1974): 107-18.

38. Malcolm Little, *The Autobiography of Malcolm X* (New York: Grove Press, 1965); George Jackson, *Soledad Brother: The Prison Letters of George Jackson* (New York: Coward-McCann, 1970); and Eldridge Cleaver, *Soul on Ice* (New York: McGraw-Hill, 1968).

39. James B. Jacobs, "Stratification and Conflict Among Prison Inmates," *Journal of Criminal Law and Criminology* 66 (December 1976): 478, 480, 481.

40. Daniel L. Skoler and Ralph Loewenstein, "Minorities in Correction—Nondiscrimination, Equal Opportunity, and Legal Issues," *Crime and Delinquency* 20 (October 1974): 339.

41. Roger A. Roffman and Charles Froland, "Drug and Alcohol Dependencies in Prison, A Review of the Response," *Crime and Delinquency* 22 (July 1976): 363.

42. Ronald L. Akers, Norman S. Hayner, and Werner Gruninger, "Homosexual and Drug Behavior in Prison: A Test of the Functional and Importation Models of the Inmate System," *Social Problems* 21 (Winter 1974): 7.

43. Raymond Irizarry, "Drugs, Institutions and Mental Health: A Prophetic View," *American Journal of Correction* 33 (November-December 1971): 26.

44. Neil M. Singer, "The Value of Inmate Manpower," *Journal of Research in Crime and Delinquency* 13 (January 1976): 10, 12.

45. Rinker Buck, "The Prisons, As Always, Are Short on Real Reform," *The New York Times*, August 29, 1976.

46. Ronald C. Huff, "Prisoners' Union: A Challenge for State Corrections," *State Government* 48 (Summer 1975): 145-46. See also Ronald C. Huff, "Unionization Behind The Walls," *Criminology* 12 (August 1974): 175-93.

47. Ibid., pp. 145, 147.

48. Gilbert F. McMahon, "The Normal Prisoner in Medical Research," *Journal of Clinical Pharmacology* 71 (February-March 1972): 72.

49. See for example, F. Ayd, "Drug Studies in Prison Volunteers," *Southern Medical Journal* 65 (April 1972): 440; W.J. Estelle, Jr., "The Changing Profile and Conditions Surrounding Clinical Research in Prisons," *Clinical Pharmacology and Therapeutics* 13 (1972): 831-32; and John D. Arnold, Daniel C. Martin, and Sarah E. Smith, "A Study of One Prison Population and Its Response to Medical Research," *Annuals of the New York Academy of Sciences* 169 (1970): 463-70.

50. Peter B. Meyer, *Drug Experiments on Prisoners, Ethical, Economic, or Exploitative?* (Lexington, Mass.: Lexington Books, 1976).

51. For a description of the Mexican system, see John A. Price, "Private Enterprise in a Prison, The Free Market Economy of La Mesa Penitenciaria," *Crime and Delinquency* 19 (April 1973): 218-27.

52. J.E. Baker, *The Right to Participate: Inmate Involvement in Prison Administration* (Meuchen, N.J.: Scarecrow, 1974).

53. Tom Murton, "Inmate Self-Government," *University of San Francisco Law Review* 6 (October 1971): 87-101.

54. Virginia McArthur, "Inmate Grievance Mechanisms: A Survey of American Prisons," *Federal Probation* 38 (December 1974): 44.

55. Stephen, *Survey of Inmates*, p. 28.

56. Hans W. Mattick, "The Prosaic Sources of Prison Violence," in J. Sussman, ed., *Crime and Justice, 1971-1972* (New York: AMS Press, 1974).

57. H.H.A. Cooper, "Self-Mutilation by Peruvian Prisoners," *International Journal of Offender Therapy* 15 (1971), 180.

58. David Fogel, *"We Are The Living Proof", The Justice Model For Corrections* (Cincinnati, O.: W.H. Anderson, 1975).

59. Alan C. Straus and Robert Sherwin, "Inmate Rioters and Non-Rioters— A Comparative Analysis," *American Journal of Correction* 37 (May-June, July-August 1975): 34-35, 54-58.

60. Howard Bidna, "Effects of Increased Security on Prison Violence," *Journal of Criminal Justice* 3 (1975): 34-35.

61. Gary Butenhoff and Norman Knight, "An Investigation Into the Effects of Incarceration on Marriage and Possible Causes of Divorce," unpublished manuscript, Washington State Penitentiary, Walla Walla, 1972.

162

62. Stanley L. Brodsky, *Families and Friends of Men in Prison, The Uncertain Relationship* (Lexington, Mass.: Lexington Books, 1975).

63. Stephen, *Survey of Inmates*, pp. 2-3, 32.

64. Columbus B. Hopper, *Sex in Prison* (Baton Rouge: Louisiana State University Press, 1969).

65. Norman S. Hayner, "Attitudes Toward Conjugal Visits For Prisoners," *Federal Probation* 36 (March 1972): 46-47.

66. Price, "Private Enterprise," p. 224.

67. Azmy Ishak Ibrahim, "Deviant Sexual Behavior in Men's Prisons," *Crime and Delinquency* 20 (January 1974): 41.

68. Anthony M. Scacco, *Rape In Prison* (Springfield, Ill.: Charles C. Thomas, 1975).

69. Stuart Adams, "Correctional Agency Perceptions of the Usefulness of Research," *American Journal of Correction* 37 (July-August 1975): 24, 26.

70. John R. Ray and V.E. Yarbrough, "Effects of Institutionalization on Juvenile Delinquents," *American Journal of Correction* 36 (May-June 1974): 28.

71. Robert Martinson, "What Works? Questions and Answers About Prison Reform," *Public Interest* 35 (April 1974): 49.

72. D.A. Sargeant, "Confinement and Ego Regression: Some Consequences of Enforced Passivity," *International Journal of Psychiatry in Medicine* 5 (1974): 144, 150.

73. Philip G. Zimbardo, Craig Haney, and Curtis Banks, "Interpersonal Dynamics in a Simulated Prison," unpublished manuscript, Stanford University, undated.

74. See Andrew Hopkins, "Imprisonment and Recidivism: A Quasi-Experimental Study," *Journal of Research in Crime and Delinquency* 13 (January 1976). Also see Andrew Hopkins, "Return to Crime: A Quasi-Experimental Study of the Effects of Imprisonment and Its Alternatives," unpublished Ph.D. dissertation, University of Connecticut, Storrs, 1975.

75. David Shichor, "People-changing-People-processing Organizations," paper presented at the Pacific Sociological Meeting, San Diego, March 1976, pp. 15-16.

76. Vicki L. Rose and Pamela J. Riley, "Political Efficacy, Correctional Policies and Prison Reform: A Survey of Attitudes and Public Opinion," paper presented at the 1976 meeting of the Pacific Sociological Association, San Diego, March 1976, pp. 9, 10, 26.

77. Board of Directors, NCCD, "The Nondangerous Offender Should Not be Imprisoned," *Crime and Delinquency* 21 (October 1975): 315.

78. "Green Mountain Post Boy," *Vermont Life* 30 (1975).

79. Lloyd E. Ohlin, Alden D. Miller, and Robert B. Coates, "Radical

Correctional Reform: A Case Study of the Massachusetts Youth Correctional System," *Harvard Educational Review* 44 (February 1974): 79-100.

80. Michael S. Serrill, "Juvenile Corrections in Massachusetts," *Corrections Magazine* 2 (November-December 1975): 3.

81. Perhaps the best list of prison functions is provided by Charles E. Reasons and Russell L. Kaplan, "Tear Down the Walls? Some Functions of Prisons," *Crime and Delinquency* 21 (October 1975): 360-72.

82. Charles W. Thomas, Robin J. Cage, and Samuel C. Foster, "Public Opinion on Criminal Law and Legal Sanctions: An Examination of Two Conceptual Models," *Journal of Criminal Law and Criminology* 67 (March 1976): 111-15.

83. Gordon P. Waldo, Theodore G. Chiricos, and Leonard E. Dobrin, "Community Contact and Inmate Attitudes, An Experimental Assessment of Work Release," *Criminology* 11 (November 1973): 355-72.

84. Martha Wheeler, "The Current Status of Women in Prisons," *Criminal Justice and Behavior* 1 (December 1974): 375-78.

85. Freda Adler, *Sisters in Crime: The Rise of the New Female Criminal* (New York: McGraw-Hill, 1975).

86. T.E. Hannum, J.W. Menne, E.L. Betz, and L. Rans, "Differences in Female Prisoner Characteristics—1960 to 1970," *Corrective and Social Psychiatry and Journal of Applied Behavior Therapy* 19 (1973): 39-41.

87. Joann B. Morton, "Women Offenders: Fiction and Facts," *American Journal of Correction* 38 (July-August 1976): 36.

Chapter 7
## Conclusions and Policy Recommendations

1. As examples of the noncorrectional literature on therapeutic communities, see Maxwell Jones, *Beyond the Therapeutic Community* (New Haven, Conn.: Yale University Press, 1968), and Jean J. Rossi and William J. Filstead, *The Therapeutic Community* (New York: Behavioral Publications, 1973).

2. Robert R. Carkhuff, *Helping and Human Relations*, Vol. II (New York: Holt, Rinehart and Winston, 1969), pp. 21-25.

3. Ibid., p. 7.

# Index

# Index

Adamek, Raymond J., 81, 92
Adler, Freda, 121, 122
Admas, W. Thomas, 93
Administrative changes, effect of, 18, 19, 27, 28
Akers, Ronald L., 14, 57, 68, 111
Alcohol, 26, 27, 33, 110, 111
Alexander, Elizabeth S., 53
Argot, prisoner, 1, 4, 49, 68, 69, 76, 79-81
Ash, Ellis, 2, 3, 31
Atchley, Robert C., 43
Attitudes, of administrators toward research, 117; of female prisoners, 81, 84, 90; of incarcerated boys, 93, 95-98; of incarcerated men, 2, 4, 7-9, 11-13, 16, 17, 19, 20, 25, 27, 29, 30, 32, 36, 43, 46-49, 51-57, 59-61, 67-69, 74, 76, 90, 104, 106, 121
Austin, Penelope, 86
Austin, W.T., 64
Australia, prisoners in, 80, 81

Baker, J.E., 113
Baker, Ross K., 108
Balogh, Joseph K., 57-58
Banks, Curtis, 119
Barker, Gordon H., 93
Barth, Ernest A., 85
Bartkeme, Kenwood, 12
Bartollas, Clemens, 94, 99-102
Bates, F.L., 64
Beit-Hallahmi, Benjamin, 72
Bendix, Reinhard, 11
Bennett, L.A., 56
Berk, Bernard, 39-41
Beto, Dan R., 42
Betz, E.L., 122
Bidna, Howard, 115
Biological theories of criminal behavior, 2, 86
Black prisoners, 17, 32, 33, 42, 43, 58, 60, 67-74, 78, 79, 84, 88, 100, 107-110, 114, 115
Bloch, Herbert A., 14
Bogan, J., 96
Bohlander, Edward, Jr., 58
Bondeson, Vlla, 81
Bowker, Lee H., 53, 54, 56
Boys, institutions for, 93-102
Brodey, Robert, 56
Brodsky, Stanley L., 58, 115, 116
Brody, Stuart A., 107-108
Brown, Andrew W., 2
Brown, B.S., 58
Buck, Rinker, 112
Buffum, Peter C., 68
Burdman, Milton, 109
Burgess, Ernest W., 43
Burkhart, Kathryn W., 86
Burns, Henry, Jr., 60
Butenhoff, Gary, 115

Caffrey, Thomas A., 98
Cage, Robin J., 57, 121
Canada, prisons in, 25, 26, 38, 39, 75, 76
Carkhuff, Robert R., 126
Carroll, Leo, 67, 68
Carter, Barbara, 86, 91
Cassel, R.N., 79
Cavan, Ruth S., 17
Cavior, Helene E., 86
Cavior, Norman, 86
Censoriousness, 37, 71
Chandler, Edna W., 86
Chandler, J., 104
Chiricos, Theodore G., 121
Claghorn, James R., 42
Clayton, J., 79
Cleaner, Eldridge, 109
Clemmer, Donald, 3-7, 30, 31, 45, 48, 61, 76, 84
Climent, Carlos E., 86
Cline, Hugh F., 37, 38, 75, 76
Cloward, Richard, 21, 22, 28, 35, 51

167

Waldo, Gordon P., 53, 121
Wallace, Robert, 43
Ward, David A., 46, 58, 59, 81-83, 88
Watkins, John C., 28
Weber, Max, 32, 137
Weeks, Ashley, 93
Weinberg, S. Kirson, 7
Wellford, Charles, 44, 96
Wenk, Ernst A., 64
Wentz, D.J., 86
Wheeler, Martha, 121
Wheeler, Stanton, 9, 20, 21, 29, 30, 34, 35, 43, 44, 48, 58, 59, 75, 76, 84, 97
Wieder, Lawrence D., 66
Williams, Virginia L., 61, 62, 91
Wilmer, Daniel M., 46, 58, 59, 81-83, 88

Wilsnack, Richard W., 72
Wilson, G., 96
Wilson, John M., 53
Wilson, Thomas P., 33
Winfree, L. Thomas, 98
Wolfson, Wendy, 72-73
Wood, B., 96
Wright, Eric O., 108
Wright, James C., 8
Wulbert, Roland, 39, 40

Yarbrough, V.E., 97, 118

Zalba, S., 80
Zald, Mayer N., 95
Zemans, Eugene S., 17
Zimbardo, Phillip G., 64, 119
Zingraff, Matthew T., 98

# About the Author

**Lee H. Bowker** is associate professor and coordinator of the criminal justice program at the University of Wisconsin-Milwaukee. He received the M.A. from the University of Pennsylvania and the Ph.D. from Washington State University. *Prisoner Subcultures* is his third book, and he has also published numerous journal articles, book reviews, and technical reports in the areas of criminology, corrections, drug use and abuse, race relations, and sex roles. In addition to his research on prisoner subcultures, Professor Bowker's criminal justice activities have included an analysis of police-community relations in a rural community, the evaluation of a juvenile justice diversion project, and the direction of the social therapy program—a therapeutic community for violent drug abusers at the Washington State Penitentiary.

M

I